ALTITUDE ADJUSTMENT

Altitude Adjustment

A Quest for Love, Home, and Meaning in the Tetons

Mary Beth Baptiste

TWODOT®

Guilford, Connecticut
Helena, Montana
An imprint of Globe Pequot Press

A · TWODOT® · BOOK

Copyright © 2014 by Mary Elizabeth Baptiste

Excerpts on pages 1, 179, and 229 from "Last night, as I was sleeping" by Antonio Machado, from *Times Alone,* tr. (Wesleyan University Press, 1983). © Antonio Machado. © 1983 Translation by Robert Bly. Reprinted by permission of Wesleyan University Press.
Excerpt on pages 104–05 from *Teewinot: A Year in the Teton Range* © 2000 by Jack Turner. Reprinted by permission of Thomas Dunne Books. All rights reserved.
Excerpt on page 132 from *Pilgrim at Tinker Creek* by Annie Dillard. © 1974. Reprinted by permission of HarperCollins Publishers.
Lyrics to "Sweet Wyoming Home" on page 160 reprinted by permission of Bill Staines, © 1976 by Mineral River Music, BMI.

Project Editor: Lauren Brancato
Layout: Chris Mongillo

Library of Congress Cataloging-in-Publication Data

Baptiste, Mary Elizabeth, 1953- author.
  Altitude adjustment : reflections on leaving home and finding my inner / Mary Elizabeth Baptiste.
    pages cm
  Summary: "A recent divorce from a marriage of fifteen years, Mary Elizabeth Baptiste makes the decision to fulfill a life goal to work at Grand Teton National Park. Finally settled in Moose, Wyoming, she begins life anew and attempts to reconcile her past with the wide future ahead of her"— Provided by publisher.
  ISBN 978-0-7627-9134-7 (paperback)
  1. Baptiste, Mary Elizabeth, 1953—-Homes and haunts—Wyoming—Teton County. 2. Naturalists—Wyoming—Teton County—Anecdotes. 3. Natural history—Wyoming—Grand Teton National Park. 4. Grand Teton National Park (Wyo.) I. Title.
  QH31.B196A3 2013
  508.09787'55—dc23
  [B]
                                                              2013035416

Printed in the United States of America

10 9 8 7 6 5 4 3 2 1

For my best friend and partner, Richard

and

In memory of

Dad
Joseph F. Baptiste
1930–2013

and

Nan
Mary Silvia Medeiros
1904–1999

Amor Para Sempre

TABLE OF CONTENTS

CONTENTS

Prologue

Woodswoman

A twist of the binoculars' focus wheel and I gasp: two toddler-sized black bear cubs, one brown and one black, twined together high up in a spruce tree fifty yards away. I scan the ground for the mother. In a nearby huckleberry patch, her cinnamon-colored rump bobs like a swatch of scruffy hide on a clothesline.

It unnerves me, this lack of boundaries. Every animal, scat, or track I find brings a new fear—a mother bear will charge, a moose will explode from the brush and trample, something *out there* will break through and annihilate me into dust. I long for an owl's head-turning ability so I can take it all in and see what's coming before it gets me.

I turn and dash on tiptoes down the trail, my imagination conjuring up a multitude of lurking predators.

This is how I remember those first years on my own in a strange place: thimblefuls of fake courage thrown at a conflagration of fear.

Part 1: Water of a New Life

Last night, as I was sleeping,
I dreamt—marvellous error!—
that a spring was breaking
out in my heart.
I said: Along which secret aqueduct,
Oh water, are you coming to me,
water of a new life
that I have never drunk?

—Antonio Machado
(Translated by Robert Bly)

First Glimpse

August 1981. The odometer on the VW Rabbit rolls over 100,000 miles as we head north from Rock Springs on Wyoming Highway 89. A hundred desolate miles on a black highway. Herds of pronghorn antelope facing west. A tumultuous storm, a rainbow. A meander through Jackson as traffic crawls around a staged cowboy shoot-out in the town square. Stops at Fred's Market for peanut butter and apples, the A&W for root beer and burgers.

We continue driving north, sniffing sharp, wet sage. Miriam reclines in the passenger's seat, a *Ms.* magazine folded open to the "No Comment" page on her lap. Strands of her rain-straight hair flap out the window.

My heart drums, my mind burns luminous. Three days ago, when I first saw that haphazard rim of peaks beyond Denver's foothills, I knew I was home. Creeping up the Trail Ridge Road in Rocky Mountain National Park, I embraced every mountain and stream, checking them off on the map like completed items on a to-do list.

Now, as we climb a curving hill past the National Fish Hatchery, Miriam bolts upright. "*Jeez-Lou-eez,* will you look at *that.*" Before us, smug with audacious power, the Teton range surges from the valley floor and the green-black forests, snagging cloud wisps as it rips through a meek cobalt sky.

From somewhere long forgotten the words *Santa Barbara* spring into my head. This is the saint my Portuguese grandmother invokes during storms. At the first turnout I park the car and leap out. My head swirls, blood charges through my veins, nerves prickle and blaze. I push and thrash, trying to tear through the dull dimensions of my current life and catapult into another. But it isn't time yet.

I want to sing, dance, run. I want to know it all. I want to sprint naked into the mountains, streak pine pitch through my hair, slip my fingers into rock crevices, slither-glide with trout over creek riffles. I want to sleep curled against a bear's belly, its fur tickling my spine, and ride a moose through the forest like Lady Godiva. I want to scale the highest peak, splay out my arms, crack open my lungs in an all-out sacrificial scream: *I'm yours forever.* I want to stand up there, feet rooted in silver rock, and touch the moon.

Promising a raw freedom previously unimaginable to me, the serrated peaks challenge me to take the risks that will bring purpose and depth to my humdrum suburban life. *I belong here.* But it's bigger than me. Orders of magnitude bigger. Through my head flow the words of Aldo Leopold: "A thing is right when it tends to preserve the integrity, stability, and beauty of the biotic community." I strive to live this tenet. As a mountain woodswoman, I could.

"The mountains are calling," wrote John Muir, "and I must go." In a flash I see the irrepressible, gleaming kernel that I've always both sought and avoided: For my life to matter, for me to do the work I'm meant to do in the world, I have to spend my days in mountains and forests like these, among people committed to their flourishing.

And all they ask in return is a simple renunciation of everything I've ever known to be true.

There/Here

May 1992. Wide-eyed and deflated, I clutch the steering wheel of my Toyota Corolla wagon, rain drumming on the roof, and peer out at my new home, #447 in the Beaver Creek Employee Housing Compound at Grand Teton National Park. Splintered steps tilt into the dented white and green trailer. Around its base, rusted sections of corrugated metal form a patchy apron. The roof undulates. I can't erase from my mind an image of the home I've left, my Massachusetts Cape, with its cedar shingles and wraparound porch, under the trees on Red Maple Lane.

It's been eleven years since I came here with Miriam, and now I'm back, reeling from the shatters of divorce, for a seasonal job with Grand Teton's Division of Science and Resource Management, "S&RM." Doubts consume me. Can I really do this job? My master's degree in wildlife management is fifteen years old, making me, at thirty-nine, nearly a generation older than the average seasonal park worker. My parents said, "You're looking for something, Mary, but I doubt you're ever going to find it."

A part of me believed them. My greatest fear—worse than dying—is that I'll not find that vague something I seek, and that my parents turn out to be right after all.

And now my new home is this squalid hellhole. I assumed Grand Teton employees would live in tidy quarters like the houses I'd seen at Shenandoah National Park where I did my master's research. Or at least in thirties-era Civilian Conservation Corps houses like the one I stayed in there, drafty but comfortable, near Matthew's Arm Campground. I expected better from Grand Teton. I dared to hope for something attractive, built of logs of course, where I'd put up curtains and raise a kitten.

For courage I pat my jacket pocket. Inside is a bundle of five twenty-dollar bills wrapped around a Miraculous Medal of the Virgin Mary. When I visited my grandmother to say goodbye, she'd stood before me, all four-feet-eleven of her. On a chain around her neck was the tiny gold *figa* charm, a clenched fist with the forefinger curled around the thumb, that she wore to chase away *quebrantos*, Portuguese curses. Taking note of this innocent superstition, I felt myself slipping into a pool of sorrow. As we both dabbed handkerchiefs to our eyes, she pressed the money and medal into my hand. "Keep this with you, Mary. *Nossa Senhora* will always protect you." I balked at the amount of cash. "That's a lot of money, Nan. You might need it." But she shook her head, the decision made. "I want you to have it. Because you're my granddaughter, and I love you."

Standing on the landing with rain dripping down my collar, I utter a prayer to the cosmos that she won't ever see this place. As I fumble the key in the lock, the floor beneath my feet shifts; I adjust my stance to avoid a spongy section of wood. The door jerks open. Standing inside is a young woman with crimped blue-black hair and a face etched with boredom. She's dressed in jeans and a mint green sweatshirt appliquéd with a panda bear.

"You have to pull the door toward you while you turn the knob," she says, holding out a fragile hand. "You must be Mary Beth. I'm Brenda." Her hand feels like a sock filled with matchsticks.

Tik-tik-tik. A ceiling panel, stained tea-colored, has sagged into a bowl shape. Water oozes at the bottom of the bowl and elongates into blobs that snap off and drop into a utility bucket on the floor.

Brenda rolls her head. "The ceiling leak just started today. I've been cleaning. The fridge needs defrosting, but I washed the kitchen floor and vacuumed the carpet."

She tells me she attends college in Salt Lake City and is spending the summer working in the park's Concessions office. It's just a place to do an internship; she has no interest in getting out to explore the park. She's engaged, and her fiancé and her mother will be visiting later in the summer. "Maybe by then," she says, "you'll know someone you can stay with so we can use your room. You have the front bedroom."

I shrug, not knowing what to make of her. The kitchen and living room, separated by a gold-flecked Formica counter, lead to a bedroom—a cell, really—with dark seventies paneling, a twin bed frame with a stained mattress, a closet, and a built-in set of drawers under a recessed mirror. Both windows are cracked; a dusty bulb erupts from the ceiling like a pimple.

Brenda continues, "I guess if you put up some curtains and get a lamp it won't be so bad." She walks back to her room and shuts the door. I hear rock music playing, the lyrics rife with "His loves," "Jesuses," and "the Fathers."

I check out the bathroom. Lacework of water stains on the ceiling. Bare bulb over the sink. Fist-sized hole in the paneling near the mirror, which has a bull's-eye ding in its center. Grimy patina around the base of the tub. I have trouble determining the intended color of the toilet bowl. Dust bunnies coat the shelves of an envelope-sized closet.

As rain pummels the roof, the rhythm of the kitchen drip speeds up to an allegro tempo. Outside, spruce spires sashay in the wind. When I checked in at the park's Personnel Office, a chunky woman with a sullen, moonlike face told me it's been raining here for two months. But the mountains are still snow-covered, and drifts persevere on the north sides of buildings and under the evergreens.

I carry my two pans, two plates, two cups, and spangle of silverware to the kitchen, whose floor swoops like the Lincoln Park Fun House. A moth-eaten curtain is suspended over the window with string and thumbtacks. Opening cabinets, I see that Brenda either runs a moonlight catering business or had a wedding shower before she came and brought every gift with her. A popcorn popper and gallon jug of popcorn. Bundt pans. Toaster oven. Crock pot. Heavy-duty mixer. Electric frying pan. Place settings for eight. Four copper-bottomed Revere Ware pans. Ten plastic tumblers. Five CorningWare casserole dishes.

In six two-shelved cabinets, only one shelf is empty. As I slide my dishes onto it, something darts through my peripheral vision. A mouse scurries out from under the stove and runs a lap around the living room. "Oh, no!" I say with a laugh.

Brenda runs out.

"We have tenants," I say, pointing.

Her upper lip tugs upward. "*Sheesh*. I found droppings in the cupboards when I was cleaning. We'll have to get Maintenance to come and get rid of them." She stomps back to her room, muttering, "What a dump. The furniture doesn't even *match*."

Judging from the condition of the place, I doubt Maintenance could keep rodents out of it. The trailer has more holes than a sponge, and I'm sure the walls provide plenty of dark spaces and snarly insulation for nesting material.

I sit down on a kitchen chair. Out the window, beyond the ring of evergreens encircling the trailer, all I see is gray. Somewhere beyond this bleakness is that mountain range, that golden Grail into which I've poured all hope for my future. For the Tetons I've fled a fifteen-year marriage, a home in the suburbs, a job as a mental health therapist. And I've alienated my family.

Just then, Emerson's words from "Self-Reliance" pop into my mind. "Trust thyself: every heart vibrates to that iron string."

I straighten. *I'm in the Rocky Mountains.* Through the window I spot movement at the base of the fir tree in the yard. Huddled under the droopy branches, a rabbit wags its ears to shed water. No, not a rabbit, I realize, noticing the shaggy feet. A hare—a snowshoe hare.

Part of me fizzes with excitement; part of me feels I'm stepping off a cliff. I can't imagine what lies ahead. I draw out three brass keys from my pocket and set them on the table before me. One for my house trailer, one for the S&RM office, and a master key for the locks on the park's gates and backcountry cabins. I slip the keys on my key ring and jingle it. *The sound of belonging.* Can this really be happening? True, I've traded an upscale New England Cape for a ratty trailer and a General Delivery mailing address. But after a lifetime of yearning to be in the Rockies, I now live in Moose, Wyoming, and hold the keys to Grand Teton National Park in my hand.

3

Baggage

In Vila Franca do Campo on the island of São Miguel, Azores, ten levels of steps lead up to *Igreja da Nossa Senhora do Paz,* Our Lady of Peace Church. Rising vertiginously up a cliffside, the steps are decorated at each level with a blue and white tile depicting some sacred event in the life of the Virgin Mother. I imagine the climb symbolizes the noble, pious, but difficult life: Don't dally in the dirt below, keep your head up, shoulder your load, and head up the steps, one by one. Keep Mother Mary in your sights. With a bit of luck and a daily lap around a rosary, the ascent should buy you a one-way passage to Heaven when the time comes.

Early in my life I willingly walked steps like these, tracing each ceramic tile with my fingers and thinking, *Yes, yes, yes,* my whole known world confirmed, seeing ahead of me only a broadening cornucopia of nurturing family and traditions. In time, right in the center of that open basket, my husband Bill appeared, hand outstretched, showing me the way.

But there was something tugging at me, something born in a roiling, metallic fog that obscured any viable path. Powerful yet invisible, it prodded me with sharp pricks.

Who knows how a life's dream coalesces in a child's heart? My mother says that, while he milked his cows, my grandfather, the son of Azorean immigrants, sang, "You know Wyoming will be your new home," but I have no recollection of that. Over and over I probe memories of my early years. But when I try to trace the origin of my westward-leaning dream, it's like the mystery of the Big Bang—I can follow it back to within a fraction of a second after my awareness of it, but I can't get to the other side.

During the winter of the year I would turn six, don a white veil, fold my hands, and thrust out my tongue for First Communion, my father's job took him to Arco, Idaho, and then to Jackson Hole. He returned home with dozens of slides of mountain snowscapes and elk. Holding up each slide to a lamp, I peered at the regal, full-necked animals and spears of mountains—the Rocky Mountains, Dad called them. I trembled with what I can now only describe as longing. When Dad set up the projector and ran through the slides on the silver screen, I stared, transfixed. At dinner he asked Mom, "What do you think about moving to Idaho? I could get a drafting job at the engineering lab there." Heart bobbing in my chest, I held my breath until she answered, a forkful of peas poised in midair, her mouth webbed in fear, "*What?* But our *families*. . . . Besides, my father would never let us go." Dad said nothing, only looked relieved that his wife had talked some sense into him. I sank into my chair, crushed.

Then there was the book I'd pulled from a wobbly bookcase in Nan's attic. I thought the title was *Dot and Dash on the Dude Ranch,* but when I Google the title I get *Dot and Dash in the North Woods* and *Dot and Dash at the Seashore,* but no dude ranch. I do remember a cherry-cheeked girl and a black and white terrier, dusty paddocks, creamy saddles, horses, campfires. Mountains sharp as lancets, summer snow, Christmas tree smells all around. There was, of course, that ultimate of nests, a log cabin, rooted and inviting, in the shadows. Mom found me in tears on my bed one day. I told her I was crying because I doubted I would ever live in a place like that.

Why would a scene in a book elicit such strong emotion in a young girl? And why feelings of sadness and hopelessness rather than joyful anticipation?

The answer lies in my family machinery. Near the turn of the twentieth century, my great-grandparents on both sides fled poverty and despair and sailed to America seeking more prosperous lives. One line hailed from the gritty streets of Dublin. The other three came from Faial, São Jorge, and Terceira, three of Portugal's nine Azorean Islands, Gulf Stream–warmed beauties fabled to be the tips of the sunken continent of Atlantis.

I can only imagine the desperation that led my great-grandmother Rosa to set sail from Terceira in 1899 carrying a *valisa* filled with a peasant's treasures. Maybe she was fleeing her husband, or maybe he sent her to seek a better life—no one knows—all we know is she came without him. I suspect dawn was breaking through the fog, and dewy webs still clung to the weeds underfoot as she stepped down the path from her mud and thatch house for the last time. Leaving milk buckets on the doorsteps of neighboring shacks, tearful friends and relatives probably ran to her with outstretched arms to offer kisses, wishes, and prayers for safe passage. Some might have slipped a coin or a bit of bread into her threadbare pocket as they accompanied her to the boat dock, where the smells of fish and seaweed hung in the air. Gulls cawed from pier posts, lines snapped on masts. I hope she traveled with someone familiar to her, but we don't know that either. What we do know is that Rosa was pregnant with my grandfather, my dad's father, when she said *Adeus* to her family and stepped up the gangplank to board the ship. As the island and the only life she'd ever known shrank in the distance behind her, she must have turned her youthful eyes to the choppy seas ahead, rubbed her belly, and prayed for the nascent life inside her.

Our family history is full of stories like this, told and retold, of grand and mournful leave-takings from the Old Country, assumed to be, for all involved, as final as death. My family knows little more about Grandpa's roots. "His father was in the Portuguese navy," Dad once told us, "and he used to send her money. But Grandpa's parents never saw each other again, and Grandpa never knew his father."

Generations ago in my family, it was acceptable, even necessary, for the young to leave spouses and parents—to plunge into the dark unknown and cross the Atlantic on a ship, throwing away everything familiar for the chance of a better life in America. That finger of land that curves into the Atlantic—Cape Cod—beckoned to them. Having heard of thriving dairy farms and textile factories seeking workers, they boarded ships bound, not for Ellis Island, but for the port of New Bedford, the nineteenth-century whaling city of *Moby Dick* fame. Some found jobs in the mills and rented tenement houses they eventually purchased. Others spread out into neighboring Dartmouth and Westport to farm waterlogged soil full of stones.

It should have been easy for me, with intrepid ancestors like these, to leave home and family and everything familiar to pursue a deep-rooted dream. But my ancestors' dreams were the forced consequences of desperate lives. They made the painful decision to leave home to survive. They gambled on the future and it paid off. In this bountiful New World, where hard work finally reaped rewards, my family could safely abandon its pioneering spirit, sending taproots clear down to the center of the earth and creating an empire. Ensuing generations were welcomed into a microcosm of Old World values—hard work, church, extended family. Held close and protected, children were assured they would never have to suffer the hardships of their ancestors.

My maternal grandparents and their siblings, after working years as domestics and tenant farmers, eventually saved up enough cash to purchase a fifty-acre dairy farm, whose rambling farmhouse became home to various relatives and friends who needed work and a place to live. Thirteen people shared the house throughout my mother's childhood. When my parents married they lived "at the farm," with Mom's parents, her father's unmarried sisters *Ti' Elena* and *Tia* Mame, her Azorean grandmother *Vavó*, and a number of farm hands who slept in the attic. I was born into this fold, into the arms of not just one mother, but five.

Never alone, never lonely. Had we been the sort of family that had reunions, we might have put those words on buttons and worn them on our jacket lapels. But families with grandparents, aunts, uncles, sisters, brothers, children, and grandchildren all living within a six-mile radius hardly need reunions.

There were daily phone calls and Sunday visits after church. Holiday dinners in sweltering tenements on makeshift plywood tables and folding chairs. Christmas carols sung on curved stairwells at someone's door. Baked custards when someone was sick, delivered warm in Pyrex dishes. Bags of Circus Peanuts—those marshmallow confections of a color never seen in nature—brought over just because *Ti' Elena* saw them on the Brach's display at Stop & Shop and remembered, "Mary Elizabeth likes those. And Nancy likes Squirrel Chews."

There was always someone to call to help lug a sofa to a third floor tenement or wriggle a new washing machine down the cellar stairs. Always someone to call for a household emergency, with many episodes remembered and woven into the family tapestry, told over and over, one person's thread taken up seamlessly by another.

"Remember when Yvette and Frank's kerosene heater blew up . . ."

" . . . and she called Charlie?"

"Where was Frank?"

"It was a Saturday. Frank was working at the post office. Charlie was off from the mill . . ."

" . . . so he walked over."

"Yeah . . ."

" . . .'cause he just lived down the street . . ."

" . . . Mosher Street."

"That's right. So poor Charlie walks in the house. It's full of smoke, and everything's coated with greasy black soot."

"What a mess . . ."

" . . . the furniture, the lights, the curtains."

"And in the middle of all this, Yvette's pounding cross-handed on the piano."

"And the three girls are dancing . . ."

" . . . in frilly pink dresses, all filthy . . ."

" . . . their arms and faces black with soot."

"Charlie said it looked like a minstrel show."

I've heard this story countless times in my life. Every time I join in the peals of laughter floating down like petals on a spring breeze. Along with the laughter was also the unspoken certainty that the family would always be there to bolster us through life's grimmer times. But I chose to relinquish all that. I didn't play by the family rules. I was the one with the crazy dream and the shameless gall to pursue it. This time, as I venture off the familiar path into this new world, this new life of my own creation, I walk alone, and it terrifies me.

4

The Price

My first day on the job, I wake up at dawn, still on Eastern time. I lie in bed and rehash. I do this often now, in the deep, inscrutable hours of sheet-churning nights, and relive heart-slashing scripts.

Some day I'll remember this trying time with humor, labeling it "My Big Fat Portuguese Divorce." But now I still hear my father's scalding-crimson rage: *What's this bullshit about divorce? Just when are you gonna bloody grow up? This is gonna kill your grandmother.* (My sweet Nan! How could he say that?) I feel my heart's syncopation, notice the words tumbling around my brain like tennis shoes in a dryer, hear how lame they sounded when they came out: *We've had problems for years, Dad.*

Yeah . . . yeah. Your mother and I have had some problems, but we've worked them out. We didn't split up because she's a terrific woman. I draw in great gulps of air. *This isn't about you, Dad.* And I hear his reply: *You're being selfish. I don't want to hear any more of this.* Then came the anticlimactic *tuddle-unk* followed by blank quiet, and I remember how surprised I was that his slamming down the phone sounded so benign on my end of the line.

And Mom. *You expect too much from life. Sure, Bill's a little greenhorn-ish at times, but he's a good man. These dreams of yours are too far-fetched.* Then, the steely set of her chin. *Good luck, Mary, 'cause you're gonna need it.*

Next, the more poignant reactions from our family's first generation—Nan and my two great-aunts—the tears, the pleas, the clutching at chests. *Please, Mary, don't leave Bill. Please. Please don't.* Holding my ground before these frail women, women I'd never crossed before in my life.

My heart thuds through a breastbone damp with sweat. *How much is a dream worth?* I'm not the type of person who can shrug off the pain I've caused people and proceed unruffled through life. It rasps at my heart and causes me endless rumination, anxiety, and sleeplessness. Could I have stayed and made it work? Followed the family path, been happy in Massachusetts with Bill somehow?

Do you know how many women would give their right arm for what you have? As I recall, both Bill and my father had said this. What's wrong with me? Why couldn't I be happy tearing recipes from *Woman's Day*, spooning out Gerber's, and writing occasional checks to environmental organizations?

When I hear my teeth crunch together, I decide *enough*, leap out of bed, and flip on the light. On my dresser, amid photos of my family, long-gone pets, and grinning children I've counseled, is a card from Miriam—a cartoon of a squat girl in copious skirts and a sunbonnet. She's peering at a signpost with two arrows: the right-pointing one reads YOUR LIFE, the one pointing left, NO LONGER AN OPTION.

I've died and entered an afterlife. The old one is gone. Over. Yet, the old still combs the new, leaving stubborn ruts.

After breakfast I pull on my hiking boots and go outside to explore. As I creak open the door, the snowshoe hare hops by our picnic table. The morning brightens, but piles of pewter-colored clouds still hide the mountains. The silence is so compelling that I feel the need to tiptoe.

The housing complex consists of two elliptical streets at right angles to each other. My trailer is located in a row of similar trailers in various states of disrepair. Across the street are five or six mobile homes that belong to the retirees who work for the Moose concessions—the store and gas station near the post office—and the Jenny Lake Store. Several tired green bungalows line the northeast side. I immediately recognize them—Grand Teton's own CCC barracks houses. Even with listing roofs and sagging doors, they seem luxurious compared to the trailers. Beyond them I find a phone booth and a row of garages.

On the other oval, protected by tall pines, sit some log cabins. Most are modest, maybe two-bedroom structures. Two are huge two-story spectacles and could hardly be called "cabins." I later learn that these log buildings house some of the permanent park staff—the trails chief, the landscape architect, the electrician.

Throaty calls bellow through the morning, and I look up to see two sandhill cranes, wings flapping like quilts. Beyond them the rubble of the Gros Ventre Slide gouges the mountainside far to the east.

Surrounded by Engelmann spruces, the S&RM building makes a classic picture: logs weathered to a sepia color, rustic porch, peaked roof, mullioned windows. A green Volkswagen Beetle chugs into the parking lot, and a bearded man in a Park Service uniform unfolds himself from the driver's seat. His legs are so long I'm convinced he drives with his feet pressed against the grille.

I approach him. "I'm starting work here today. I'm Mary Beth."

He offers a massive hand. "Tim Nichols. Come on in." I connect the name with the telephone voice that offered me this job.

The inside of the building smells musty, with an overlay of some other faint, rotten-y odor, definitely organic. Tim's office is crowded with bookshelves, two desks, and a drafting table. Every horizontal surface is covered with documents and papers. Red lights flash on both telephones.

"Oh, man," he says. "More messages. Just can't keep up with 'em."

He scoops papers off a chair and invites me to sit, then he reclines in his chair, arms bent behind his head, feet plunked straight out. Dried mud crusts his boots; blades of grass are mashed in the grommets.

"We have three more seasonals due in today," he says. "A woman named Rachel, and two kids just out of high school that we hired as bio assistants. We really didn't need them, but they're sons of the superintendent's friends. You'll all be on the weed crew, with you as the chief."

I've never been called a "chief" before. Already I'm thinking cones-of-silence, shoe phones, and "*Missed it by that much.*" But *weeds?*

Reading my mind, Tim tacks on an afterthought. "But don't worry. We've got you lined up for some wildlife work, too. Trumpeter swans . . ."

Tim's sentence dies away and his dark eyes widen as a young beauty walks in. Rachel is in her early twenties, with corn-silk hair falling in a loose braid down her back. Her open face flaunts an earthy rawness—unrestrained, self-satisfied, woods-wise. I know at first glance she's that breezy woodswoman I long to be, comfortable in the backcountry from years of experience.

As she peels off her gray sweatshirt, the eighteen-year-olds walk in—Robert and Chris. Their eyes track Rachel unselfconsciously from her dazzling mane to her sturdy Asolo-clad feet, with an extended pause at her plump breasts barely contained by a second-skin tank top. I step backward, away from the light pouring in the window, hoping to hide the silver strands in my chocolate brown ponytail.

Once more the front door squeaks open and clunks shut. Footsteps. Making eye contact only with the floor, a towering guy with wavy, coal-colored hair and flecks of gray in his goatee strides into the office. Mid-thirties. A brooder, I think, noting the accordion-crimped forehead.

"Hey, it's the boss," Tim says, straightening. "Jace Callaway. Jace—our new seasonals."

Jace still studies the floor as he shakes hands with each of us. His handshake is trying-too-hard firm. After introductions he sits at one of the desks and opens an Environmental Impact Statement the size of a deep-dish casserole.

I inhale to calm the jitters in my midsection. Jace Callaway is a stunner. The ache of recent divorce haunts me as my gaze gravitates to his left hand, to the thin gold band.

Tim leads us out for a tour of the office. In the next room a fleshy, bald man in a Park Service dress uniform waves at us as he drones into a phone. Tim hurries us by. "That was the chief of S&RM, Mandell Thompson," he says.

We follow Tim through a central room whose walls are lined with maps, overstuffed bookshelves, desks, and a bank of cubbyholes being used as employee mail slots. In an adjacent office a thin-haired, heavy-set man in jeans and a plaid shirt sits back in an office chair with crossed arms and a thick document open on his lap. I swear he's asleep. Tim ushers us past with no explanation.

We come to another room stuffed with cupboards, tables, a refrigerator, and two upright freezers. Two thirty-something guys peer around a metal cabinet.

Tim introduces them as Glen and Mark, also seasonals, tall with the trim musculature of athletes. (What *is* it about this place? I've yet to meet an average-looking guy. They're all jaw-dropping hunks.) Mark's face sports a friendly grin. "Welcome to paradise," he says.

Tim explains that while they help out with all S&RM projects, Mark and Glen are raptor biologists—red-tailed hawks, great gray owls, bald eagles, peregrine falcons.

Tim opens a freezer door. "This is where we store the road kills that we use to bait the bear traps. And anything else we find interesting." Rifling through frosted plastic bags, he draws out an elk leg, a partially decomposed antelope head, a whole coyote pup, three unidentifiable songbirds, and a red-tailed hawk. The rank odor I'd noticed on entering the building is no longer a mystery. It stirs up long-forgotten college memories, my sinuses prickling with the smell of formalin—carving out a rat's ovaries and the gastrocnemius muscle in a frog's leg, smuggling a partially dissected cat in a plastic bag into my dorm room so I could work on it after lab hours. Then later, in grad school, kneeling in brittle fall leaves to collect the sour-smelling contents of a deer's stomach at a hunter check station. I can't deny this love of the putrid that's so characteristic of bio majors.

Tim leans around the freezers muttering, "Should be one more back here someplace . . . Julian?" In a far corner of the room, in a cave carved out among gray cabinets, we find a rangy guy slouched at his desk and focused on his computer screen. Beside him another desk is piled with books and documents. For a few minutes we all stand behind him and stare at his hair. It's frizzy and auburn, tied with a rubber band into a ponytail barely longer than a question mark.

"This is Julian Stewart. He's a PhD student at U of M up in Missoula," Tim says. Still the guy doesn't acknowledge us. With an oblique smile, Tim continues, "Julian does his best work when he's asleep." Then he raps on a metal cabinet and shouts, "*Julian.*"

"*EE-yah.*" Julian's chair dips backward; his arms flail as he scrambles for balance. Then he swivels his chair around, leans back, and plants an ankle on the opposite knee. Sour-faced, he angles his arms across his chest and plows a thumb through his beard.

Good save, I think. Like Jace, Julian sports a cleft between his brows as deep as the Marianas Trench. He wears understated wire-rims and seems fully aware of his craggy handsomeness. But Julian seems to have the social graces of a mollusk. "Yut. Yut. Yut. Yut," he says, giving each of our hands an uninterested shake.

"Tell 'em about your research," Tim says.

"Hm-m-m, let's see." Julian blinks, then points and straightens his foot. "I'm studying predator-prey interactions in the park. Mainly the big carnivores— grizzly bear, mountain lion, lynx—and their prey—moose, bighorn sheep, elk, deer, pronghorn. And I help Jace, Mark, and Glen with some raptor work, too— eagles, peregrines, red-tails." His tone is matter-of-fact, as if he's describing the daily tasks of a vacuum cleaner salesman.

"*Way* cool," Robert says.

Back in his office Tim reaches into a plastic grocery bag and hands each of us two aluminum traps the size of Animal Cracker boxes. "You might need these for your trailer mice. Just don't let them go in the backyard, or they'll beat you home." He shows us the spring mechanism on the trap doors. "They like oatmeal and peanut butter.

"And here are you guys's radios. And remember: You lose a radio? You sign over your firstborn child to Uncle Sam, along with your choice of limbs." His laugh is wheezy as he passes out hand-held Motorola radios, chargers, and cards listing all the park employees with their radio call numbers. "We're the three hundreds. Mandell's 3-1-0, Jace is 3-1-1, and on down the line."

I heft the radio in my hand. *Ah, the trappings.* Like the reassuring tinkle of keys in my pocket, this radio is opening a door to my dream.

The phone rings but Tim makes no move to answer it. Instead, he picks up a letter from his desk and seems to get lost in it.

Chris offers half of his granola bar to Rachel. She accepts it, beaming like sunrise. This small gesture of kindness between them, so innocent, ripples me with longing.

Chris faces me. "So where are you from, Mary Beth?"

"Dartmouth, Massachusetts," I say. Nobody knows the town of Dartmouth. Everyone confuses it with the Ivy League college in Hanover, New Hampshire. So I start to explain. "It's on the southeast coast, a suburb of New Bedford, the whaling city . . ."

"No kidding! I know Dartmouth."

"You *do?*"

"You know Pauline Persons?"

I lift. "*Pauline?* Sure. We graduated from high school together." I'm grooving on that cozy jolt of familiarity and common ground. Even though he's still a teenager, we know someone in common. Maybe I won't feel so out of place here after all.

Chris pops the last of the granola bar into his mouth. "She's my stepmother," he says.

5

Places

On a day drenched in burly yellow light, Tim sends Rachel, Robert, Chris, and me to the Seasonal Naturalist orientation. I'm eager to start learning about this new home of mine, and traveling around the park in a bus with those in the know should be a slick way to do it. And relaxed, too. While the naturalists will have to quickly learn a barrage of facts they can present to the public in campfire programs, we biologists will have plenty of time to assimilate the new knowledge in our more solitary work environment.

I'm energetic and bubbly today. No pining over my recent losses. Today I feel I can move forward and embrace this new life with courage and flair.

We meet the naturalists milling around the bus outside park headquarters. Just as I expected: a bunch of college kids. But then another group emerges from the building, people closer to my age and showing more wear on their faces. They are the long-term seasonal naturalists—Jackie Skaggs, Linelle Wagner, Katy Duffy, Don Cushman. With years of experience among them, they return year after year to this park that they love, and interpret its resources to millions of visitors.

As the bus heads north, Jackie, whose generous curves accent her gray uniform shirt, points out the peaks: the Grand Teton with its northward list, Middle Teton with its dike of igneous rock seeming to split it vertically in two, the hard-to-see South Teton. And the lesser known but just as prominent Nez Perce, Teewinot, Mount Owen, Buck Mountain, Static Peak. Between the mountains are the canyons I would come to know and love: Granite, Open, Death, Cascade, Paintbrush.

Jackie explains that French trappers came through here in the 1800s and named the mountains *Les Trois Tetons*, the three breasts. They'd also been called "Pilot Knobs" by explorers who sighted them as landmarks as they came over Union Pass. The Shoshoni Indians called the mountains "Hoary Headed Fathers." Jackson Hole was named in 1829 for David Jackson, a partner of Jedediah Smith in the Rocky Mountain Fur Company. The trappers called a valley ringed by mountains a "hole." First called Jackson's Hole, the name was later shortened to Jackson Hole.

The first white man to visit the area was supposedly John Colter, another fur trapper. Most historians believe he came over Togwotee Pass to the northeast, and departed over Teton Pass to the southwest in the winter of 1807–1808. Colter Bay was named for him, as was Colter Canyon on the west side of Jackson Lake.

At 13,770 feet, the Grand Teton isn't as high as the famed Colorado "fourteeners," but the Teton view is unique because these mountains loom up seven thousand feet above the valley floor. In Colorado, smaller foothills slope up to the high peaks. The Tetons have no foothills because of the unique geology of the Jackson Hole Valley.

"The Teton Fault lies along the base of the mountains," Jackie says, holding her hands up, fingertips to fingertips, "and the valley, over time, is sinking." She slips one hand under the other. "This causes an uplift in the mountains, making them appear even higher."

Gazing at the jagged crests, I think of my ancestors on Faial and São Jorge, looking across the sea to the nearby island of Pico, whose namesake mountain rises seven thousand feet above the ocean. But unlike the stark Grand, Pico is rife with hydrangeas and belladonna lilies, and its volcanic summit continually vents sulfur gas.

The bus winds up Pacific Creek Road to Emma Matilda Lake, where Katy steps up smiling, binoculars in hand. Salty black curls flounce under her felt ranger hat. "Let's find some birds," she says, leading us off the bus.

We walk through different habitat types—lodgepole pine, aspen, sagebrush, willow wetland—and Katy identifies every bird we see. Standing behind her, Don raises his hand above her head and points downward. "Now you know why we call her 'the Bird Lady of Grand Teton.'"

I scribble. Yellow-rumped warbler. Red-tailed hawk. Swainson's thrush. Ruby-crowned kinglet. Three-toed woodpecker. I've got a lot to learn. Years ago when I studied ornithology at Virginia Tech, I discovered I lacked the bird identification gene. Give me something stationary, like plants. Dendrology had been a snap, even in the prolific eastern forests.

"*Look.* There . . ." Binoculars at her eyes, Katy dips one hand in front of her, imitating the flight pattern of a raptor just above the sagebrush. "Northern harrier. See the white rump? That's the thing to watch for. And see how it flies? It stays low, looking for prey. They used to call them 'marsh hawks.'"

Ah, marsh hawks I remember. Now they're changing bird names on me. I glance at the youthful faces around me.

Near a willow thicket we find a shady lunch spot. Rachel and I sit together and compare notes as we eat. Munching on a Kit Kat, Chris stretches out on the ground at Rachel's feet. Soft-eyed, he gazes at her. "Awesome, huh?" he asks.

I'm not sure whether he means Rachel or the scenery.

"It *is* awesome," she says. "I'm so happy to be back in the Tetons."

"So you worked here before?"

"Not for the park. I waited tables at Colter Bay for the Lodge Company."

I bristle. That could have been me. My senior year in college, I heard about summer job openings with a concessions company in Montana's Glacier National Park. It was the first I'd ever heard about summer work in national parks. On a whim I applied and was offered a hostess job at the Lake Mac-Donald Lodge Restaurant. My parents and then-fiancé were incredulous that, with my new biology degree, I'd consider doing something so asinine. (A similar reaction beset my cousin and college classmate Meg's decision to take a job picking strawberries on Cape Cod that summer.) My father piled me into the Pontiac Catalina and drove me to an interview at a botany laboratory within commuting distance of home. I got the job, and my Rocky Mountain bug went untreated.

"*Cool,* Rachel." Chris's eyebrows peak. "You must know all the ins and outs of the park. Hey, let's go on a hike sometime. You could show me around."

"*Sure.*" Rachel nods, her face an open door. "That sounds like fun."

God, she's falling for this? Yesterday she was telling me she has a boyfriend.

Robert approaches and collapses to the ground beside us.

"So where are you guys from?" I ask.

Chris is from Connecticut; Robert, Texas. They both graduated from high school this year. Chris is headed to Yale; Robert has no plans. As I learn more about them, I like them more.

Chris turns to me. "So, Mary Beth, what's this like for you?"

"What do you mean?"

"I mean, starting out again as a single woman in a place like this, at *your* age."

My cheeks burn. This little twit is going to be a cramp in my side. "It's *great*, Chris," I say, one eye pinching with unabashed sarcasm. "I had incredible adventures in the seventies, and I get to have them again now."

I lean on my elbow and listen to the warblers twittering through the willows. I'm steamed. If I'm going to be the *grande dame* of S&RM, then, by golly, I'll have to prove myself.

At the end of the day, I borrow an armload of field guides from the office bookshelves and head out. Sunlight boils down the canyons. Hugging the books to my chest, I spot Glen and Jace unloading field gear from a tan Bronco in the parking lot. I stride over to them, but they don't look up.

"Hi, guys," I say, with a wide grin.

Jace's face sweeps in my direction, but I never see his eyes. "Hey." He swings a backpack over one shoulder, then leans back into the truck. When he emerges, he's holding a spotting scope in one hand and a clipboard in the other. His mouth seems frozen in apathy. I wonder if some congenital defect has left him lacking a few smiling muscles.

On the driver's side Glen battles with something behind the seat. "*Damn*," he says, forcing. Looks to me like a backpack strap has snagged in the seat track.

"Need some help?" I ask.

"Nope," says Glen.

"Got it," Jace says.

I keep on. "Been out in the field?" *Duh*. It's obvious, I know, but I'm exhausting my supply of communication starters.

Having extricated the pack, Glen loops his binoculars over his neck. "Raptor surveys" squeaks from his constricted throat. He kicks the truck door shut and follows Jace to the building.

I skip around to catch up. "Find anything?"

"Yep."

When they enter the building, neither looks back to hold open the door for me. I stand on the porch and watch the heavy door slam on their heels.

Where I come from we'd call this behavior rude. I should feel put off and insulted, but I don't yet. I'm still too full of the day, eager to get out in the field tomorrow. But between the office and my trailer, something alights on my shoulder and I begin to feel its weight. Jace and Glen, I realize, hold their knowledge and experience in tightly clamped fists, and none of us seasonals would be able to pry it out of them.

Have I wound up in a place where edgy individualism trumps kindness? Have I focused on *place* at the expense of the human element in my new world?

I was once a "wildlifer" grad student—enamored of animals, forests, mountains—working hard to be tough and strong, qualities that would secure my place in that world. All the nurturing that brought me there was invisible to me. But when I became a counselor, I leaped to another level. Compassion, thoughtfulness, and respect now bloom as the perennial flowers that sprout through life's churning mud.

The cost of this life change suddenly seems exorbitant. I think of my Nan as she fingers her three daily rosaries (one each for my mother, my sister, and me), my parents, ex-husband, great-aunts, all distraught over the choice I've made. Have I turned my back on the people who love me to come to a place without heart? This place of indestructible youth, robust health, and unsquelched desires is foreign to me. The world I've left behind of traditions, obligations, and expectations now seems paltry and quaint, as if it were lifted from the pages of a Louisa May Alcott novel. I feel I belong in neither world. I'm on some gaseous planet with no footing to ground me.

The weight on my shoulder finds its way into my skull, turns cold, and presses at my eyeballs. *Too late . . . too late . . . too late.* The words strum through my brain like an off-key chant.

Despite the strains of gospel music leaking out from Brenda's closed door, the trailer feels like a tomb when I enter. I rush to my room and collapse on the bed. On the far wall I've pinned a poster—a photo of thunderheads over Mounts Owen and Teewinot with the words, "God Bless Wyoming, and Keep It Wild." This was the last entry in the diary of fifteen-year-old Helen Mettler, who fell to her death in Avalanche Canyon in 1925.

My insides heave as I descend into the nether realm of *saudade*.

❦

To Azoreans, death is never far away—just out of view, a mere breath-puff beyond one's peripheral vision. It might be because these islands have a habit of grinding around and turning themselves inside out.

Atlantis theories aside, current wisdom maintains that the islands formed from water-cooled lava that seeped from a crack in the ocean floor to create the undersea mountain range known as the Mid-Atlantic Ridge. The Azores are the tips of these mountains peeking above the water surface. Running the entire length of the Atlantic Ocean, the Mid-Atlantic Ridge consists of nearly a hundred volcanoes, some active and some dormant. Pico Alto, on the island of Pico, is the highest of these volcanoes at 7,711 feet. All of the Azorean islands have central *caldeiras,* craters, and many have hot springs. Enterprising residents of the town of Furnas, São Miguel, cook pots of meat and vegetable stew, *cozido,* in underground ovens heated by the island's hot springs.

Throughout recorded history, earthquakes and volcanic eruptions have sporadically rocked the Azores, often burying entire villages within seconds and taking many lives. On my ancestral island of Faial stands a half-buried lighthouse at the Vulcão dos Capelinhos, a barren stretch of volcanic soil now being used by nesting shearwaters. Over the course of a year, 1957-1958, while over two hundred earthquakes rumbled, submarine volcanoes spewed more than thirty million tons of black ash and flaming lava high into the air. Some of this boiled-up material formed a new island that was connected to Faial by an isthmus, adding more than a square mile to the island's area. So many homes and farms were destroyed by the eruption that then-senator John F. Kennedy of Massachusetts and Senator John Pastore of Rhode Island sponsored the "Azorean Refugee Act," which enabled many Azoreans to emigrate to the United States.

The silver lining is that volcanic outflows bring fertility to island soils. Anything grows. Shrubs and flowers—azaleas, hydrangeas, lilies, irises, roses—grow in island fields, and Azoreans cultivate a staggering variety of vegetables, fruits, and grains.

But the history of violent upheavals has imprinted itself into the collective consciousness of the Azorean people, resulting in a strange mix of optimism for plentiful harvests and fatalism about life events. Those who choose to live there do so with courage, determination, fierce devotion to family, and a dogged belief that religious faith will protect them beyond death.

No doubt arising from this cultural fatalism is the emotion of *saudade,* a word that's considered untranslatable into English. As I understand it, *saudade* is an anguished longing for people, times, or places that are no longer in one's life, or even a wishful dreaming about events that never occurred. Compared to nostalgia, which is limited, *saudade* is a persistent melancholy that pervades the present and extends to the future.

Saudade begat the Creature, as I've come to call it, the family curse, along with the songs and stories and blind devotion. Insidious and cunning, it stalks the generations, permeating our family culture with the burning question: *What's the use?* When things don't go well, when uncontrollable circumstances dash hopes, when people disappoint, a terrifying beast forms out of the fog and haunts us. Slights and tragedies are coddled, watered, and sunlit. We lace them together like dark, flamboyant flowers and wear them with pride around our necks—leis of pain.

True to *saudade*, the past I pine for never really existed. Although based on innocent love, my marriage was not the boatload of emotional riches every woman yearns for. I felt stifled and bored, and I wanted a bigger life. But what I'm beginning to learn is this: Just being married—even unhappily—kept the Creature at bay for fifteen years. Bill was always there, a safety net, when hardships came. Now I'm on my own.

And something's going to crash; I just know it. Like the Azoreans who never know when their island's *caldeira* might blow and spit molten lava over the rim, I worry that, even if the Teton fault doesn't scrape into "The Big One," a pebble might fall into this groove of mine that seems to fit so well. Everything I've fought for might turn out to be nothing but gossamer fluff.

I can't give in to it. Determined to outwit the Creature, I pull myself up and head outside for a walk.

Down the street is a tan and white trailer in similar condition to mine. As I approach, I catch a whiff of lighter fluid as charcoal burns in a hibachi grill on the picnic table. The trailer's side window slides open and a voice calls out. "Hi, Mary Beth."

If I've learned only one thing through this drama it's this: The universe blows holes into your darkest moments so light can flood in.

"*Rachel.* You live here?"

The door opens to an angelic vision. Even in drab gray shorts and a faded blue T-shirt, Rachel's sunny hair and radiant smile chase the Creature back into its lair.

"I think we got the *House Beautiful* trailers," she says.

I notice she, too, has a bucket on her floor to catch drips.

"For sure." I laugh. "There'll be a special decorating issue out this summer featuring our two trailers right alongside the Biltmore and Rockefeller mansions."

Her head drops back into an unselfconscious cackle, then she gestures toward the kitchen. "Mary Beth, this is Eric."

Slicing cucumbers at the counter is a towering Nordic in a Grand Teton Lodge Company polo shirt. "So you're Mary Beth. Rachel's been telling me about you."

The boyfriend. *Man.* Sheaf of sundrenched hair. Eyes clear and bottomless as oceans. All sinew and muscle. I just want to gawk at his virile beauty, but I control myself. I feel very single.

"Hey, do you have plans for dinner, Mary Beth?" Rachel asks.

"Uh, well . . . no."

"Eric caught some trout today. We're going to grill it." She hefts a dense loaf off the counter. "I got this great bread from the Bunnery, and we'll have salad, too. Why don't you join us?"

What? Back home meals are planned out well in advance, and only your parents or grandparents invite you to stay for dinner if you happen to drop by while they're cooking it. A dinner invitation is made days, preferably a week, in advance, with guests offering to bring a dish. I actually think of refusing. *You don't have enough. . . . You weren't expecting company. . . . I don't want to eat all your food. . . . I'll have my canned soup, and I'll be fine.* The "I don't want to be a bother" drivel that the women in my family excel at.

Someone's tossing you a life preserver—for God's sake, grab it. "Thanks, Rachel, I'd love to," I say. "I've got some potatoes at home. I could bring them over."

"Cool," Rachel says. "We'll make potato salad."

We cook and eat and chat in the yard until the scent of fir hovers on the night chill and stars dot the blackening sky. Chris and Robert stroll by, and Rachel invites them over to toast marshmallows on sticks we find under the trees.

It's after eleven when I return to my trailer. *I can get into this after-hours mingling with coworkers,* I think as I brush my teeth and snug into bed. Even *saudade* and the Creature can't haunt me tonight. My dreams are of the blue-globed hydrangeas that edge the rim of Faial's *caldeira*.

6

Learning Curve

Tim invites us to an "office social" at his house in Moose where I meet his wife, Jennifer, and their two toddlers, Sophie and Tommy. Jace and his wife, Janet, are there with their three-year-old, Elsa. Glen and Mark bring perky, suntanned wives; Glen and his wife pass a pink-clad baby back and forth between them. When the food is ready, the moms corral the kids in the living room, while Rachel and I escape to the yard to sample elk and antelope meat, and talk wildlife and environmental conservation with the guys. The conversation resonates with me, and I feel smart, relaxed yet stimulated.

The next morning we follow Dr. Richard Shaw, a botany professor from Utah State University and the author of a book I just bought at the visitor center, *Plants of Yellowstone and Grand Teton National Parks*. Starting at the Death Canyon Trailhead, we hike the shady trail to the Phelps Lake Overlook.

When those callused edges of your heart have been recently flayed off, leaving behind a raw, thirsty, beating pulp, it's your brain that heals them by absorbing details. Those plants I learned in my first years at Grand Teton have stayed with me, unlike any I've tried to learn since.

Artemisia tridentata, big sagebrush
Balsamorhiza sagittata, arrowleaf balsamroot
Smilacina racemosa, false solomon's seal
Streptopus amplexifolius, claspleaf twisted-stalk
Viola canadensis, Canada violet
Arnica cordifolia, heartleaf arnica

I already know most of the trees: the deciduous aspen, cottonwood, serviceberry, and hawthorn; and the evergreen subalpine fir, blue and Engelmann spruces, lodgepole and limber pines, Douglas fir. The purple-coned whitebark pine, whose calorie-rich nuts help fatten grizzly bears for the winter, lives only at elevations above 8,500 feet. One of the world's largest whitebark pines, Dr. Shaw explains, grows in Cascade Canyon. Nearly six feet in diameter, this tree is probably four hundred years old.

To us, now, these forests, save for occasional cleansing fires, will thrive forever. We walk, exuberant, through the moist shade, blessedly ignorant that, in just a few years, huge swaths of our beloved western pine forests will succumb to bark beetle infestations. Entire mountainsides will rust over with dead trees. The outbreak will begin in the lodgepole forests, but over time, rising global temperatures will enable the beetles to spread to higher elevations, and whitebark pines, already weakened by the blister rust fungus, will also start to die. In less than two decades, four million acres of conifer forests in Wyoming and Colorado will be decimated, the trunks of individual trees sporting the beetles' telltale plugs of sap called "pitch tubes."

After a wildflower walk along the Snake River, we slosh through a knee-deep creek in our hiking boots. Back on dry ground, we pour cupfuls of water from our boots. Then we wring out our socks, paste them back on our feet, and slip back into soggy boots. But the day is warm and dry, and I'm loving this forest scene with birdsong bubbling all around and easy banter with my coworkers.

We head to a cabin belonging to Mardy Murie, noted darling of the environmental movement. On the way I learn that Mardy grew up in Alaska and was the first woman to graduate from the University of Alaska in Fairbanks. She married her illustrious husband, biologist Olaus Murie, in 1924, and for their honeymoon, the couple traveled by dogsled through the arctic wilderness studying Alaskan caribou. Next they moved here to Jackson Hole, where Olaus was assigned by his employer, the US Bureau of Biological Survey, to study the Jackson Hole elk herd. Mardy and their children assisted Olaus with his elk studies in the Absaroka Range near Yellowstone and in Moose Basin, an area I will come to love in Grand Teton's northern wilderness. In 1950, when Olaus became president of the Wilderness Society, this cabin on whose porch we now gather served as the unofficial Wilderness Society headquarters.

Mardy Murie, now nearly ninety, sits in a wicker chair on the porch and gazes westward at the mountains. Dressed in white pants, teal blouse, and navy cardigan, she's a stately woman with effervescent snowy hair and sky blue eyes.

Park spokeswoman Linda Olson talks of Mardy's accomplishments. She wrote two books—*Two in the Far North* about her experiences in Alaska, and *Wapiti Wilderness,* jointly written with Olaus, about living, working, and raising their family in Jackson Hole. After Olaus's death in 1963, Mardy continued to work for passage of the Wilderness Act and the Alaska National Interest Lands Conservation Act. She was invited to Washington, DC, in 1964 to witness President Lyndon Johnson sign the Wilderness Act, which protected millions of acres of wilderness throughout the country. Sixteen years later, she stood beside President Carter as he signed the Alaska Lands Act into law. Her tireless conservation work has won her many awards, including the Audubon Medal, the John Muir Award, and the Robert Marshall Conservation Award.

With yearning hearts, we crowd around her, disciples to guru, hungry for bits of wisdom that will tie it all together for us. But while Linda chatters on, Mardy is silent, her eyes focused on the mountains until Jackie takes Mardy's hand and looks into her eyes. "I understand you and Olaus liked to dance," she says.

Mardy's face lights up. "We *loved* to dance. We danced in the cabin in Alaska. And when we lived on the elk refuge we went dancing in Jackson."

While her story fuels my fires of environmentalism, I feel sad hearing of her rich life. She's been widowed for nearly thirty years and now faces the losses of old age. She was born in 1902, just two years before my own grandmother. I wish I could have known her twenty years ago.

Someone asks her, "If you could live your life over, what would you do differently?"

Her stare settles on the cottonwoods beyond the meadow that is her front yard. "I'd be more radical about the environment," she says.

———

"You're into all these fringe causes, Mary. No wonder you don't have any *normal* friends."

This is what Bill said to me when I pulled out a canvas bag at a Piggly Wiggly Market in Virginia years ago. The checkout clerk looked for a price tag on it, to ring it up with my groceries.

"Oh, no," I said. "I brought that to carry my groceries so you don't have to put them in a paper bag. I'm saving trees, see?" I pointed at the logo on the front of the bag—a leafy maple with the words SAVE A TREE printed above it.

The clerk, a plump woman with a prominent gap between her front teeth, raised her eyebrows and slid the sack behind her to the bagger, a gangly teenage boy. He twirled the bag on the rubber belt until he figured out it had handles.

Bill's comment about my friends referred to the hippie-leaning environmentalists I'd met in grad school who participated in the first Earth Day, abhorred high fashion, and shunned traditional gender stereotypes.

So years later when I run into Katy after work one day at Moose's main attraction, Dornan's store and bar, and we sit on the wooden step out front and talk about the earth's losses—forests, clean water, wildlife, arable land—and when she says that human overpopulation is the greatest threat to the planet, and having more than one or two kids these days is like reaching into the candy jar and taking more than your share, I know I've found my tribe.

Taking cues from Katy, Rachel, and other woodswomen I meet, I stop shaving, relinquish fussy fetishes of mainstream culture like deodorant and blow dryers, and start braiding my shoulder-length hair.

But after a few weeks, my legs look like those of the swarthy Portuguese fishermen that undoubtedly pepper my ancestry. And my hair, unlike Rachel's tractable mane, will not stay in a braid. Instead, it radiates and tangles like the hibernaculum of garter snakes under the Snake River bridge.

But while some rituals of the culture must stay, I find myself beaming as this new life of mine unfolds.

7

Digging In

Clouds scud over the horizon around the Kelly Hayfields, and gusts beat up dust devils around Robert, Rachel, and me. I've never experienced such a vast, flat, treeless space, and it humbles me. Pronghorn antelope, curious about our pickup truck, amble close enough to sniff us, then pronk away, their hooves gouging the dry earth. Riding the wind are shrill whistles of western meadowlarks, hoarse shrieks of sandhill cranes.

Nearby, three white-footed *Peromyscus,* deer mice, explore their new prairie home, courtesy of a government-sponsored move from our Beaver Creek trailers in the back of our truck. Chances are good they'll become part of the food chain before we reset the traps in our trailers tonight.

Far to the south a herd of horses gallops; even at this distance, we feel the earth shudder beneath their hooves. These horses, and the cattle summering at the Elk Ranch and other park areas, are the reason I'm here. A historic deal with local ranchers to allow grazing in the park spawned an ongoing clash between park biologists and the ranching community. Exotic plants introduced by seeds lodged in tire treads or carried by livestock and birds are quick to invade disturbed soil, such as grazed pastures, roadsides, and ditch banks. Years of grazing in the Kelly Hayfields have helped establish a thriving population of exotic weeds that drive out native plants.

Rachel and I kneel on the ground with our bible *Weeds of the West* between us. In square-meter plots bounded by Rebar stakes and string, we count musk thistle rosettes. Our counts will provide baseline data for a scientific study to test the effectiveness of different herbicides.

Tim brought us here yesterday to show us how to identify musk thistle, one of Grand Teton's most common and invasive weeds. Native to southern Europe and western Asia, *Carduus nutans,* or CANU as we abbreviate it, was accidentally introduced to the United States in the early 1900s. A biennial, CANU needs two years to complete its life cycle. Year one brings shiny rosettes of lobed leaves tipped with fine spines. In its second year pink blossoms shoot up on prickly tall stems, then go to seed. Musk thistle joins more than twenty thousand plant species in one of the world's largest plant families, Asteraceae, the sunflower family, or the "composites." Its siblings include native sunflower, yarrow, aster, and balsamroot, and other exotics like western salsify, oxeye daisy, dandelion, and tansy.

As a breeze rolls in, I sniff a dry, acrid smell. Rachel tips her head, inhales, and coughs. "Ooh, *skanky,*" she says.

I jump up, windmill my arms. "Robert! Stop! You're upwind of us and the herbicide's blowing this way."

Robert wheels around. "*What?*" He looks cartoonish in a white paper suit, Texas Rangers ball cap, safety goggles, and a red bandanna covering his mouth and nose, bandito-style. He was supposed to help us count plants, but he kept losing track and having to start over whenever he reached triple-digit numbers. So we sent him into the hayfields with a sloshing container of 2,4-D herbicide in a backpack sprayer. Unsure of his ability to identify the rosettes, I found an area far from our plots with little else but musk thistle growing. Apparently, he's strayed closer to us.

"Why don't you spray over there, beyond the plots?" I gesture to an area downwind, beyond a decrepit shed.

Rachel shakes her head. "Clueless wonder."

"Hey! Ya see that?" Robert yells.

" . . . ninety-seven, ninety-eight, ninety-nine, one hundred. *What?*" Rachel mashes down the already counted rosettes with one gloved hand.

"I don't know. Some big bird." He points at a raptor sailing low over the sagebrush.

I recognize the white rump patch. "Harrier," I say.

"How much longer do we gotta be out here?" Robert asks, walking back toward us, dragging the sprayer wand on the ground. He whips off his goggles. The bandanna hangs limp around his neck like a sunburnt snakeskin.

"Until we finish counting."

"Geez. I'm tired. We partied again last night. Didn't get to bed till two."

"3-1-5, 3-1-2." Tim's calling me on the radio.

I pull out the radio from my belt holster. "3-1-5."

"I just picked up a coupla cartons from R&R for you and Rachel. They were delivered to the Maintenance building so I brought 'em up to the office."

"*Yee-ha!*" Rachel squeals. "Our uniforms."

"Thanks, Tim," I say.

As I delve back into the counting, I hear singing. Imitating Ritchie Valens, Robert croons "Oh, Donna" into a chin-high musk thistle stalk like it's a vintage Ed Sullivan microphone. He gyrates his body under the weight of the backpack sprayer.

"Oh, *jeez*. . . ." I grab my stomach in a giggling fit.

We hurry through the rest of the counting, then roll into the front seat of the dented, bilious green pickup we've christened "Nellie." I grasp the steering wheel, press down the clutch, turn the key. Nothing happens. I release the clutch, then press it down farther. Still nothing.

"*Dammit*, Nellie," Rachel says.

We fish out jumper cables from the tool box and raise the truck hood. *Yugh, what's this?* A desiccated elk jaw sitting on the engine block. I pincer it out with thumb and forefinger and hurl it away while Rachel calls Dispatch to ask if anyone's working nearby who could give us a jump. Soon a Park Service truck approaches on the two-track. It's Doug Bonner from Maintenance. "I was heading down the Antelope Flats Road and heard your call," he says.

Back at the office we tear into our cartons. In mine are a pair of Vasque Sundowner hiking boots, two pairs of green denim jeans, a ball cap, three gray shirts, a dark green fleece jacket, and a Gore-Tex rain jacket. The shirts, cap, and jackets all sport the NPS arrowhead patch.

I finger one embroidered patch. Smooth mounds of brown, white, and green threads form a silhouette of a bison against a background of snow-capped mountains and conifer spires. Written in blocky white letters above the mountains are the words "National Park Service."

Tim hands us each a pair of official green NPS coveralls. "No more tissue paper suits. You got the real thing now." He drags a tome off a bookshelf and hands it to Rachel. "For your reading pleasure," he says.

She sits in an office chair with NPS-43, *Uniform Wear Standards*, on her lap. "Listen to this, Mary Beth," she says, forefinger poised on a page. "'Shirt sleeves should be no more than one-half inch beyond coat sleeve ends. . . . Pens and pencils must not visibly protrude more than a quarter inch from the tops of pockets. . . . Bottoms of pants must hang no lower than the top of the heel and no higher than three inches above the ground. . . . Pants bottoms should be as close to parallel with the ground as possible . . .'"

"Oh my *God*." I read over her shoulder. "'Socks must not sag. . . . Excess strap on gaiters must be tucked in and not left dangling. . . . Name tags are worn over the right pocket. They must be level, centered and one-eighth of an inch (the width of a nickel) above the top of the pocket flap . . .'" Wrinkling my nose, I look at Rachel. "Is this for real?"

"And how about 'Beards must be long enough to indicate that the beard is intentional rather than giving the appearance that the wearer has been negligent in shaving.'" She crows in laughter. "And listen to this: 'Any form of haircut which draws more attention than the uniform and detracts from the wearer's authority is prohibited.'"

It's our first experience with a pompous government document, and we're folded over laughing when Tim walks in.

"So, Tim," I say, "this means I can't get a mohawk?"

His muffled laugh is accompanied by rhythmic lifts of his shoulders. "If I see your socks sagging, you're outta here."

"Is that a beard, Tim?" Rachel asks. "Or have you been negligent in shaving? Mary Beth, pass me that ruler."

Just then Jace enters, eyes downcast, a manila envelope in one hand. He attempts a smile, but his face seems cast in plaster. With a staccato, ill-at-ease motion he places the envelope in one of the mail cubbies. His name pin appears to be exactly a nickel's width above his pocket flap.

Tim points to a flyer tacked above the mailboxes. "Hey, I don't know if you're interested, but there's a barn dance next Friday night." He flips his thumb eastward. "At the Hunter Barn in Kelly."

Jace dips his hands into his pockets. "Yeah. I heard about it." Turtlelike, he draws his neck down into a pit between his shoulders, then turns on his heels and walks out.

"The Spring Fling is next weekend?" Rachel's eyes light up. "Mary Beth, you'd love it. We *have* to go."

"What's a barn dance?"

"It's a country dance in an old barn," Rachel says. "With live, old-timey music."

I'm charmed by the idea.

"The park employee association puts it on every summer," Tim says. "It's always a good time."

"A *great* time," Rachel says.

Tim checks his watch. "I guess it's quittin' time, but here's what's on tap for tomorrow. I'm taking the wonderboys up to Flagg Ranch to pull mullein. Rachel, you need to help Julian with a peregrine survey. And Mary Beth, I'd like you to spray some weeds at Jenny Lake."

Dumping spaghetti into a colander that evening, I happen to look out the window as Chris and Robert walk by and knock on Rachel's door. My curious streak takes over, and I rush to another window for a better view. The door opens and her bright smile welcomes them in. To these hormone-driven teenagers, Rachel must seem not only supremely hot, but close enough in age as to be accessible.

At the hayfields this afternoon, Rachel told me that she and Eric broke it off and are now just "good friends." No hurt feelings, just time to move on. I'm curious: Does that mean they sleep with other people now? Because I spent my whole adult life with the same man, these questions about relationships plague me. What would it be like to sleep with someone else?

Mom and Dad call later. "Bill's sure having a hard time," Dad says. "It's pathetic to see him bumping around that house all alone." Then Mom gets on the phone. "You're such a militant feminist," she says, "that no man would ever want you again."

I admit I did things that annoyed Bill—like keeping my maiden name and wearing second-hand clothes out to dinner. On the other hand, I'm a modern woman and an environmentalist; I recycle. Was I wrong to ignore his embarrassment? Should I have abandoned my strongest convictions to keep him happy? What do we owe our husbands to maintain marital stability? (It never occurs to me to ask, "What do our husbands owe us?")

Feeling remorseful, I call Bill. "Don't expect me to stay single," he says, "because you know I hate being alone."

His comment irritates me. Of course I don't expect him to stay single. Then I understand what he's getting at. "Are you dating someone?"

"Well, since you asked . . ."

Leah Buckley is a shapely redhead from our high school class who lives in the neighborhood with her two kids. I shouldn't be surprised. Bill loves kids. He's getting on with his life.

There's an empty space inside my heart. It's bowl-shaped and diamond-hard.

8

Hopping on Board

"You're always supposed to put your husband first, even before your children. A priest told me that."

This is what I overheard Granny tell Mom one day when I was in the third grade. I got squirmy-gutted as my eyes flashed in horror. Would she really choose Dad over us if something bad happened? My imagination took flight. We'd all be on a boat when a gale wind would come up, flinging Dad, Nancy, and me into the thrashing sea. Mom would stand on the deck with one life preserver. Her frantic gaze would go from one to the other of us, but in the end, she'd throw the ring to Dad, leaving Nancy and me gulping water, going down, down, down to live with the fishes. (Why not just put cement boots on us now and get it over with?) Then she and Dad would buy a rose-covered cottage on Nantucket, and they'd putter the harbors in an outboard-powered dinghy and live on bluefish and quahogs and clams. And when she died she would still go to heaven after letting her children drown, because the priest said your husband comes first.

There was no doubt in my mind that if Dad had *really* wanted to move to Idaho, all he had to do was say so, and I would have been a western girl. At first there would have been many rosaries and novenas said, but the move would have eventually been blessed, accepted as God's will, because this is how the world works: Men chart the course and women step in line behind them. There was only one way I could both follow my dream and stay in the family's good graces at the same time: *Hop on board.* In my mind a task materialized: Find a fetching man with the same dream. Someone strong and self-reliant, a hunter-gatherer, who lives in a log cabin in the mountains. Any mountains would do, as long as they were rock-topped and sprinkled with snow all year.

The year I turned thirteen, my family rented a cottage in New Hampshire for a week in July. Finally I was heading to the mountains! I was twitchy and restless as we wound in our green Rambler through clapboard-and-shutter towns and pine shadows. Cigarette smoke filled the car. Nancy cuddled one of her Breyer's ponies. On the radio someone was talking about riots in New Jersey, and President Johnson gave some boring speech.

At dusk we arrived at the cottage. Low-wattage lamps barely lit a chilly room with two double beds and a stone fireplace. I joined Dad on the screened porch that overlooked Lake Winnipesaukee and the mountains beyond. The moon trailed a silver ribbon over the water.

"Nice moon, eh, Maeh?" Dad said. He meant "Mare" but his Massachusetts accent lopped off the "r." Between his fingers a Tareyton glowed, a ruby bit in the near darkness.

"Yeah." Looking up at him in the moonlight, I saw his frown, like maybe he forgot something at home. A soft squeak slid through his lips as he pulled on the cigarette. "What's the matter, Dad?" I asked.

"Oh, nothing. I was just thinking about those lakes in Jackson Hole and how beautiful they must be in the summer."

With his mention of Jackson Hole, I remembered the slides of the elk and the snowy mountains. Then I thought of the summer scenery in *The Sound of Music,* which had burst onto the movie scene a few months earlier, and how the staggering Alps, the rock-edged lakes, and the green meadows thick with edelweiss had captivated me.

"Mm-m-m," I said, nodding. I got it. I understood what he meant.

Each morning that week we packed ham and cheese sandwiches and Fluffernutters, gooey messes of peanut butter and Marshmallow Fluff on Sunbeam Bread, and hit the tourist traps: Storyland, the Flume, Old Man of the Mountain. We drove the Kancamagus Highway through dark woods speckled with sunlight. At Clark's Trading Post, dull-eyed black bears shimmied up poles to a platform where they lounged and stretched to our delight. To us they were live teddy bears, lovable and pitiable in their clumsy bodies. But all these things felt like trying to quench a troubling thirst by catching snowflakes on my tongue. Nose pressed to the car window, I admired the wavy-soft mountains and longed to be in them.

Sipping a bottle of Narragansett beer one night on the cottage porch, Dad waved his pointy forefinger, injured years ago in a hunting accident. "Hey, *goils,* whaddya say tomorrow we hit the Polar Caves?" he asked, emerald eyes glinting through a smoky spiral. He always made me laugh when he talked like Moe Howard.

I stared out at the lake. Turquoise hills corduroyed beyond the opposite shore. They weren't the Alps or the Rockies, but they still called me. I needed to be *in* them. I wanted to walk through their trees and drink water from their streams. Caves weren't mountains, but maybe going down into a cave might get me closer to whatever was calling me.

The next day we followed my dream boy, a sandy-haired tour guide named Peter, through cave formations called "Orange Crush" and "Lemon Squeeze." It was *him*. I knew immediately that Peter would one day become that mountain man I'd fantasized about. He'd been working at these caves all summer just hoping for a girl like me to come along, someone who would hop on board and follow him into the mountains. I ran my fingers through my pixie haircut and hoped he'd notice my red plaid pants and cool boat shoes.

But my family was messing it all up. My face burned with embarrassment as my mother wriggled through the passages in her pedal pushers and that stupid aqua kerchief wrapped around her head. Then I wanted to die when Dad told Peter his beer belly couldn't fit through a narrow chute. If only I'd been there without them, and without my little sister tagging along with her goofy pigtails and those god-awful blue Keds. What must Peter have thought when he saw these people I was with? It was only because of them that I couldn't tell Peter about our shared destiny. They were keeping me from fulfilling my life's dream.

That night we sat on the porch again while Mom cooked dinner in the kitchenette. As I peered at the hills across the lake, they seemed to move farther and farther away. In my hands, I folded and unfolded a Polar Caves brochure with a photo of a blond boy crooked around a passage near the Lemon Squeeze. He looked a little like Peter, but not exactly.

"Heah, Maeh," Dad said, handing me a slice of cheese on a Saltine. I took it, but it tasted like cardboard in my mouth. I grumbled.

"Whatsa matter with you? You sick or something?"

"*No.*" I slumped down in a chair and opened the brochure for the fiftieth time. Why couldn't they just leave me alone? Didn't they realize they had ruined my life?

※

"How did you ever end up with a man like Bill?"

This question comes often, and it's a question I even ask myself. The answer is this: I married Bill because I loved him. Loved him in the way a young person loves—unambiguously, and within the confines of the unseen framework of the time.

The second of February, a Wednesday, 1972. My friends and I had rushed from the cafeteria back to Boland Hall, the women's dorm, across our small campus of Stonehill College, south of Boston. Clenched in our hands were torn sheets of notebook paper jotted with cryptic notes: John—July 17, Jeff—Oct. 31, Frank—May 19, Steve—Jan. 15, Bill—Aug. 9.

Later, dressed in jeans and sweaters or frumpy housecoats and fuzzy slippers, we filed down to the dorm lobby and clustered around the black and white console TV, paper slips moist in our clenched fists. I squeezed between two girls on the sofa; others flopped in chairs or lolled on the faded carpet. Still others lined the walls and stuffed the doorways.

"Okay, everybody," someone said as she turned up the TV volume. "This is it."

Expressionless men in military uniforms stared out from the screen. "This lottery," one of them began, "is a lottery of birthdates for men born in 1953. Men with numbers less than 120 will have a higher likelihood to be called for active military duty in 1973."

Our mouths hung open. Was it coming down to this? Your future being decided by the day you were born? You really had no more control over your life than that? On the screen a man with a mole over his lip reached into a drum and drew out the first piece of paper. "Number 1," he said. "March 6."

A frantic rush as we searched our notes. Relief. No match yet.

"Number 2—March 7. Number 3—August 3 . . ."

I breathed a deep sigh. So far so good. There were, after all, 365 days in a year. Chances were good our friends wouldn't be called until far into the lottery.

" . . . Number 7—August 9. Number 8—August 17 . . ."

"*Shit!*" I screamed, waving my paper slip. "It's Bill—he's August 9. He's only Number 7." Bill Ferreira's face loomed in my mind, his mellow eyes and fine cheekbones. He and I had graduated together from Dartmouth High School. We'd both come from farm families, and our mothers had also graduated from Dartmouth High. Bill was sweet and familiar, and now he was going off to fight a war in Southeast Asia.

"Number 9—October 25. Number 10—October 31 . . ."

"That's Jeff."

As the numbers droned on, shrieks of recognition erupted from the group.

When it was over a petite girl smashed her cigarette in an ashtray, stood up, and turned off the TV. She turned to face us, butterscotch eyes brimming. "I *hate* this goddamn war," she said. We looked away, rose to our feet, and trudged back to our rooms. No one spoke. There were some sniffles and muffled sobs, but the loudest sound was the shuffling of feet on carpet.

A group of us gathered in someone's room. Elton John's *Friends* album was set on the turntable; a candle was lit and stuck into the neck of a wine bottle. Hugging our knees, we sat shoulder to shoulder on the floor between the two slide-out beds. We were thinking of all those boys, our classmates. Some pushy and pompous, some bespectacled and bookish. Some muscled and gorgeous, others pimply-faced and thin-chested. Some sexy and irresistible, some irritating and hopelessly "square." But right then, every one of them wormed into our hearts and became precious, like brothers, like pets. These were the young men we sat next to in biology class, the boys who made our eyes roll when they jabbered, the kids who danced like scarecrows, the guys we had crushes on. Which of them would become "casualties" in a stifling jungle on the other side of the world?

As Elton's clear nasal voice sang about friends becoming lovers, my focus reset and I entered a carefree dream of a world without military drafts and wars. My heart cracked as I imagined myself hiking up a mountain trail wearing cutoff jeans, with a bandanna around my hair and a rucksack on my back. Higher, higher, higher, striding out full and strong, Pot o' Glossed lips kissing the sunlight, sucking in a symphony of pungent forest smells, endless youth, forever vibrant. And with me—a *friend,* a dashing *male* friend. Sharing the lead, we walk through the krummholz trees, above timberline and onto a rocky summit with snow lingering in the shady spots. And this *friend,* this capable male *friend,* climbs onto a ledge above, turns, and holds out his hand, palm up and vulnerable. There's a dreaminess in his eyes and a soft upturning of the lips, a silent invitation . . .

Lover. Lover. Lover.

Every day we heard news of the day's "casualties" in Vietnam. We all knew someone—brother, cousin, friend, neighbor—who was fighting, MIA, or had died. We were conflicted about the anti-war rallies. Our fathers and uncles had fought in World War II, and had instilled in us similar feelings of patriotic duty.

"We can't just pull out of Vietnam," my father had said. "The Communists would take over all of Southeast Asia. Just like what the Soviet Union did in Eastern Europe in the forties. There'd be a bloodbath."

But for the first time in my life, I was parting ways with my father's political views. Vietnam was different from the World Wars. What were we fighting for? We'd lost sight of it. All I knew was that an eerie black hole in Southeast Asia was sucking down our young men, and what is dwindling becomes valuable. Simple supply-and-demand economics.

July that same year. The Edge Nightclub, Pawtucket, Rhode Island. We were nineteen. We loved pounding rock 'n' roll, we loved to dance, and we loved being legal adults. In Rhode Island in 1972, we were legal adults.

Electric guitars blared and drums thumped through amplifiers. We sipped rum and Cokes and beers and pressed our forearms into the table.

"Number 7, that's me," Bill was saying with a nervous chuckle. "Never won anything in my life, but I just got lucky."

"I'm right behind ya at 10," Jeff said, sipping his drink. Wiry reddish eyebrows shaded his eyes. "And no more student deferments either."

"So what does this mean?" someone asked. "Will you definitely be called?"

"The army already mailed us appointments for our physicals," Bill said. "August 8, in Boston." He combed his fingers through the loose coils of his brown hair.

Oh my God, I thought. The draft would end the following January, but we didn't know that. I felt woozy as I saw Jeff and Bill wading through muck in combat boots and helmets, carrying rifles, dodging land mines and sniper fire, and shooting, no, killing people. *Killing* people.

"I have that day off, too," Bill said. "Was looking forward to a round of golf." *Golf? Oh, jeez.*

The band's lead vocalist blasted the intro to "Joy to the World."

Bill stood up, took my elbow. On the dance floor the music drew me in. I could have sworn Three Dog Night was on that stage. Every muscle and nerve in my body reverberated with that driving bass guitar. Legs pumping, I swung my arms, tossed my hair, ground my shoulders. I gave everything I had to the dancing—it was big, mindless, exuberant.

Bill twisted self-consciously and pumped his arms like the Pips. This didn't seem his milieu, but he gave it his best try.

I wiped beads of sweat from my nose as the song ended. We stayed on the dance floor as dreamy guitar triads signaled the beginning of Chicago's "Colour My World."

When Bill drew me to him for the slow dance, I melted into his warmth. Sparks shot through my chest, even if he did play golf. Suddenly he wasn't just another Portuguese kid from Dartmouth High. We weren't scaling a mountain peak, but nonetheless, there was that gentle outstretched hand and the unspoken invitation . . .

Lover. Lover. Lover.

9

Evolution

On ground streaked with early morning shadows, I seek out the culprits—filigreed rosettes of spotted knapweed, *Centaurea maculosa*. A native of Eurasia, CEMA is a knee-high spindly plant with brushy pink flowers. It hitched a ride to the United States with alfalfa and clover seed to become a huge rangeland weed problem, overrunning native plants in Wyoming, Montana, and other western states.

I'm at South Jenny Lake this morning, before the concessions open. I got an early start to pick up the spraying gear from the S&RM garage behind the office—no easy task because, for me, opening the dungeonlike garage door is like lifting the *Titanic,* and I've had a stitch in my sacrum ever since.

I mosey around with the backpack sprayer. Made of orange plastic, it's heavier than I expected, with three gallons of liquid at about eight pounds a gallon. And ungainly, too—when it sloshes, I list like an unbalanced barge. With the pressure pump handle on my left side and sprayer wand on my right, I walk around the vegetated areas, pumping absentmindedly. When I see a knapweed rosette, I take aim and squeeze the handle of the wand. Out sprays a shot of blue liquid, a diluted solution of the herbicide Banvel. The blue dye dries and leaves color on the plant, showing me the ones I've already sprayed.

I pause after every three or four sprays to straighten my back or to tug at some part of my new NPS coveralls. Tim ordered a pair about two sizes too small for me, and they fit like what my mother would call a *tripa,* the gut lining used as a casing for *morcela,* Portuguese blood sausage.

Jenny Lake is a mirror this morning; the upside-down reflections of the peaks are so vivid I imagine there's a second inverted spine of mountains dipping into the water.

But I'm only half here. Last night in a dream, the house on Red Maple Lane emerged from a summery haze buzzing with cicadas. Not much had changed, except a lush lawn now grew in place of the overgrown pasture to the north that was to become my vegetable garden. Some men drove up the driveway in a pickup truck, to do some landscaping, they said. They asked me where they should start. "I don't live here anymore," I said, flustered. Bill appeared on the porch. "There's something I've been saving," he said. I followed him into the house to the den where he reached behind a bookcase and handed me a glass vial with a rubber stopper. Inside was my gold wedding band, immersed in cleaning fluid. "I'm keeping it from tarnishing," he said. We both cried hot, bloated tears.

More tears press against my eyelids now. Being in this spectacular place by myself at this hour unnerves me. The parking lots are empty except for a few cars that probably belong to backpackers. I feel like one of the few remaining living characters in *The Andromeda Strain* or *The Stand,* searching for some confirmation that life goes on, that someone else is around to witness this great beauty. It's that old "If a tree falls in the forest" question: If I'm the only one here to see these stoic mountains, do they—do *I*—truly exist?

Furthermore, I hate traipsing around the park spraying herbicide. This *is* a national park, for God's sake, protected land and wildlife. Toxic chemicals have no place here. Aldo Leopold should lunge from his grave and pound us all to pieces with a lodgepole. And besides, I look like an escaped convict in this garb—coveralls with goggles and an Atom Ant respirator. Tim assures us that bandannas tied around our faces are protection enough against the herbicide, as long as we don't "inhale the stuff." But I don't buy that.

Rounding the path by the Jenny Lake boat dock, I spot two middle-aged men in Teton Boating caps walking ahead of me. They're heading to the dock to prepare for the daily onslaught of tourists eager to ride the tubby wooden boats across Jenny Lake and hike to the park's popular attractions, Hidden Falls and Inspiration Point.

Damn! While *I'm* relieved to see human activity, I sure as hell don't want anyone to see *me.* Ducking into the brush, I lean forward and pretend to be so absorbed in my work that I don't see anything but weeds—weeds—weeds.

The sun creeps higher. Cars drone through the lots. Time to quit before I get assaulted with the typical "*Whatareyouspraying?*" question by visitors. ("Knapweed," I've learned to answer as I rush away.) Plunking the sprayer into Nellie's bed, I walk into the sagebrush to look for some of the wildflowers Dick Shaw taught us.

I recognize Indian paintbrush, lupine, and lingering yellow fritillaries, now turning reddish. Armfuls of arrowleaf balsamroot, mats of peachy buckwheat. And something I didn't expect—the dissected leaves and sorrel-colored, cup-shaped flowers of the rare Brown's peony. But I don't dawdle, because traffic's picking up, and I want to protect the flowers. I straighten and move on, not giving any hint that I've found something unusual and lovely.

I never know what will set me off these days. When a Toyota diesel pickup truck just like Bill's turns into the lot and the exhaust fumes reach me, I crumble. Memories of Saturday chores with my ex-husband shoot me in the gut.

"It's pretty impossible, unless you have someone waiting in the wings." This is what my cousin Meg once said about leaving long-term marriages, unless they were beyond hope. You know, like riddled with violence or addiction.

There was no one waiting in our wings, but I didn't believe her. Besides, I didn't want the stigma. "She left Bill for *him?*" But I couldn't just *leave* either. Meg and I had been struggling for years, trying to find our way through less-than-ideal couplings, but we were ensconced. Not only in what Robert James Waller called "the inertia of protracted custom," but also in the clinging-ivy vestiges of our Catholic upbringing, our daisy chain families, and the instilled honor of commitment. We'd grown through our twenties and thirties with these glittering gems of men, hardworking, handsome, ideal "catches." Mine even spoke Portuguese, which gained him *muitos* points on my mother's family scorecard. These men had stood at our sides at every family event and smiled beside us in all the photos from the mid-seventies on.

If you spend nineteen years with a guy, then move far away to a place where no one knows about it, did it really happen?

I crouch beneath a cottonwood tree, and all the pain I've been avoiding these past weeks floats back to me on the lingering diesel fumes. Wracking sobs that need to be wept spurt out. Tears spill to the ground, leaving dark spots in the dust.

———

Nineteen years, fifteen of them married, indelibly burned, now and forever part of me, the source of this emotional limp, this tinted monocle through which I will view the rest of my life.

When I was married my world was outlined, like the Sunday comics. Cheerios for breakfast, sandwiches for lunch, meat and potatoes for dinner.

Eight-to-five jobs, weekend chores, family visits. Pictionary or Trivial Pursuit with friends (Bill's friends) on Friday nights. *Cheers, M*A*S*H, LA Law, SNL.*

I'd fallen into this life down a water slide chute. It was the only chute in sight at the time, and once I unclipped my heels from the ridge and launched myself through the gate, there was no flipping around onto my belly and scrabbling back up to the top. I skidded down until I plopped with a white splash into the pool. Once in the pool, I played the game.

My mother would go to my father, sitting in his TV room with a Narragansett beer, and ask, "What do you want for supper?"

"How about meat loaf?"

She sautéed onions and garlic, mixed in ground beef and tomato juice, and shaped it into a loaf for *him*. For *her*, she made a separate loaf, no onions, because they triggered her migraines. She boiled and mashed potatoes, heated up a can of Veg-All. When she drew the two loaves from the oven, sizzly-brown and steamy, Dad called out, "*Theresa!* I'd rather have hot dogs." So, back to the freezer she'd go for two red-gray tubes and put them on to boil. At the table Dad said, "The potatoes are a little lumpy." She called the next day to tell me about this incident, bitter bile rasping in her throat as she spoke. "I've had a terrible headache today," she said. "I must have got a piece of onion in my meat loaf by mistake."

I soaked dried beans overnight. After work the next day, I cooked the beans—*chicka-chicka-chicka*—in the pressure cooker, then poured them into a pot with onions and garlic, threw in chopped celery and carrots, broccoli and zucchini, pinches of salt, pepper, dried parsley.

When Bill came in from the office, he asked, "What's cookin'?" Lifting the lid off the pot, he peered inside and contorted his mouth. "What's this shit?"

"This *shit* is vegetable soup," I snapped.

"You *know* the only vegetables I eat are peas and corn."

(How well I knew this: Bill was the only person I knew who'd leave a salad bar with a saucer of croutons. Nothing else.)

Remembering meat loaf and hot dogs, I vowed I wouldn't stand for this. "Then make something else."

As I stormed from the kitchen, he opened the freezer and thunked a pepperoni pizza on the counter.

But the next night while chicken and potatoes baked, I made a salad for me and heated up canned peas for Bill.

During the night he nudged me. "You're gnashing your teeth," he said.

———

Thinking, always thinking. I would sit in a wicker rocker on our front porch, ruminating about my wildlife classmates who, after graduation, packed everything they owned in junk-heap cars and headed to Colorado, Montana, or Idaho for government jobs or PhD programs with fresh, eager wives in tow.

Bill's friend Steve landed a job in Seward, Alaska, and I was spurting-geyser jealous. Steve was heading to the Last Frontier with his pretty bride, Evelyn, whose idea of frontier was any place beyond the outer walls of a retail establishment. Steve puffed out his barrel chest and boasted about filling his Bronco with canned goods in preparation for the rumbling journey to Dawson Creek, British Columbia, and then on the Alcan Highway to Delta Junction, Alaska.

"Fifteen hundred miles of dirt road through the wilderness," he said. "Can you imagine it, Bill?"

Blowhard, I thought.

Steve continued, "Of course, Evvy's not too pleased about this. She hates the idea of leaving Massachusetts and being away from her family."

What a waste! My insides frilled and frothed. *Why can't Bill get a job in Alaska?*

———

With Karla Bonoff and Linda Ronstadt belting out feminist angst from my cassette player, I'd berate myself: *If I were a real feminist, like I pretend to be, I wouldn't wait for Bill. I'd just do it. I'd live my own life. I'd do as Louisa May Alcott did and "paddle my own canoe."*

Then I'd head inside to start dinner.

———

Only Miriam knew my life was missing something big. As grad students at Virginia Tech in the seventies, we shared an apartment, big dreams, and *Ms.* magazine. At her suggestion I opened a savings account in my name only and began saving a few dollars from every weekly paycheck for traveling. Miriam said, "It's fine if Bill doesn't like to travel. But he can't stop you from going on your own. Who says husbands and wives have to do everything together?"

Her logic comforted me. But Miriam swam in a different pool. Her parents had divorced years earlier. She'd learned to see the world differently.

Nonetheless, as my travel account built up, I felt high on power. Finally I summoned up the courage to tell Bill I was going on a trip to the Rocky Mountains.

His eyebrows clenched into a stern V. "I can't believe you'd be so selfish as to go without me."

"Then come with me."

"Pffuh. I have to work for a living, Mary. I don't have time to go flitting all over the country." His tone was clipped, ball-and-chain.

I croaked, "Then I'll go with Miriam."

"My *God,* Mary," he said, "are you *never* going to let this go? This . . . this . . ." He flapped his hands, juggling for the right word. "This *obsession* with the West? I don't get it. I've told you again and again, I'm *not* moving out west."

My heartbeat thundered down into my gut. "I'm not asking you to move. I just want to visit."

"Yeah, and then what?" His eyes drilled into mine as his head teetered back and forth. "You call me and tell me you've found this perfect place in the mountains and you can't wait for us to move out there?"

He knew me too well. Heat pulsed in my temples. "That's *ridiculous.*"

Storming out of the house, he slammed the door so hard my miniature Pairpoint Glass plates rattled in the windows. I called Miriam. "Of course he's going to react like that," she said. "You've never stood up to him."

The night before Miriam and I left, my in-laws called, ostensibly to wish me a "good trip." But then they asked to talk to Bill. They wanted to tell him, I knew, how dreadful and frightening this was, his wife driving across the country with a woman friend, and what if the car blew up or what if they got attacked by bears, sharpshooters, or ax murderers, but above all, *what will people think?* I overheard Bill say, "She's got this in her head, and there's no talking her out of it."

Miriam and I tooled over frost-heaved highways across the Great Plains, camping each night in KOAs. She told me her husband had checked out everything in the car and changed or topped off all the fluids, then he'd gone to the hardware store to buy her some things for the trip. One of them was the noisy gadget we clipped to the car battery every night to inflate the air mattresses. My mouth dropped in disbelief and envy.

I was shocked how easy it was to drive across the country: You just fill up your car with gas and start driving. Why was this so hard? But I knew the answer, and it had nothing to do with car fluids.

Outside Salina, Kansas, the Rabbit's muffler blew out and we roared into the Midas lot sounding like the Hell's Angels. Between Salina and Hays a hammering wind sucked Miriam's pillow out the car window. Through the rearview mirror it looked like a withered pig lying in the middle of the parched highway.

In Grand Teton National Park, Miriam photographed me on the shore of Jackson Lake. "You're in your element," she said, peering into the camera lens.

We stayed at Colter Bay with George Angelo, a high school classmate of Bill's and mine, who'd been working at the park as a seasonal ranger since college. Miriam and I slept on two sofas in the living room of the trailer he shared with another ranger. We giggled at the incongruity of being in the Tetons and hearing George's Massachusetts accent peppered with Portuguese phrases.

"Heah, Mary," he said, handing me a baking dish from the cupboard. "Use this *panela* for the lasagna."

The squeaky door woke us one night when George came home late from an ambulance run to Jackson. "Ooh—I woke you up," he said. "Sorry." He sat on the arm of Miriam's sofa to chat with us, his Smokey Bear hat perched on his knee.

I told him about my experience on Highway 89 when the Tetons first came into view. "These mountains do something to me, George."

"I know what you mean. My folks think I'm nuts to drive out every June. I could make a lot more money teaching summuh school, but I love it out heah."

"I'm jealous."

He chewed the inside of his cheek. "You know, with your wildlife degree, you could easily get a seasonal job in Science & Resource Management."

Neurons crackled in my brain, but I rolled my eyes because the idea seemed so far-fetched.

In the morning when I awoke to the *chomp-chomp-chomp* of cold cereal being munched at the kitchen table, I burrowed deeper into my sleeping bag. A seasonal job? In Science & Resource Management? Thoughts somersaulted and dropped like confetti, but they eluded any recognizable pattern of possibility.

Near Montana's Flathead Lake, I ate a pound of cherries, an act I came to regret. Miriam was driving, and for once we were silent. We'd discussed my situation for eleven days straight. By now the answer was so obvious we just quit talking about it. I knew the solution. I only needed the courage to pull it off, and to deal with the consequences. After eating the last cherry, I balled up the paper bag and tossed it into the backseat. Already my stomach was rebelling.

Back home, Bill sulked. "I had to do all the laundry while you were gone," he said. "The house is a sty. The garden's overgrown with weeds. You left a lemon or something in the fridge, and it rotted to hell. I had to scrub it down with baking soda to get rid of the stench."

Words rat-a-tatted out of his mouth like bullets from an Uzi.

＊

But still, I stayed on—for eleven more years. What was I waiting for? Did I really think Bill would look at me one day, glassy-eyed, and say, "Ya know, honey, I saw some photos of the Rocky Mountains, and you're right—they do seem fantastic. Let's go out and visit. Maybe I could check out job possibilities there, and you could finally put your wildlife degree to use."

It was far more likely that the moon would break loose and divot and thud through our front yard like an errant bowling ball.

I rolled into my parents' driveway one Saturday to a classic Rockwell setting: the white Cape huddled behind oaks and maples, the petunia-lined walkway. In the windows of my old room in the northeast dormer were the same crisp organdy curtains that had hung there since my childhood. I knew that, under the twin mattress, a brittle palm frond from Palm Sunday still protected the occasional sleeping visitor from harm.

Before I got to the door, Mom called from their tiny trailer parked out back. "Back heah, Deah. We're packing for Florida."

I negotiated the narrow steps into the trailer. The world closed in, but comfortably so. I could stand in the middle of the room and touch all the kitchen appliances, the bathroom door, and the convertible table-bed. Everything scaled down and in its place, no excess.

Mom was cutting shoeboxes and stapling the ends to shorten them.

My face scrunched. "What the hell . . . ?"

"I'm going to put the glasses and stuff in them so they won't slide around in the cabinets while we're driving," she said, her mouth spreading into her lopsided grin. Her fingers reddened as she crunched the stapler around two slices of cardboard. "The dahn boxes are just an inch too long to fit in the cabinets."

"Hi, love." Dad planted a clumsy kiss on my cheek as he squeezed into the trailer carrying a worn box labeled FLORIDA ORANGES. He set the box on the table and began to draw out miles of wire of various widths and colors. The way his brow thickened and lowered as he worked told me I'd faded into his background for the moment. I didn't ask about the wire. I just smiled at their absorption in the stuff of their lives, their shared interests, their anticipation of an adventure together. I envied their humor and willingness to dive into the mundane with the only goal of pleasure, the pursuit of joy for its own sake.

I wanted to tell them: "I'm suffocating in my skin. My marriage is disintegrating. I want to escape to the Rocky Mountains." I wanted them to take my hands and say, *Oh, sweetheart. Let's have tea and talk about this.* But I knew that wouldn't happen. Besides, I didn't want to ruin this moment. I didn't want to bring chaos and pain into their thrifty, ordered, satisfied lives. Instead, I took the scissors to another shoebox, snipped it just so, and held it for Mom to click in the staples.

❦

I waited so long because I treasured those kindnesses that pass, as unnoticed as sleeping breaths, between husbands and wives. When Bill's father said, "I took your mother to her doctor's appointment." When a friend said, "Peggy likes mysteries so we watch *Murder, She Wrote* on Sunday nights." When Bill left a glass of juice and a multivitamin on the counter for me each morning before he showered.

I still notice such things, and I'm enamored of them. They're the gentle tickings of the marriage clock, the unconscious, everyday interactions that are missed and cherished only after the clock stops.

At a graveside service my great-aunt told the new widow, "When they bury your husband, a piece of you goes in the hole with him."

I already knew this, even when my marriage clock still ticked. I didn't want to fragment myself. I stayed on.

But another clock ticked. I was approaching forty. I didn't want to be forty, fifty, sixty, and still longing for an unlived life. Loneliness, a minister once said, is when we must change and no one else changes with us.

It was time. And I had to do it alone.

I once stood with Bill at an altar and said, "I do." Fifteen years later I stood with him in Probate Court and, citing irreconcilable differences, said the equivalent of "I don't." Walking down the courthouse steps, I felt a giddiness feathering around my chest. I drove to Demarest Lloyd, a seaside state park, where a golden retriever left his human far down the beach and joined me as I walked.

Wind blew cold off the water, and waves lapped slush onto a rim of snow at the shoreline. That night my cousin Meg, her six-year-old son, Tristan, and I cracked open fortune cookies at a Chinese restaurant. You are on top of the world, my fortune read. Tristan, eyes glinting like agates, said, "It's true, Mary. You really are on top of the world!"

But from the top the only way in any direction is down, and down points into dark, swirling depths. Between those "I do" and "I don't" bookends of public proclamations are volumes of drama, romance, tragedy, and comedy. The stories of my whole adult life are contained in these tomes: neat, safe, acceptable stories with predictable endings, until now. I have huge holes to fill. I haven't just left a husband to pursue a lifelong dream. I've taken a sledgehammer to the Vila Franca do Campo tiles, thumbed my nose at *Nossa Senhora*, and kissed goodbye the promise of eternal peace in the afterlife.

10

Trying Out

Thirty-six degrees when I leave Beaver Creek on a Saturday morning, the mountains still thick with leftover snow. But by the time I get to Jackson, nearly five hundred feet lower in elevation and farther from the high mountains' influence, the sun's heat has coaxed grasses to green and trees to bud. In the Elk Refuge pond north of town, mallard ducks and Canada geese dabble for underwater treats, their rear ends tilted up like feathered pyramids.

I park Darcy near the town square. (Since my divorce, I've started naming inanimate objects.) Gracing each corner of the square is an arch built from antlers dropped by elk on the refuge. Pausing under one arch, I look into the profusion of wired-together antlers, their bleached tips staggered in every direction, and I get this idea in my head: I want to see all four arches, from every angle. So I head diagonally across the square to exit through another arch, then walk the perimeter to a third where I go back into the square, cross to the fourth, and so on.

As I pass once, then twice, a bristle-haired man looks up from his conversation with a young man in Patagonia fleece. The two of them watch as I pass for the third time in my quest to see the four arches. I'm sure they're thinking I've lost something critical to my mental stability. But no matter. I continue across the square and through the fourth arch.

I want to say to them, *This is what women making a new life do: We try everything out, see what fits.*

I'd rather be out with other single friends, other divorced women my age and maybe a guy or two, enjoying breakfast in town, hitting the trails for a hike this afternoon, getting together at someone's house to cook dinner and watch a video tonight. No pairing off yet. Just social times with friends. We'd fill each other's lives, chase away loneliness. But I live with a college student who rarely leaves her bed, and the people I've met are either married, young and footloose, or they're rugged individualists who think they don't need anybody. I haven't found a welcoming group yet.

Besides, I see Bill's face everywhere I look. I hate to admit it, but I'm lost without a partner. It's still so new—this waking up alone each morning in a twin bed between my old college dorm sheets, realizing there's no "other side of the bed" and no warm body there to reach out to. And coming home in the afternoons to a might-as-well-be-empty house—with no one to ask after, no one to share stories with, no one to cook dinner for or eat with—is all virgin territory to me. Being married and ensconced in nearby family had filled my psyche with well-worn thoughts, well-rehearsed behaviors. Now, deep inside me is a shapeless void. Emptiness is not the normal way of things. It's a bland, foreign condition that begs to be filled. But how to fill it? And with what?

Weekends are the worst. This morning, after a night of thrashing, I finally got up to do yoga at six, then made pancakes. Brenda slept on. The trailer was clean enough. And *very* quiet—smotheringly so—a pressing, opaque silence.

After washing the dishes, I looked around the kitchen. Panic smoldered in my stomach. What to do next? *Be present*, I told myself, but it felt distressingly self-indulgent. I watched the lemony morning light saturate the table, the chairs, the refrigerator. *How lovely*, I thought, not really believing it, because the encroaching light only accentuated the kitchen's shabbiness.

Get out in nature. Pulling on jacket and boots, I wandered into the woods behind Beaver Creek. The snow was so hard I could walk on its surface without post-holing. I saw two twitchy-eared mule deer, heard birdcalls I couldn't identify. The flourish of sunlight through the forest was rich and lovely. But still I felt empty. I decided it was a good day to go to "town," to Jackson.

No plans. I'm on an adventure today. I leave the square and walk along East Broadway. When the traffic starts to annoy me, I cross the street and head south on King Street. I find Shades Café, where I lounge at a pizza-pan-sized table with a cup of herb tea and a banana muffin, and peruse the *Jackson Daily Guide*.

Down the street I find the tiny building of weathered logs that is the Teton County Library. The air inside smells of old wood and yellowed paper. I get a library card and check out *Wapiti Wilderness*, by Margaret and Olaus Murie.

By the time I get back to the car, the sun's heat pounds my back. When I check my watch, I'm surprised that only two hours have passed since I left the trailer. I'm not ready to head back yet. So I leave my jacket and the library book in the car and take off walking again.

CATTLE KATE SOLD HERE. The sign intrigues me as I dawdle along Deloney. Above the sign, I spy a dress on a mannequin. Now I'm no clotheshorse, judging by this faded maroon river driver shirt I'm wearing and the patch sewn on one knee of my jeans. But this dress transcends fashion. Black and gray calico print, mid-calf length, princess style, with long tapered sleeves softly gathered at the shoulders and a dash of silver ribbon at the collar. It's dressy, but in a western, casual style. If I ever have any reason to dress up, I think, this is the style for me.

Miniature brass bells tinkle around the door as I enter the boutique. Inside are the smells of wealth: buttery leather, tangy-fresh fabrics, a hint of gardenia from a high-end potpourri. The piped-in music is Native American flute. This is no Cherry's in downtown New Bedford, or even Jordan Marsh or Filene's in Boston. This is more like the Packet, in Dartmouth's harbor village of Padanaram, that ritzy, nautical-themed store frequented by upper-crust New Yorkers summering in the private seaside developments of Nonquitt and Ricketson's Point.

As I glance around, my gut cools and a voice grates in my ear: *Who do you think you are?* Thighs tense, I'm tempted to bolt. But instead I smile at the approaching young woman with octagonal glasses and leafy dark hair. "Can I help you with something?"

"The black print dress in the window?"

She nods and leads me by a display of shirts inlaid with Indian beads and porcupine quills. My eyes round, and I can't resist skimming my finger over the quills as I pass.

"The Cattle Kate," says the clerk, glancing over her shoulder.

"Uh-huh," I say, as if I already have several more in my closet. "The Cattle Kate."

On a rack she finds the dress in my size, and I carry it draped over my forearms, a gift for a queen, to the dressing room. When I toss it over my head, the fresh cotton floats cool and breezy before absorbing my body's warmth and settling around me like a quilt. As I zip it up, it becomes another layer of skin over my torso. In the mirror is a woman from another age. A wise, timeless woman of substance, a woman with impeccable taste and classic style. It's *the* dress a woodswoman would wear for the occasional night out—understated, yet elegant—and it becomes me unlike anything I've ever worn before. Before I left Massachusetts I gave away all my dresses and skirts from my previous life. But I decide here and now, if I'm going to own one dress, this will be it.

I finger the price tag and balk. There's that nagging voice again: *If this isn't a pathetic case of retail therapy, I don't know what is.* But I ignore it. I head out to the cashier and snap my VISA card on the glass counter.

This dress, I decide, is my divorce present to myself. I sign my name and tear out the carbon copy receipt. Declining an unrecyclable plastic bag, I stride out into the blinding sun with my new Cattle Kate rolled under one arm.

11

Animal Nature

Antelope bitterbrush snags our green jeans as Tim and I climb the broad hill overlooking Spencer Pond. Ochre clouds seal the sky, and a threatening smear obliterates the highest summits. There was frost on my picnic table when I left for work at eight this morning. With the temperature now hovering around forty-five, summer seems a figment, but brilliant patches of lupine and arrow-leaved balsamroot reassure me.

Tim suddenly stops short and jams his palms downward. Following his example, I collapse behind a clump of sagebrush, yanking binoculars to my eyes.

In the pond below, two trumpeter swans swim in tandem, pausing here and there to nibble vegetation. I notice contrasts and incongruities. Explosively white bodies. Ebony bills striped with coral near the hinge. Heads stained reddish from dipping in the mineral-rich water. Graceful necks as long as their bodies but no thicker than two finger-widths.

I'm awestruck, as I always am whenever I see an animal or plant I've never seen before in the wild. Each one is a piece of the wilderness puzzle. I want so hard to fit into this puzzle, for my edges to easily slip into the proper place, a perfect fit, no bumps or excess or holes left unfilled. But I don't know if I ever will. If, indeed, any human being ever will. Nature is already perfect without us. She doesn't need us. In fact, we just seem to screw things up.

Tim tells me about trumpeter swans, *Cygnus buccinator*. They are monogamous until death, and couples return to the same territory every year.

"There's the nest," he whispers, pointing to a pile of sticks atop a mat of vegetation in the water. "Looks like one of 'em's heading there now. That must be the pen, the female; the male's called a cob."

I jot down "pen = ♀, cob = ♂" in my field notebook as the pen climbs onto the nest mound, nudges through it with her bill, and settles down into incubating position.

"When should the eggs hatch?" I ask.

"In a week and a half or so. Incubation usually lasts thirty-four or thirty-five days. I first saw her on the nest on the 26th of May, but she may have been laying eggs and incubating for a few days before that."

Tim explains that trumpeter swans once thrived throughout the continent, but when civilization moved west, much of their habitat disappeared. Fashion contributed to further losses when swanskin powder puffs came into vogue. The Migratory Bird Treaty Act of 1918 helped protect swans that migrated between Canada and the United States, but even so, by the early 1920s, swan populations were nearly decimated. The US Fish and Wildlife Service established Red Rocks National Wildlife Refuge in southwestern Montana as a sanctuary for trumpeter swans.

"As a whole—how are they doing now?" I'm eager for news that the birds are well established, secure, and likely to thrive far into the future.

A gust of wind leans into us, and Tim claps both hands on his head to anchor his ball cap. "They're slowly gaining ground, but it could be better." Grand Teton trumpeters, he explains, are part of the Tri-State Population, which consists of Montana, Idaho, and Wyoming birds. Federal protection has resulted in more birds, especially in Canadian flocks. But now there's a new issue: Over time the Tri-State birds seem to have lost their innate urge to migrate to their traditional winter range far to the south. For some reason, they now converge on ponds just a few miles south of here in the National Elk Refuge.

"So we have all the Rocky Mountain trumpeters spending winters in the Greater Yellowstone Area," he says. "The Canadian birds still fly down here, like they always have. But now the Tri-State swans stay too."

As swan numbers increase, so does pressure on winter range. With limited food and severe weather, crowding makes the swans more susceptible to starvation and disease.

"We can't ever let our guard down, can we?" I say.

"Never." He slips his binoculars into their leather case.

I write in my notebook:

Spencer Pond—6/15/92. 1125-1215. ~50°. Cloudy, windy.
Nesting pair. Both swans swimming, feeding, then ♀ climbs on nest,

pokes around with bill, settles down to incubating position. ♂ swimming, feeding nearby, vigilant.

In addition to Spencer Pond, I'll monitor five other swan breeding territories in the park this summer. Periodically, the Wyoming Game and Fish Department will check some more remote sites by airplane. Tim says he's already seen pens brooding at five of my six territories. The sixth, Elk Ranch Reservoir, seems this year to be just a hangout where immature, unpartnered swans gather to feed, swim, and loaf. Water levels there vary from week to week thanks to Herbie Doyle's adjustments to the Spread Creek dam. A park employee, Herbie regulates irrigation flows for the Elk Ranch's grazing allotments.

"The swans'd be a lot better off if he'd just quit fiddlin' with it," Tim says. "But your park master key unlocks the padlock on the weir. If the water ever looks too high or too low, go ahead and adjust it."

The swans endear themselves to me, and as the expected hatching times approach, I make time in my work schedule to check them several times a week, even on weekends. I imagine myself a mother/midwife, fingers on the pulses of my pregnant daughters, aware of any abnormalities, documenting any inauspicious events, ready and anxious to usher the next generation into the world.

On the 24th of June, in seventy-three degrees of blessed sunshine, I climb the rise overlooking Spencer Pond and am greeted with a sight that sends me sprawling to the ground. One swan swims back and forth, as if on guard. The other stands and preens on one side of the nest. In the center of the nest, I see with my naked eye a writhing pile of gray fluff.

Three cygnets appear through binoculars. *Triplets!* But all I see is a blur, because I just can't stop these happy tears.

Spencer Pond—6/24/92. 0915-1015. 73°. Clear, windless.
Hot damn! I'm a grandmother! 3 downy cygnets on the nest. ♀ preens on nest, then climbs down into water. ♂ climbs up and takes her place on nest. He's looking around, vigilant. ♀ swims and feeds nearby for fifteen minutes, then climbs back on nest as ♂ dips back into water and swims around.

As they roll and topple over each other, my heart beats a joyful rhythm.

"*Great news,*" Tim says when I spout my hatching announcement at the office. "Keep checking on them, though. Let's hope they all make it." He rummages through papers on his desk and hands me a blue flyer. "And since you'll be monitoring herps, too, you should go to this. Chuck Peterson's giving a talk at the Blackrock Ranger Station tomorrow. He's the herp dude from Idaho State."

"Herps" are amphibians and reptiles, "herpetofauna." Other than netting polliwogs from the brook behind the pigpen at the farm and slinging an occasional garter snake from my garden, I have no experience with herps. Just so I don't seem totally clueless in front of this Peterson guy, I take Baxter and Stone's book, *Amphibians and Reptiles of Wyoming*, home to study before the talk.

But when I meet Chuck at the presentation, I realize my worries were unfounded. Soft-bodied and bearded, with a Buster Brown haircut and aviator glasses, he welcomes us warmly. He's wearing rumpled tan Dockers and a plaid shirt. Standing beside two Styrofoam coolers, their lids punctured with holes, he asks someone to dim the lights for his slide presentation.

I pencil details about Grand Teton's four amphibian species in my field notebook.

Rana pretiosa, spotted frog—brownish-green with black spots, orangy coloring on underside of lower torso and legs.

Pseudacris triseriata, chorus frog—tinier and more slender than spotted frog, tan or light green with three stripes down the back. Call sounds like dragging a thumbnail over a comb.

Bufo boreas boreas, boreal toad—warty skin, white line down the back, blocky shape.

Ambystoma tigrinum, spotted salamander. Look for it near housing areas—they like window wells, garages, basements.

"Then there's the non-native bullfrog, *Rana catesbiana,*" Chuck says, "but it's only found in the Kelly Warm Springs, where it was introduced. It's too cold for it anywhere else here."

I glance around the audience. Sitting close to Chuck are many young, sunburnt faces—new seasonals from Moose and Colter Bay, sparkle-eyed Rachel flanked by Robert and Chris. There are the naturalists—Linelle, Katy, Jackie, and Don—and a few gray-haired Jackson residents. In the back of the room,

Jace, Glen, Julian, and Tim stand with deadpan faces and arms locked over their chests. Julian checks his watch more than once.

"Okay," Chuck says, setting down the projector's remote and turning on the lights. "Now for the reptiles."

He rubs his hands together as if he were about to tackle a juicy steak, then opens a cooler and draws out a striped snake that loops around his forearm. "Anyone recognize this?"

Sure looks like a garter snake to me.

"It's a garter snake, but check this out." Grasping the snake's head and tail, he stretches it out to full length, just over a foot. Along its stripes are scarlet spots. "This is *Thamnophis sirtalis,* the valley garter snake." He reaches into the other cooler. "And this guy is *Thamnophis elegans,* the wandering garter snake." This one's lighter in color and doesn't have the red spots.

"We also have a little boa constrictor here, the rubber boa, *Charina bottae.*"

Boa constrictor? He's got to be kidding.

"It's a beautiful little snake," he continues, "light brown to olive green, but hardly ever seen." He passes around an eight-by-ten photo of a rubber boa. "If you ever see one in your travels around the park, be sure and fill out a wildlife sighting form."

Aptly named, I think. It looks like an olive brown rubber hose with the ends sealed. The head doesn't look any different from the hind end.

Chuck next launches into the worldwide amphibian decline. This is, of course, years before we know about the deadly chytrid fungus that we biologists, in our desperate searches for amphibians, were unknowingly spreading from pond to pond on our waders. Eight years from now, chytrid fungus will be found on dying boreal toads at the National Elk Refuge just down the road.

But right now, we're looking beyond ourselves to the usual environmental disasters: loss of wetland habitat, pollution and acid rain, the greenhouse effect and its resultant warming of the earth. Researchers in Oregon's Cascade Range will soon find that egg masses of western toads, of which our boreal toad is a subspecies, will fare better when protected by ultraviolet-filtering shades. This result will suggest that amphibian declines may be partly caused by increased UV radiation related to the thinning ozone layer.

The boreal toad and the leopard frog, Chuck explains, have already disappeared from 85 percent of sites where they historically occurred in Colorado and eastern Wyoming. Numbers of boreal toads in the park are down from historic records. And once abundant along the shores of String Lake, the leopard frog, *Rana pipiens,* the frog we all dissected in high school biology labs, hasn't been observed in the Tetons since 1953, and is now believed to be extirpated here. I sadly remember all those helpless frogs I pithed and sliced open years ago.

The talk winds down and everyone heads to the platters of zucchini bread and cookies in the back of the room. I introduce myself to Chuck. He pumps my hand and gives me his card. "Call me anytime you have questions," he says, thumbing his glasses higher on the bridge of his nose. "I'm so happy you'll be helping out with this."

His hearty welcome makes me smile from a deep place.

12

Teton Two-Step

Rachel will be here in twenty minutes to pick me up for the Spring Fling, and I'm bug-eyed giddy.

I'm decked out in my new Cattle Kate for its maiden voyage. My flat-heeled, ankle-high leather boots are, I think, the perfect complement to the dress. Eyeing myself up and down in the mirror, I think, *Is that really me?* The dress transforms me, as it should, considering I paid a trendy Jackson boutique half a week's salary for it. But the hair ... oh my *God* ...

The hair is, as usual after a wash, webby and flyaway, a mess of *farripas,* as Nan would call it. What to do with the hair? This is serious. Way beyond fine-tuning with dabs of the hairbrush. It needs something big.

Brenda's door is ajar. When I knock and peer inside, I find her stretched face-down on the bed with her nose in an Agatha Christie novel and a yellow-patterned box of Whitman's chocolates beside her on the quilt.

"Can I borrow your curling iron, Brenda?"

"Sure. It's in the bathroom closet."

"Aren't you coming to the Spring Fling? It starts in half an hour."

"Oh, no," she says, waving a lump of chocolate between thumb and forefinger. "I don't dance." Biting into the candy, she pouts back into her book.

You poor thing, I think. *Dancing fills the soul.*

Wrapping hanks of hair around the rod, I recall my cousin Karen's wedding years ago, a typical bash of a family party in a hotel hall. While my sister, cousins, aunts, and I sang, shimmied, and spun to Elvis's "Jailhouse Rock," Granny and her sister Kate, both with halos of white hair, shuffled by together in a souped-up foxtrot. Beyond the dance floor our husbands sipped drinks at a table. After a while the DJ packed up, and hotel workers dimmed lights and upturned chairs. With coats thrown over their arms, the guys milled along the back wall. But we women, unwilling to end the night yet, gravitated to Aunt Rita as she pulled our sweaty arms into a circle and sang out in her gravelly voice, *"You put your right foot in, you put your right foot out . . . "*

We all joined in the shaking it all about and turning ourselves around, held aloft on those happy kites of laughter and belonging. I turned and grinned at the husbands, all laughing except mine, who stood out among the others, arms like two hammers pressed across his chest, his face a shield of boredom and disapproval.

"Oh," I said, running to him and grabbing my coat. "I guess we need to go."

"We should have left an hour ago," Bill said, glowering. "But why quit now, Mary? You've got at least a half dozen more body parts to go."

Chuckling, I take a brush to my hair and slip on a leather headband. Twirling my skirt, I romp around the living room. I have so much to be happy about— I'm out of that suffocating marriage and finally living in the Rockies, the *Tetons*. I love my work. Three baby swans are beginning their lives at Spencer Pond. And I'm going dancing tonight. I am rich beyond *belief.*

A clatter at the door and Rachel's standing in my kitchen in a flared denim skirt, western-style fringed jacket, and cowboy boots. Her hair falls in sun-yellow sheets around her shoulders; behind one ear is tucked a thin braid woven with beads and two dangling feathers.

Next to her breezy getup, my Cattle Kate seems bland, almost frumpy.

But her jaw falls when she sees me. *"Mary Beth.* You look beautiful! *Wow.* What an *awesome* dress."

"Oh," I say, flustered. "Thanks. But look at *you . . .*"

She waves me silent. "This is my roommate's skirt. And I found this jacket at Browse & Buy, the thrift store in Jackson."

She's an unconscious beauty. The best kind.

It's still light out when we head east on the Antelope Flats Road, but a plump snowberry of a moon bulges over Sleeping Indian. A short-lived alpenglow blushes the peaks. Although we're just a week out from the summer solstice, the now familiar sundown chill fills the valley.

My feet jiggle on the floor of Rachel's VW Rabbit. I love to dance, but my dancing has never evolved beyond rock 'n' roll hip-grinding. I don't know the first thing about western-style dancing. And have I ever been to a dance without Bill? I honestly can't remember.

"You're gonna love the Spring Fling, Mary Beth," Rachel says, downshifting and turning up the dirt road to the Hunter Barn. "We always have such a great time. And the steps are easy, so don't worry. You'll catch on fast." She peers into the rear view mirror. "Hey, is that Bob behind us?"

I turn around. I've just met Bob Wemple, the park engineer, in the past week. "It *is*. And there's a *dog* in the passenger's seat." Leaning out the open window, I wave back at the white Toyota pickup with a pink kayak jutting askew from the bed and a dog's nose sticking out the window.

"That's *hilarious*," Rachel says, looking at me round-eyed.

"Wyoming blind date."

Rachel parks in the grass alongside other subcompact cars and pickup trucks. A lone bison snuffles and chuffs through the nearby meadow. Stark against the mountain skyline, the barn looms ahead: two stories of weathered wood, with a pair of elk antlers splayed under the gambrel roof. Horse stalls below, windowless room above, probably once used for hay storage, but now primed for the rhythmic tread of boots on its splintered floor. At the top of a flight of rickety steps, Rick Lichtenhan, a seasonal Trail Crew worker, collects tickets at the double doors, now propped open and spewing amber light.

As Bob climbs out of his truck, a jackal-like dog with bat ears dives out beside him. "Rachel, Mary Beth." He nods. "This is Maggie."

I wrap my arms around Maggie, whose breath smells as if she's been chewing on a long-dead animal. *Dogs at a dance. I love it!*

Rachel takes my arm and holds me back as Bob leads Maggie into the barn. "I have to pee," she whispers. "But I don't want to use those Porta-Johns."

"Me neither. Let's find a place in the trees."

We duck into the aspens behind the barn and wade through knee-high grass. I hike up my dress, drop my drawers, and squat, transferring my weight from one foot to the other to dodge grass awns. Rachel is in the same position beside me as we laugh and ogle the mountain view. I wonder if anyone else has ever worn a Cattle Kate while peeing in the woods?

Fluffing up our skirts to dislodge bits of chaff, we saunter back to the parking area and greet friends. We notice the naturalists Jackie and Katy, and from our office, Chris, Robert, Tim and his wife, Jennifer. No Jace, Julian, Glen, or Mark. They must be holed up at home reading the *Journal of Wildlife Management*.

We follow blue jeans, calico skirts, and cowboy hats over packed dirt to the barn. On this fresh night brimming with eager promise, I inhale a cool dusk full of lingering smells of hay and manure. I clutch up my skirt, skip up the steps, and hand my ticket to Rick. Once inside, we meld into a wooden space charged by ardent faces. Along one wall Bob arranges an armful of hay he's brought from the ground floor to fashion a bed for Maggie, while the band "Shelley and Kelly" tunes up fiddles, mandolins, and guitars.

As Chris corners Rachel, I glance around the room seeking familiar faces. Curls bobbing and pretty face aglow, Katy approaches, her hand cupping the elbow of a wiry, blond man with aviator glasses and an impish, welcoming face.

"Mary Beth," she says. "This is my husband, Patrick Matheny."

He pumps my hand. "Katy's told me about you. It's good to finally meet you. You're in for a *great* time tonight. Save me a dance, will ya?"

My first reaction is a nervous giggle. I think of saying, "*Save* you a dance? I'll be so bored from standing around that I'd jump at the chance," but instead I reply, "Sure."

A couple close to my age approaches, both sporting thick hair to their shoulder blades, the woman's chestnut and straight, the man's dark and corkscrewed.

Katy introduces them as Elaine, who works in the Concessions Office at the park, and Jack, a ranger with the Forest Service. I feel an energy from Elaine and know immediately she and I will be friends.

"The Tetons," Elaine says, sea-green eyes going dreamy, "are the center of the universe." She squeezes my arm. "But you already know that."

She's right. I do.

The band starts with the lively "Take Me Back to Tulsa." Stiff bodies line the walls; eyes dart about self-consciously. Finally Katy and Patrick venture onto the dance floor and launch into an energetic western swing. A stream of people follows. I spot Elaine's flowery yellow skirt snaking around Jack's lanky legs and Tim's big grin towering above the crowd.

Relieved of his ticket collecting duties, Rick, his face eager and childlike, holds out his hand to me. *I guess this is how it's done.*

"Wanna dance this one?" He blinks.

I melt into the barely remembered feel of a male hand pressed into my shoulder blade, steadying me with strength and warmth and guiding me onto the dance floor. I turn to face him. Under burnt-brown hair, he's frowning down at me, as if trying hard to do this right. I want to reassure him, *You'll do fine! I don't know how to do this either.* When he holds out both his hands, mine fall into them, a sweet acquiescence.

I put my brain on hold and follow his lead. Step together, step apart. Step together, step apart. I twirl on my toes and we circle around each other, my fingers twisting in his, the Cattle Kate shuffing sensuously around my legs. The rhythm thumps through my body. Soon I'm sporting a broad grin that stays pasted to my face long after the music stops.

From her hay bed, head up and eyes alert, Maggie watches the festivities. Between dances I scratch her neck. She stretches out one paw, inviting me to keep it up.

Plucking a sprig of hay from his shirt collar, Bob strides over and asks me to dance as the band begins to play a waltz tune. But on the dance floor he pauses. "I don't like all these steps," he says. "I just do what I want to do." He takes one of my hands, steps backward and forward, whips me about like a lariat until my head's spinning.

When the band plays "Cotton-Eye Joe," people line up in groups of four, arms around waists, radiating from the center of the floor like wheel spokes. As they stomp around the circle, Elaine, Jack, and Dennis from Dornan's guide me into their line. At first the steps to "Cotton-Eye Joe" confuse me, but I watch the row of adept feet beside me and Simon-say my way through until the progression stamps itself into my brain circuitry. By the song's middle, I'm beaming, head held high, kicking and hopping along with the other hot bodies around me.

After a break for snacks and drinks, the band strikes up "All My Exes Live in Texas."

Patrick stands before me. With his right hand behind his back, he bows ceremoniously and presents me his left. The song is slower than a swing tune, and I don't recognize the rhythm.

"What is this?" I ask, crinkly-eyed.

"It's a two-step."

"Huh?"

"It's easy. Just follow my hand." Scooping me up, he clasps my right hand in his left and metronomes it back and forth—quick-quick, slow-slow, quick-quick, slow-slow—in time with the music. Laughing together, we ratchet around the dance floor like windup toys.

I'm drawn, brimming and bursting, into the long night, astonished that, unlike in my high school and college wallflower days, men I've only recently met approach me for dances.

Two hours into the three-hour affair, I skim across the dance floor with George Angelo, my Dartmouth High classmate, down from Colter Bay for the dance. I'm so shaky-happy to dance with someone I've known for twenty years that I chatter nonstop, trying to enhance the connection. I tell him my dad's parents used to win dance competitions at the Lincoln Park Ballroom, and that my cousin Tillie loved to polka with my other grandfather at the Dartmouth Grange dances. George is the only person in the Tetons who would know Lincoln Park and the Dartmouth Grange, and I so want him to show interest and maybe a hint of nostalgia. But as I blather on, George looks straight ahead, steering us clear of other dancers. "Yup, uh-huh," he says. "Isn't this a blast?"

As we pass the snack counter, a tall guy with a muscular back reaches into a cooler for a Coke. I'd recognize that comma-sized ponytail anywhere. Julian hands the soda to a man in a black cowboy hat and places a dollar in the cash box. The next time George and I circle around, Julian's huddled against the back wall, hands pocketed, head screwed forward, eyebrows woven together. When the music stops, I go over. Spotting me, Maggie rises from her bed and follows.

"*Julian.* What are *you* doing here?"

"Thought I'd help out selling the drinks," he says. His shoulder spasms.

I lean over to scratch Maggie's ears, then nod toward the counter. "I can take over for a while if you want to dance."

He cringes. "Oh, hmph. *I* don't dance."

The way he says it sounds like an affront—like I should have known he'd never lower himself to do something so trivial and unproductive as dancing. But the flicker of insult dies quickly. It's his issue, not mine.

"You don't know what you're missing," I say, turning away.

Why is he even here? I wonder. He's clearly out of his element. It's probably because he wants to observe from the sidelines—not get involved in this risky behavior—but gawk at those who do. All at once I admire Rick, Jack, Patrick, Bob, Tim—all the guys who blunder and jolt over the dance floor, defying self-consciousness. They don't even think about it. They *do*. They jive and twirl and stomp in the delight of the here-and-now. Like George, who refused to delve into the past with me and simply enjoyed the moment.

I glance around when the last song starts. Rick stands nearby. When I make smiling eye contact, he proffers his hand. *I think I just asked a man to dance and he accepted. I'm learning a new language.*

Shelley begins a thin, haunting tune on her violin. Rick listens. "Waltz," he says. Then he leads me in a real waltz, the kind I've seen in movies—one-two-three, one-two-three—as he whispers the count in rhythm.

The song flows pointedly, a ribbon of water winding downhill from a high bluff. Kelly's guitar joins in, a tributary, and twines flawlessly with the violin melody.

"What a beautiful song," I say, turning under Rick's outstretched arm.

"It's called 'Ashokan Farewell,'" he says. "It was written for the PBS Civil War documentary."

The song seems classic and genuine, as if it were written during the Civil War, not for a TV reenactment. As if it were inspired a hundred and thirty years ago while a war tore the country apart, and people came together to give themselves over to music and dance to forget, to hope and place their faith in the precious things of beauty that endure beyond hardship.

My eyes close around a dream of surrender. The music floats me round and round and far into the past. A hundred years ago, I imagine, cowboys and ranch women waltzed like this on rough-hewn barn floors all over the West, to a violin, a guitar, maybe a washtub bass. Sixty years ago, I see Mardy Murie, her thick braid bundled high on her head, smiling at Olaus as they glide across the dance floor in a log hall on the Jackson Town Square.

Inhaling warm air thick with sweat, I dance. We dance. For the sheer joy of it. Right now, the pain of my divorce seems as insignificant as the shreds of hay embedded in the soles of my shoes.

As the final strains of the waltz fade away, Rick pumps my hand and thanks me.

"Thank *you*, Rick. You lead really well."

He reddens. "Uh, well, thanks."

I'm full of gratitude for him and for all these men and women who take chances, who risk looking foolish and clumsy on a dance floor and love it anyway.

Reluctant to leave, Rachel and I help load up the remaining snacks and sodas into boxes and carry them out to Bob's truck. He'll return them to a storage area for the next event the Grand Teton Employee Association sponsors. Cavorting around the parking area, we sing, "Take Me Back to Tulsa."

Rachel drives the empty road, silver in moonlight, alert for the shining twin disks of elk, coyote, or moose eyes in the headlights.

Back in my trailer Brenda's door is closed, with no outline of light around it. I slip out of the Cattle Kate, now limp with the heat of western swing, waltz, two-step. Inside the collar a white tag reads: MACHINE WASH COLD WITH SIMILAR COLORS. LINE DRY OUT BACK, AWAY FROM LIVESTOCK. I drop the dress into my laundry bag and flop into bed.

Still counting "1-2-3, 1-2-3," I waltz into sleep to "Ashokan Farewell."

13

Bliss

I'm drunk on the Tetons.

Varied, unpredictable days tumble along, and the groove suits me. The job is like summer camp sprinkled with Three Stooges routines. Nellie's battery still conks out every time we park for more than an hour, I still struggle with the S&RM garage doors, and Rachel's and my efforts one day to load a boat onto a trailer at the Jenny Lake boat ramp could win a comedy award. My boots are caked with mud, and I often wear the same shirt more than once before I wash it. Counseling work, where I wore fresh, pressed blouses and pantyhose, and stressed through days filled with addicts, acting-out kids, and indifferent parents, becomes so remote in my memory that I wonder if I only dreamt it.

For the first time in my life, I feel my day-to-day life is in sync with my environmental convictions—that the ultimate goal of my actions is, as Leopold urged, to preserve the complex web of natural life around me.

Our office is studying wildlife diversity in the woods around Beaver Creek where the park's fire management folks are clearing vegetation to reduce fire hazard. I head up the hill behind the housing area, trundling an orange-wheeled gadget over the ground to measure distances between sampling locations. I soon figure out that the tool is meant to be used on pavement. The floor of this lodgepole forest is thick with grouse whortleberry bushes, ankle-high shrubs that will eventually produce sweet red berries the size of BBs. But right now the little suckers seem to have no other purpose than to tangle in my measuring wheel. Add in the rocks, blowdowns, and rotting logs, and my measuring project becomes a tooth-gritting, cussing fiasco.

At four-thirty one morning Tim and I head out to do a breeding bird count. We drive straight to the park's north boundary, then head back south, stopping at each of fifty stations a half-mile apart to listen and watch for three minutes.

We stand in a gauzy silence pierced only by occasional peeps, twitters, and trills. I hesitate to breathe, afraid it will cause some disturbance and ruin our survey. I man the stopwatch and clipboard, making notes as Tim spins on his feet, points, and murmurs, "Three-toed woodpecker ... robin ... green-tailed towhee ... another robin ... western tanager ..." He zips around. "And *there*—yellow-rumped warbler."

Rachel and I stop in Tim's office after lunch one day. "You two wanna help me take that heron to the vet's?" he asks. "That heron" is a great blue heron with a broken wing that he found in a ditch the night before and placed in a dog pen in his backyard. We carry the bird in a crate, past the quizzical looks of serene cat owners in the vet's waiting room. Leaving later with the heron wrapped in a shoulder bandage, we have a newfound sympathy for the frogs and fish it spears with its awl-sharp bill.

The Spring Fling seems to have opened up my world, and my spare time fills up. I meet Elaine in the restroom at headquarters one day, where we chat for much longer than we should on government time. As we part she invites me out to breakfast with her and Jack on the weekend. They pick me up at eight on Saturday, and we drive to Jackson under a pristine sky. While we're eating and enjoying the Bunnery's woodsy ambience, park naturalist Linelle comes in and suggests we float down the Snake River on her raft. When? *Now*. Why not? We drive back to Moose for gear, leave one car at Deadman's Bar, and pile into another for the twelve-mile drive north to Pacific Creek. On a white cloud of a raft we coast down the river, Linelle oaring us around logjams and sand bars. Bald eagles perch in cottonwood branches overhead, and beavers loll on the shore, their pelts iridescent in the sunlight. To me it's a rapturous ride on a cloud.

A rap on the trailer door at seven one morning, and Rachel's standing on the stoop in knitted slippers and a knee-length nightshirt with a sweater thrown over her shoulders.

"Mary Beth, I bought some blueberries last night. Do you have any yogurt? Come over and we'll have blueberry pancakes. We'll be done in time for work."

It doesn't occur to me to say no, even though I've just finished a bowl of oatmeal and I still have to wash my hair. Instead I tie it into a ponytail and follow her with a quart of Yoplait under my arm.

I love this fluidity, this blurring of boundaries. With friends to share both special and mundane times, I feel I can do anything, weather any storm. I feel I've known them all my life. We're almost as enmeshed as my family, only instead of placing our devotions with the church, these humble disciples worship the earth, especially this park and its mountains and wildlife.

On a hike into Death Canyon, Rachel and I climb over the Phelps Lake moraine and down to the shore choked with prehistoric-looking false-hellebore—head-high poisonous plants with pleated leaves as long as my forearm. Then through an aromatic conifer forest under ragged cliffs. Up the switchbacks by the roaring creek, spray shooting over mottled boulders. Higher, higher, higher—my lungs drink in air rich with essences of fir, water, light. More, more, more—I can't get enough of it. Boots tramping in rhythm in the dirt, we share stories about families, long-ago hurts and joys, lost loves. We wince in pain, shriek in laughter. Dual energies of common passions and sisterly empathy arc between us.

Above the switchbacks an olive-sided flycatcher calls, *Quick—three beers!* Rachel and I stop to rest, drinking from the same water bottle and nibbling the same apple. Here the creek flattens, and the canyon opens to a U-shaped trough fringed with subalpine fir and Engelmann spruce. Beyond the trees are the snow-curried Mounts Bannon and Jedediah Smith. Just past the Death Canyon patrol cabin, slush covers the trail, soon deepening to snow. We hear a faraway *peent,* the warning call of a pika, the round-eared rabbit cousin that lives in high-elevation rock fields. I gleam with the realization that I'm in pika habitat just a few hours after I've left my trailer.

The cold sprouts goosebumps on my arms, but a steady fire burns in the pit of my stomach. When we tire of post-holing to our knees in snow, we turn back, stopping for lunch on a crescent of sand by the creek. Hearing a splash, we ogle a moose cow and calf as they step into the water from the willows on the opposite shore.

On our way down Rachel spots a black bear high up Stewart's Draw. "Let's just watch it for a while," she says. We duck under cover of some lodgepole pines and pass her binoculars between us. Cumin-colored with a white blot on its chest, the bear walks pigeon-toed to a log, noses the length of it, then hooks it with a clumsy paw and flips it over. Its tongue unfurls in a sweep for insects.

Later we slurp ice cream sandwiches on the porch at Dornan's. A bald eagle sprints by, following the Snake River. By now we're so deep-gut tired and high on this life that we just let it soak in.

That evening after a shower I wander north from Beaver Creek and ruffle my fingers through my wet hair. Droplets scatter into the sagebrush, and onto some stubby plants I recognize as yellow toadflax. Butter-and-eggs, we called them back east, referring to the odd-shaped yellow flowers with yolk-colored throats. Sitting cross-legged on the ground, I pull a handful out by their roots. Their scent is rough, earthy.

I was a child, six or seven, when Nan, with barely an eighth grade education, took me to one of the fields and tugged me to my knees beside her. "Look, sweet-haht," she said. "Butter-and-eggs. Let's pick some for the house. Miss Hamilton taught me the wildflowers. She had a book with pictures." Miss Hamilton was her second grade teacher in 1911. To Nan and to me, butter-and-eggs were whimsical bits of sunshine that brightened the dreary farmhouse kitchen. Here they're noxious weeds, but that just means I can pick them and have fresh flowers on our table.

Ahead of me, a yellow-bellied marmot perches on a rock, chin raised, tail dipping as it stares me down.

I'm overcome with satisfaction that I've lived this day well, that I've both loved the earth and filled my soul with the treasures of nature and friendship, all things I drew to myself in this new life. Back in the trailer I get on the phone, as I often do in the evenings, and spend far too much time raving about this mountain paradise to various friends back east and badgering them to visit.

Later, muscles soft and tingly, I lie in my bed in the coarse twilight that the Teton midsummer stretches to nine-thirty or ten o'clock, and listen to the relaxed beating of my happy heart.

14

Female Trouble

It's nearly six on the Friday before the Fourth of July weekend when Fred Lamming from Teton County Weed and Pest drops Rachel and me off at the office. We've spent the day at the Elk Ranch doing some big guns thistle spraying with his two-hundred-gallon spray rig. I haven't checked my baby swans yet, so I run into the office and grab the first set of keys I find. Rachel joins me.

"What's that?" I ask, starting the Bronco and nodding at a brown roll in a plastic bag on the floor.

She picks up the bag and mashes the plastic against the contents. "*Hmph.* Some kinda poop." She shrugs and drops it back on the floor.

I push the speed limit up the Outside Highway. At the parking spot we grab binoculars and head out under an umbrella of bruise-colored clouds.

"Uh-oh," I say, dropping to the ground as we crest the hill above Spencer Pond. "I only see two cygnets. How many do you see?"

Rachel glasses for several minutes before answering. "Only two," she says, her voice fading.

We scan the whole perimeter of the pond, then the nest area again. Still just two cygnets.

"*Damn,*" I say, sighing.

"Maybe a hawk or owl nabbed one."

"Good for the hawk, bad for the cygnet."

I bite my lip as I write in my notebook:

Spencer—7/1/92. 1820-1900. Overcast, wind picking up. ~ 50°.
Only 2 cygnets. Parents and babies swimming and feeding near nest.
Cygnets bobbing in shallow area, imitating parents, plunging heads

underwater with butts upturned. Whole fam. meanders around to east side of pond and back to nest site.

"Getting cold," Rachel says.
Squaring our shoulders against the wind, we jog back down the hill.

～

Elaine heads out the door of my trailer and stops short. "Hey—it's *snowing*. Can you believe it?" She turns to face us, head thrown back, mouth wide in clucky laughter. "Snow on the Fourth of July. My *God*."

I switch on the porch light. Jack pokes his head out the door, and goose-feather snowflakes melt into his ponytail.

"Oh, *no*," I say. "My *swans*."

"Listen to you." Elaine pokes my shoulder. "You sound like their mother."

"I'm a grandmother," I say. "Three cygnets hatched at Spencer Pond a couple of weeks ago. We've already lost one. Don't ever tell me I don't know what it's like to worry because I never had human children."

Her eyes soften. "And human parents think they're the only ones who love and worry. *Hah*."

Jack hugs me and steps out. "Thanks again, Mary Beth. Great food. Great company." They disappear into the squall.

With Brenda gone home to Salt Lake for the weekend, I have the trailer to myself, and I love it. I scrape out the skillet and cover the salad—remnants of our rained-out Fourth of July barbecue—and pile the dishes in the sink. *Amanhã:* I'll wash them tomorrow. Tonight's for cozying in.

Curled in a ratty stuffed chair with George Winston on the tape player, I sip chamomile tea and bask in self-reliant solitude tempered by the afterglow of social times with friends. Just a few months post-divorce, I still cherish these things like glistening gems fought for and won in bloody battle.

Wrapping an afghan around my shoulders, I think about what Elaine said. I *do* feel protective and parental toward my wildlife charges. Being a biologist puts me in a unique position. Every day I observe the daily activities and behaviors of wild animals. My observations convince me that they feel and suffer as people do. Animals are sentient and vulnerable beings, just like people.

～

There'd been a miscarriage years ago—a waxy peanut flushed away with a cramp—preceded by two months of anxiety and followed by a month of fatigue. At the time I was in my counseling graduate program. When I got the result of the pregnancy test, waves of heat and disbelief washed over me, and I headed straight to Doc Whitmore, my graduate advisor. In my group therapy class some-one once compared Doc's office to a watering trough, where people routinely stopped by for a few edifying laps of compassion and validation. Relieved to find his office door partly open, I rapped and peered inside.

"Oh, *Doc*," I blubbered.

"Jeez, Mary. What's going on? Come in. Come in." Grabbing my arm, he pulled me into the office, moved a pile of papers and books from a chair, and sat me down. His blue plaid shirt was stretched sideways so the buttons ran cock-eyed. It was half tucked into his waistband with the other half bunched over his hip. Sitting in his chair, forearms on his knees, his eyes were riveted on my face.

"You won't believe it," I said, shaking.

"You're pregnant."

I gasped. "How did you know?"

He ran one hand over his spherical, balding head. "Now, Mary, I'm gonna ask you something that you don't have to answer. But I want you to think about it."

"O-*kay*." I plucked a tissue from the box on his desk, soaked through it with one prolific blow, and reached for another.

"Does this interfere with divorce plans?"

My God. I felt as if my skin had turned transparent and he could read my beating heart. Because what was in my heart hadn't even reached my head yet. I sat on my hands and bounced my heels. Air whistled through my constricted throat.

"Because if it does, Mary, I *completely* understand. I don't know if that helps, but I know you and what your dreams are, and they don't seem to involve children."

My throat relaxed. "Thanks, Doc."

"Now that being said . . ." He bowed his head to one side, forefinger in mid-air. "I do have to say one more thing. You'd make a great mother, Mary. Of boys. You should have boys. You'd have them out camping and hiking in the woods . . ."

"*Doc* . . ." I slapped my hands over my ears.

"I'm sorry, Mary. That was my agenda, and it's your life. Just know that I'm behind you in whatever you decide to do."

Now I breathed easier. He understood. One person in this world understood. What a gift.

He looked at his watch. "*Jeezy-Christmas.* My Counseling Techniques class. I'm late." He jumped out of his chair and pawed through the piles of paper and half-filled coffee mugs on the desk. "Sorry, Mary, but I gotta run. Can you come back later?"

I'd skipped down the building steps feeling lighter, despite this foreign thing growing in me that at the time felt no different from a malignancy.

My father had once said, "The only way to lead a worthwhile life is to have a coupla kids and raise 'em right." Our families lived for news of procreation. And Bill desperately wanted kids. Like our families, he felt that motherhood, the Great Legitimizer, would calm me down, anchor me, and force me into a more sedate and conventional lifestyle, one in which I didn't embarrass him by supporting unpopular political causes and taking off by myself to faraway places.

Bill also decided that I would quit my job and devote 100 percent of my time and energy to child care. Fatherhood, he believed, would firmly ensconce him in the family grotto of perpetual responsibility as the primary wage earner. Because, after all, manly Portuguese men support respectable Portuguese women whose dreams never go beyond serving them and their offspring. He also thought that, once that wrinkly pink muffin was expelled from my body and thrust into my arms, all the energy I'd been expending on my own dreams and education would stop short and redirect.

But to me, the most disastrous outcome of having this baby would be an inevitable, lifelong suffocation in this marriage, the predicament Doc had immediately grasped. Hollow-gutted, I watched my Rocky Mountain dream turn into a helium-filled balloon that, when I wasn't looking, got yanked out of my hand and was now drifting away, unreachable, into the ether. Up it would go, becoming fainter, fainter, fainter, attenuating to a wisp, and finally a figment, a floater in the eye, out of reach.

A decision was made for me. I awakened at two a.m. with contractions in my belly. A few hours later, it was over. I had my life back. But Bill was crushed. The way he saw it, my not wanting children branded me as selfish and unwilling to take on adult responsibilities. On some level I agreed with him.

But don't try to pigeonhole me into a steel-rimmed realm of possibilities. Let me nurture without reservation, regardless of species or familial relation. Now I know there are many ways to be a mother. I've loved abandoned cats, dogs, even a gigantic white goose named Samantha. I've dodged needle-sharp teeth to squirt eyedroppers full of antibiotic down squalling throats, and slid butter-smeared pills down coiling tongues. I've spent many a night jumping out of bed to plop a kitten in its litter box or to let a puppy out.

These days, as wildlife demands my psychic energy, I confess to committing zoology's most egregious sin: anthropomorphizing. Ascribing human character-istics to animals is the realm of cartoonists and Hollywood script writers, not that of "professional" wildlife biologists. But what do you get when you cross a biologist with a counselor? An empathic biologist. The kind that feels the clamp of teeth on spine when the coyote nabs the rodent, that feels the crunch of the car bumper on ribs and the scrape of pavement on flesh when she sees roadkill.

I know this tendency of mine lowers my status among my male colleagues. One of the cardinal rules of biology is that we work to ensure the survival of populations; we shouldn't concern ourselves with the fate of a few individuals. "Real" biologists are supposed to exhibit indifference about the cruelty of nature. But sensitivity and compassion imbue my view of wildlife survival with a mater-nal concern. And I dare to believe this could be a good thing.

Good or bad, my closeness to the animals I study is emotional and compas-sionate. I fear harm to them. I want them to be happy, at peace, and well fed, and to have healthy babies of their own. Isn't this what every mother wants for her own children?

Gusts of wind buffet the trailer; the walls groan. Wind seeps through the windows and ruffles the curtains. Cracking open the door, I watch petals of snow tangle in a bowl of light. The snow thrills me, but I can only think of the swans. Of the Spencer pen, cold and afraid, huddled over her nestlings, bill tucked under one wing. And the cob nearby, alert for predators. The cygnets—do they feel comfortable and at peace, as all babies should? Or, sensing their parents' alarm, do they tremble in fear?

I whisper a plea into the snowy darkness. *Bless them with courage and strength. Keep them warm and safe. Let them thrive.*

15

Heritage

Spencer—7/5/92. 0940-0950 hrs. Temp: ~45°, pouring rain.
Only 2 adults preening near nest site. No cygnets. Looks like a lifeless
gray ball of fluff on nest.

Some solid place inside me caves in. To steady myself I hunker down and hug
my knees. Closing my eyes, I let the rain drizzle down my face. While I'm hot as
a furnace, my center vibrates as if I'm in the early stages of hypothermia. Gravity seems to have drained all liquid out of my body through my feet. I don't look
down, too afraid that I'll see my own blood swirling in the puddles and flowing
down the hillside in a red-tinted runnel.

The next day is sunny and warm. Tim and I truck a canoe to the pond and
paddle to the nest where we find one dead cygnet and one intact egg. "Probably
infertile," Tim says. The lifeless body of a second cygnet floats nearby in the
water. No sign of the third cygnet, no splotches of blood or scattered feathers that
would indicate predation.

"Dad-burnit," Tim says.

"Poor babies," I say.

We load up the canoe, strap it down, and climb back into the truck. Staring
out at the Tetons, I'm almost surprised to see that they are just as vivid and lovely
as they've always been.

What do we do when we lose something we love? We cook. Comfort
food. Back in my kitchen I reach for the packet of recipe cards I brought from
home. One catches my eye: the recipe for *sopa de couves*, Portuguese kale soup,
written in my mother's graceful penmanship. I read through the ingredients.
I just bought kale at Albertson's this week, and I have potatoes, an onion,

split peas, a head of cabbage, and a can of kidney beans. I even have a jar of *pimenta moida,* crushed hot peppers canned in liquid, from deMelo's market in Dartmouth.

But, alas, no *chouriço* and no *linguiça,* those spicy, smoky Portuguese sausages that infuse life into soups, stews, and other dishes. My spellchecker underlines them with squiggly lines. When I right-click on *chouriço,* I get four choices: choric, chorizo, Chirico, and cheerio. Choric? Of or relating to a chorus, says my dictionary. For *linguiça:* linguist, languish.

What is kale soup without *chouriço?* What could replace that potluck staple, *chouriço* and peppers? What would my father rave about from Billy's Café in Fall River, if not for *chouriço* and chips—french fries—all mashed together in a Portuguese *papo seco,* a spherical hard-crusted roll, enjoyed with pickled onions and beer, while gruff-voiced men shout in broken English and slice their short fingers through air thick with cigar smoke?

And what is a *torta,* a Portuguese omelet, without onions, fresh parsley, and chopped *linguiça* beaten into the eggs? Where else but in southeastern Massachusetts is *linguiça* pizza found on the menu of every Italian restaurant? And what sandwich compares to the classic *linguiça* sandwich, fever-red thumbs of sausage split lengthwise and fried in a cast iron skillet, then jammed between slices of Portuguese bread that soak through with peppery yellow oils?

When I describe *linguiça* to Elaine and Jack, they blink. "I like the sound of that word," Jack says. "Maybe Elaine and I should have a little daughter and name her *Linguiça.*"

I sigh in resignation. My kale soup will be vegetarian. I set to chopping.

In July of 1969, when Neil Armstrong and Buzz Aldrin walked on the moon, my parents were visiting Dad's Irish side of the family in Dublin, where they enjoyed nightly *hoolies*—food, drink, and song fests—at the homes of various cousins. Mom and Dad returned exhausted, bearing scratchy linen dish towels emblazoned with "Guinness," the workplace of my older cousin, Peadar. Wanting to hear all about Ireland, I asked about the food, hoping to hear of tasty Irish dishes, unique desserts, special sauces.

But Mom's reply was lackluster. "Meat. Potatoes. Cabbage every day. Sometimes peas."

"Aw, come on, Tree," Dad said. "The breakfasts were *terrific.* Eggs and rashers."

"Rashers?"

"Like Canadian bacon."

One summer morning a year later, when Peadar and his wife, Joan, were visiting, my mother asked him what he'd like for breakfast. Round as a globe with a belt for an equator, Peadar peered confidently through his horn-rimmed glasses, eyebrows perpetually raised, and answered, "I'll have . . . a raw egg and a banana." He took his egg in a coffee cup. My sister and I watched from the doorway in horror, hands gripping our bellies, as the egg slid down his throat in one smooth gulp.

Nonetheless, the self-assured way in which my Irish relatives sang "Oh, Danny Boy" in nasal tenor voices implied that the culture need not evolve any further.

Not so on the other side. Our Portuguese heritage was an albatross around our necks in New Bedford, where our fathers frequented smoky taverns with names like *Clube Sport Madeirense,* the "Zee Club," and "Stackhouse Street." We hated all the ethnic names—Souza, Gonsalves, Medeiros. (When I married Bill Ferreira right after college, I didn't take his name, partly because of my feminist leanings, but my own name, I thought, was Portuguese enough.) No, we all wanted WASPy Old Dartmouth names everybody could spell like Winslow, Slocum, or Ricketson. Or even better, Plymouth Colony names like Alden or Standish. Even our family Irish names, Collins or Hayes, would have been better. And we wanted our parents to join the Wamsutta Club, the Padanaram Yacht Club, or the New Bedford Country Club. But no ancestor of mine ever set foot on venerable Plymouth Rock. No Mayflower bluebloods sprout from my family tree, and until my generation no university grads either.

"Hey, girls, watch this." Dad held a bar of soap and a pepper shaker in one hand as he set down a bowl of water on the coffee table.

Nancy and I flanked him on the couch.

"Ya know why Port-a-gees smell bad?"

Ha-ha-ha! Ha-ha-ha! It seemed hilarious to hear him say that. Did we know what we were laughing at? If he talked like that, surely he didn't mean *us.* He meant the "greenhorns"—the ones who just got off the boat from the Azores, the *Bacalhau Scow,* a term Dad's friends at the Zee Club coined after a Portuguese codfish dish.

"I'm gonna show you why." He shook some pepper into the water. The grains floated and spread over the surface. He pointed. "See all the Port-a-gees swimming around?"

More giggles.

"Now watch this." When he dipped the soap into the water, the pepper grains scooted away from it. "See? Port-a-gees don't take baths 'cause they're allergic to soap!"

We laughed till we collapsed lightheaded on the couch.

Who, in this new land of Brits and Scots, would ever understand this culture? One person. I call George at Colter Bay. I get the answering machine and say, "George! Can you come down to Beaver Creek tonight or tomorrow for dinner? You won't believe it but I made kale soup. Vegetarian, though. No *chouriço*, no *linguiça*. Let me know if you can make it."

But I don't hear back from George, so I eat the soup alone. One afternoon a week later, leaving the Signal Mountain Convenience Store, I hear a voice that carries me back to Antonio's Portuguese Restaurant in New Bedford's north end.

"*Eh, Ma-ri-a!*" George calls across the parking lot, with flawless Portuguese pronunciation and a perfectly rolled "r." He strolls over to hug me.

"*Jorge!*"

"Sorry I missed your *sopa de couves*. I been really busy." He tears open a package of pink Hostess Sno Balls and chomps into one. "Hey, we're having a clam boil tonight at my place. Why don't you stop by?"

My mouth waters. "You have *clams?*"

"*Well,*" he says, wiping a sprig of coconut from his lip. "They're canned clams. And hot dogs, onions, sausage, potatoes."

I play-frown. "No *linguiça*, huh?"

"No *linguiça*." He laughs. "Hey, Mary, this is *Wyoming*. We can't have everything, ya know?"

Having a plan for the evening heartens me as I map out the rest of my day. I'll check some nests, survey weed infestations along the Leeks Marina Road, just north of Colter Bay. On my way back, I'll stop at George's cabin for a quasi-clam boil with friends. For once I'll be gone from Beaver Creek this evening. We might have so much fun eating and partying at George's—maybe we'll have a campfire in the yard and walk on the lakeshore in the moonlight—that I may not get home until well after dark. I don't even have to tell anyone where I'm going or what time I'll be home. This new freedom is a tonic to me; I'm wild with its adolescent novelty. An added bonus comes when I find new cygnet twins at Christian Pond, looking perky and healthy as they swim with their parents. I'm a grandma again, and it thrills me.

A broiling, late afternoon sun beats down as I pull into George's driveway near the Dumpster. That's strange—the cabin door is closed. I knock. No answer. Knowing he always keeps it open, I walk in. The place smells of cooked food, and there's a note on the table:

Hey Mary—
    We got called out on a boating accident on Jackson Lake. Everything's cooked—help yourself to the "clam boil." There's a Sara Lee cake in the fridge too.
    Don't wait for us—it'll be a late night. —G

I lift the lid and peer into an enamel pot on the stove. The contents are cold and congealed: tan blobs in a gray slurry. I don't even heat it up, but scoop a few spoonfuls into a bowl and eat silently, standing in the kitchen.

The sink is filled with dirty dishes. I wash my bowl and spoon and leave them upside down on the counter to drain, resisting my old Portuguese wifely temptation to wash all the dishes and leave the sink squeaky clean for George.

The Sara Lee is half eaten. When I slide the remainder out of the box, crumbs cascade to the floor, but I just kick them aside. Then I sprawl across the shit-brown Naugahyde couch and eat the whole damn cake off its slimy cardboard square.

16

Stakeout

Rachel and the boys have left for the day, and I'm turning off my computer when I hear voices murmuring by the office mail slots: Jace, Glen, Julian, Tim. I strain to hear. When the words "problem," "campground," and "food-conditioned" rise above the garble, I know a bear's involved. I'm so stoked about the prospect of trapping a bear that I can't contain myself. I run out to join them. When I approach, Jace ahems, like he's got phlegm in his throat, and the other three clam up and take great interest in their shoes.

"We've got a problem bear?" I ask, bubbling.

They huddle together, hands jammed in pockets, elbows Velcroed to ribs. I realize it could take some work to break through.

"Uh, yeah."

"Where?"

Their gazes sweep the floor, then turn upward to examine the book spines on the shelf. They act as if I've asked them how much money they have in the bank. Nevertheless, I don't back down. I look at each of them until Tim finally says, "Gros Ventre Campground."

"Oh? What happened?"

Again, the incredible shrinking act. But I stare at them until Jace says, "Somebody left doughnuts on a picnic table."

"Oh, *no.*" Then I laugh. "We should call this bear Cream Puff."

They look back at me, all rigid-jawed.

I change the subject. "Are we gonna trap it?"

"Don't know yet," Jace says, as all four of them slink out of the room.

❧

"*God,* it's hot," Rachel says, pulling off her respirator. We've been spraying herbicide in some knapweed test plots north of the Gros Ventre River.

I dump my backpack sprayer on the ground and unzip my coveralls. "You said it."

Rachel's eyes twinkle with an idea. "Hey, there's gotta be a swimming hole nearby."

On a side stream we find a secluded dogleg formed by a delta of marbly gray stones and overhung by a leaning cottonwood trunk. The water is clear, about thigh-deep. We look around. Nothing but grassy fields interspersed with brushy willows and dense cottonwood stands.

Rachel sheds her coveralls, T-shirt, and jeans. In her bra and bikini panties, she drapes the coveralls and shirt over some willow branches. "Maybe some of the sweat will dry off," she says. Then, moving as if she does this all the time, she drops her underwear in a heap on the ground and wades into the stream. She turns to face me, then plunges in the water to her chin. "Oh, Mary Beth, it's *delicious.* Come on in."

Bill's words come to me, from years ago, at a pond we found in the woods in New Hampshire: *Skinny-dip? Here? You've got to be crazy.* But now, bolstered by Rachel's unselfconscious joy, I follow her lead and undress. Shoulders roasting, relishing the solar heat on my defenseless, naked body, I enter the water. It envelops me, quells the heat, and neutralizes the sickly smell of herbicide that, despite the respirator, still coats my sinuses. I'm left weightless, blessed with the most complete freedom known to humankind.

Before us, snow-topped mountains border Granite Canyon. To the south lies Rendezvous Peak, where the tram inches up the mountainside carrying tourists from Teton Village to the high alpine areas.

Grabbing the cottonwood trunk overhead with both hands, we let the stream's current trail us. Heat blisters the crown of my head while the rest of my body rides the water. This, I realize, is one of those moments I will treasure all my life.

"We should name this place," Rachel says.

"How about Dryad's Bubble? It's from *Anne of Green Gables.*"

"*Oh, yeah!* One of my favorite books of all time."

I smile, ever enchanted by the like-hearted people I find here. "Mine, too." I scissor my legs in the water. "So what d'ya think Jace would say if he found out we were skinny-dipping on government time?"

She cackles. "3-1-1! Let's just say we were on our coffee break."

When we start to chill, we stretch out to dry on the sunny stones, dress, and head back to the truck. I open the tailgate.

"*Fuck.*" I know immediately something's torn in my hand. I flop forward, pressing my hands between my knees.

"What happened?" Rachel asks, flipping off her ball cap.

"Damn piece-o'-shit truck," I say, kicking the tire. "The tailgate's always stuck. I wrenched on it and my thumb was behind it. I think it bent all the way back to my wrist."

Her eyes peel back in horror. "*Ee-ew.*"

"Something's torn inside—a tendon or a ligament. I can feel it."

"We'd better get you to the clinic."

"*Dammit.* My right hand, too."

Dr. Blue at Emerg-A-Care says I have a torn ulnar collateral ligament. "No big deal," he says. "It's like a window shade that's snapped and rolled up. It'll be a simple surgery to go in there and pull it back down."

But Dr. Peter Rork, the orthopedist, is also working at the clinic today. "I don't think it's that bad, Brent. Let's just try a cast for a month and go from there."

For the cast, the first in my life, I have a choice of colors. I pick purple. Determined to not let this get in my way, I go back to work in the afternoon. Fred Lamming is here with his sprayer rig to treat thistles and exotic morning glories along the Gros Ventre Road. As he inches the truck along the road edge, Rachel and I take turns riding shotgun in the bed and aiming at our targets with a handgun sprayer attached to a hose from the herbicide tank. After some experimenting, I find I can shoot left-handed, leaning the gun across my cast for leverage. I'm surprised how accurate my aim is. With every shot, I whoop it up and thoroughly enjoy myself.

"You're a regular Annie Oakley," Fred says with a wink.

❦

"What're ya doin' this weekend?"

Tim's question comes Thursday afternoon, while I'm entering bear sightings into the park's wildlife database. "Don't know yet. Why?"

"Jace, Glen, and Julian are all leaving town for the weekend, and I need some help tomorrow. We need to sit in the Gros Ventre Campground all night and see if we can nab that bear that's been causing all the trouble. He's having no part of the trap."

Cream Puff. "Is this the same bear that tore through an Audi sunroof and stole a Playmate cooler off the backseat?"

He starts. "How'd you know that?"

I spread the stack of bear reports on my desk and draw one out. With my cast, I've become adept at fingering things with my index and middle fingers. "Who needs opposable thumbs?" I giggle as I hand him the report. "Looks like one of the campground rangers wrote it up."

"That's the one," he says, reading the sheet. "The bear seems to be most active in the wee hours, so I'll pick you up at midnight. Bring food. Get some extra sleep tonight."

Friday night we go on a stakeout. The eastern sky blanches where moonlight seeps through thin clouds. In a closed loop of the campground, the culvert trap is set and baited with the foreleg of a road-killed elk. Creeping in our F-250 pickup with the lights off and his head out the window, Tim backs us into a campsite within view of the trap. He turns off the dome light so we'll be in complete darkness when we open the doors. We want to keep our night vision sharp for this task. It's warmer in the truck than I expected; I throw my jacket in the back of the king cab alongside the darting kit and tranquilizer gun.

Beside me is this grizzled hulk of a guy I just recently met, and I don't quite know what to make of him yet. My worst fear is we'll sit here in silence for eight friggin' hours. I'm wired, fidgety. Sitting still is not my forte. Thank goodness I can stretch my legs and flex my feet; Tim has slid the seat back as far as it will go. Unlike a college dorm mate of mine who once stayed awake all night to wait for her period to start, I've never purposely sat up all night just waiting for something to happen.

We sit, watch, listen. The Gros Ventre River hisses through the night. Every now and then Tim's park radio, barely audible on low volume, sputters. A ranger investigating a fender bender near the Jackson Lake Lodge. A disturbance at the concessions employee dorm at Colter Bay. One ranger calling Dispatch for a radio check; another signing off duty for the night.

Tim and I make small talk about the news—the recent overturn of the Exxon Valdez captain's conviction, the Clinton-Gore ticket. But I'm getting sleepy, and current events won't keep me awake. Extending my arms over my head, I ask him how he got his year-round job at Grand Teton. He tells me he worked a few summers on the Trail Crew until he got his wildlife degree, then the permanent job in S&RM opened up.

"I was lucky," he says. "Most people wait years for a permanent job to open up."

"So I shouldn't get my hopes up?"

"Best not to. Glen's hanging on for one too." He trains a flashlight beam on his wristwatch. "We should have a look-around, I guess."

In the meager light of an egg-shaped moon, we leave the truck and head in opposite directions. Feeling no fear, I tiptoe around the campground loop and into the woods. Suddenly I have to pee in the worst way. Saucer-eyed, I search the area first. Nothing unusual. Tonight the stream of liquid pouring on leaf litter sounds as robust as Victoria Falls.

I walk south to the Gros Ventre River. Eyes zigzagging, on the lookout for I don't know what—a huddling shape? a lumbering mass?—I walk until the river's roar consumes all other sounds and scan the cobbles on the shore. All clear. As I pick my way back through a willow thicket, a Canada goose honks. My heart lurches. I freeze where I am, legs kinked, hand clutching a branch overhead, breath caught in my throat. Any second now I expect to hear the snap of a twig or swish through leaves that might signal a bear nearby. I expect it so strongly that I almost create the sound in my head. But all I hear is a *scree-eek* as Tim opens the truck door. Now I'm terrified, and I rush back, not breathing until the passenger door clicks shut behind me, sealing me once again in our dark tomb.

After a while lead weights bear down on my eyelids. We fumble to pour coffee from a thermos in the dark. Although neither of us is hungry, we spread out a feast on the seat between us. Eating slowly to pass the time, we nibble chips and salsa, apples, cheese and crackers, Reese's peanut butter cups. Tim reaches into his pocket and brings out two giant carob chip cookies he made. I'm amazed we can eat all this food in the middle of the night, but there's nothing else to do, and it keeps us awake.

Our body heat steams up the truck windows. Rolling mine down, I bristle with the cold that's descended into the night. Every other night with my down sleeping bag unzipped over my bed like a triangular comforter, I miss this dramatic temperature change. I slip back into my jacket.

After another campground circuit, the quality of our interaction changes. Strained chatter fades and conversation becomes more fluid. Our low voices feather around the truck cab, uninterrupted and without distraction, focused and at full attention. When I ask Tim about his childhood, he talks about growing up in Denver and going to school with his buddies, Grand Teton maintenance workers Doug Bonner and Sam Billings. He says his father still works at the

Park Service regional office in Denver. I tell him about growing up on the farm in Massachusetts and my close extended family.

But there are other things I want to talk about. "How long have you and Jennifer been married?" I ask.

"Twelve years," he says. He turns his face in my direction, and even in the sparse light I can see how wide his eyes are. "It's so long I can't remember *not* being married."

His comment rattles me. There was a time not so long ago when I, too, couldn't remember not being married. Now the good things about being coupled consume my thoughts. Will I ever, I wonder, reach the point where singledom becomes so indelibly fixed in my psyche that I won't remember what it was like being married? Could I nestle so comfortably into single life that I'd want to stay there forever?

"I know that feeling," I say. Then some gate opens, and I pour out the whole poor-me sob story about my divorce, my family's reaction, and how now, after fifteen years of marriage, single life seems so alien.

"Bummer," he says, munching on chips.

Another hour passes, during which we venture out two more times but find nothing. Back in the truck we go silent, our heads lolling back against the headrests.

"Stay awake, Tim," I whisper.

"I'm tryin'."

Thoughts percolate through my mind, a river pouring over rocks, slowing and slowing, as if the water supply is being turned off. I imagine this is how my life will end—a relentless slowing of thoughts and a fruitless attempt to will them to quicken.

I see Herbie turning the wheel over the weir on Spread Creek, slowing the stream of water into the Elk Ranch Reservoir. I watch the swans slapping about in shallow puddles, unable to swim, mud caking on their webbed feet. *Shoo them back to deeper water. . . .* Waving my arms, I run through the muck after them until I trip and sprawl, *splat,* face down.

My head rolls to one side, and my whole body spasms. Beside me Tim's breaths are deep and prolonged. I hiccup, gobble another peanut butter cup, look through the binoculars. Tracing an arc from one side of the windshield to the other, I examine tufts of shrubs, rocks, tree trunks. Then upward to the teardrop shapes of individual cottonwood leaves in pale moonlight.

Finally a hint of ecru light waxes over the trees, a slowly opening bloom. A robin's *cheerup! cheerio! cheerup!* shatters the quiet, then the *whee-ooo* of a gray jay and the *yant-yant-yant* of a nuthatch.

Tim starts and yawns when George Angelo comes on the radio to sign off duty at five.

"Did you know George and I went to high school together?" I ask. For some reason I'm proud of this fact, proud that someone everyone knows here is part of my past.

Tim's gorilla arms stretch to the windshield. "Didn't know that. He's quite a character."

"Tell me about it."

When we head out for the last time to snoop around, I'm smiling at the sounds, the damp morning smells, and the heart-splitting beauty of them all, and the sweet perfection they weave through the hesitant, gossamer threads of dawn.

Once more we search the campground loop, the surrounding woods, the river bottom. Tim finds an old bear track behind the comfort station, but it's already caving in and filling with leaves.

"Hawkeye," I say, punching his shoulder.

He sports a big banana of a grin.

We keep walking until I spot a dark mound. "Check this out, Tim." It's a dried up pile of poop that sure looks like bear scat to me. Taking up a twig, I poke at it. "Ah, paydirt." Buried in the pile are silver bits of aluminum foil.

"That's our dude," Tim says. "Looks old, though. I'm afraid he's moved on. Let's go home and get some sleep."

I sleep like a kitten through the long light of morning.

During an employee pizza party Monday in the parking lot behind the maintenance building, we spot a crowd of people staring up into a cottonwood tree. We walk over for a closer look. There's our bear, ample backside slumped over a stout branch, sound asleep.

17

Ursine Lessons

I peer into the barred holes on the side of the culvert trap, and, for the first time in my life, stare into the eyes of a wild black bear. In typical defensive behavior, it lowers, then raises its head and blows smelly breath in my face with a "Hah!"

"*Yuck.*" I back away, laughing.

After its arboreal snooze, Cream Puff had returned to earth and climbed into the baited trap below. Tim hauled the trap back to the office and parked it in front of the garages. Drive a truck with a bear trap behind it and heads turn, no matter where you are. Before long a crowd of maintenance guys working around Beaver Creek shows up to watch us "work up" the bear.

Bending his Abe Lincoln–like body into a C-shape, Tim slides a jab stick through one of the holes and injects a dose of Ketamine-Rompun sedative into the bear's hip. When it's clearly asleep, Jace reaches into the trap and grabs hold of the loose fur at the scruff of its neck while Julian holds the hind legs. Together they drag the bear out of the trap and lay it down in a shady spot. Jace wraps a blue bandanna around its eyes to protect the dilated pupils from light.

I've never been this close to a bear before, and I'm humbled. Kneeling before it, I stroke the coarse fur with both hands from head to rump and down all four limbs, like a medicine woman shooing away bad juju.

Hinging apart the bear's hind legs, Tim announces, "Female. Let's get her in the sack and weigh her."

Julian pushes me aside and unfolds a sheet of burlap. The other guys sink to the ground, *en masse,* arms thrashing to help.

"Here. This way."

"*No*—watch her *head.*"

"Keep it down, guys. She can hear us, you know."

"Julian, pull that side under her."

I know there's a better way to do this because my mother the nurse once showed me how to make a bed around an unconscious patient. But I stand back as they wrest the bear into the middle of the burlap sheet. Tim secures the ends and attaches them to a scale, then he and Julian heft the lifting pole. At seventy-eight pounds, she's barely bigger than Hobo, my last dog.

"Pretty small. Not much tooth wear," Jace says, rolling back the bear's upper lip. "Probably a yearling."

Julian measures her length, girth, head, and foot dimensions while Tim wields a chisel and forceps and extracts a tooth. Cementum, the bonelike substance covering the roots of teeth, grows a new layer every year. When the root is sliced, the concentric layers, called cementum annulations, can be counted like tree rings to determine the bear's age.

Tim drops the tooth into a plastic bag, which he'll send to a state laboratory for slicing and analysis. Handing me a paper towel, he tells me to press it into the tooth socket until the bleeding stops. Then he squirts it with antibiotic solution.

"We'll need heart rate, respiration, and temperature," Jace says.

"I can do that," I blurt. Laying my hand on the bear's chest, I initially have to focus to differentiate between her heartbeat and mine. But soon I sense the soft *pa-poom, pa-poom, pa-poom* throbbing into my palm. I count seventy heartbeats and thirteen breaths per minute. A digital thermometer appears and I take it, but I balk when I look up and see the circle of expectant faces above me—there's my neighbor Frank Smith, who works on the Road Crew, and seasonal maintenance workers Jeff Walton and Sam Billings who've been laying carpet at one of the employee houses. Chris, Robert, and Rachel are there, too. An audience.

"I've only done this on dogs before," I say self-consciously.

"It's no different," Jace says, opening a jar of Vaseline.

I dab some on my fingertip and smear it over the end of the thermometer. Leaning forward, I lift her little tail and slip the thermometer into her rectum. Black numbers flicker, stopping at 101.8 degrees.

Tim records the data. "Everything's normal."

For some reason I'm moved to check the bear's ears. I roll back the furry flaps and examine the pink convolutions inside. When I see oily black specks, I realize what I'm looking for. "Dogs can get ear mites," I say. "Looks like she's got 'em too."

"Mm-puh," Jace says, nodding with eyebrows raised. He jots something down on the clipboard.

When Tim squeezes the handles of a nutcracker-like tagging tool, a blue ear tag crunches through the cartilage of the bear's ear. The sound makes me cringe; I pinch my own earlobe, pierced by a silver bear claw earring. I take up the clipboard and, resisting the urge to write "Cream Puff," I note instead, "Blue tag, #17."

"Okay, we're done," Tim says. He and Julian slide the snoozing bear back into the trap and pull away the burlap. "Let's hope this is the last we see of Bear Number 17."

With the trap linked to the trailer hitch of the F-250, Julian, Rachel, and I pile into the front seat and head to the John D. Rockefeller Parkway, just south of Yellowstone. Few words escape Julian's lips as he drives along the Grassy Lake Road, but Rachel and I chatter like dawn sparrows. By now we're so accustomed to Julian's, Glen's, and 3-1-1's aloofness that we've nicknamed them the SAPs—self-absorbed pricks.

When we round a curve in the dirt road, the view opens to a meadow thick with purply flowers.

"*Wow*," I say.

Rachel glows. "Blue camas. They're here every summer around this time."

I roll down the window and stick my head out into a cloud of dust. "Man," I say, shaking my head. "I still can't believe that just a few months ago I was counseling people with all kinds of problems, and now I'm helping to relocate a problem bear."

"*What?*" Julian's jaw falls. "You were a therapist?"

"Yeah, she was. She has a counseling degree, too," Rachel says. "You didn't know that, Julian?"

"Nope." His face is still as a sculpture.

Rachel, who's sporadically working on an undergraduate wildlife degree, tells us about past jobs she's had working with pronghorns and bald eagles. Insecurity taps at my ribs: She's got the experience, I've got the education. Together we make a complete wildlife biologist.

By the time we find a good release site—relatively flat, with water and cover nearby—and open the trap door, Cream Puff has regained consciousness. But she's still holding the residual effects of the sedative. She hobbles from the trap to the ground, hind legs weak and tipsy. She stumbles over logs, looks side to side, and starts to approach us. We yell and jump and clap our hands until she turns and heads to a nearby creek. After slurping some water, she shambles across the dirt road and up the hill. We watch her through binoculars until she disappears into the forest.

My heart's pounding. I've touched her. I've everted her ears to check for mites, massaged her joints and limbs, combed my fingers through her fur. Now she has to make a new life in an unfamiliar world. I can empathize.

For the ride back I take the middle of the bench seat between Rachel and Julian.

"So what are her chances, Julian?" Rachel asks.

He grimaces as he forces the shift lever into third gear. "If she stays up here and doesn't tangle with grizzlies or hunters, she should be okay."

These could be the most words strung together I've ever heard Julian say.

"Or," I say, "she might just head right back to Moose."

"True. If she does, though, she won't get many chances before they shoot her."

"They oughta shoot whoever left that doughnut out," Rachel says.

"No kidding." Julian's shoulder twitches.

Inside me a heaviness settles. Why should this bear be removed from her home range, made vulnerable in a strange place, and risk death because of human stupidity? In this interconnected, sustaining web of life on earth, why must humans always reign?

Right then a red fox sprints across the road. Julian stomps the brake, and Rachel and I brace ourselves against the dashboard. As the fox barely misses the front wheel and ducks into the ditch, its relief is my own. Spiky conifers and lacy aspens hold proud in meadows peppered with wildflowers and grazing elk. A moose emerges from a willow thicket, watches us roll by, then saunters back. We ride silently as the wilderness afternoon unfolds around us.

My past life and recent losses are an eternity away. Now, here, in this pitching truck, we're so close I can feel the warmth of Julian's thighs radiating into mine, of mine radiating into Rachel's, and back through again, one glorious, integrated circuit.

18

Harlequin Romance

Stretch. Pull. Wrench.

My shoulder joints threaten to split apart as Tim and I churn a canoe through Jackson Lake's white-crested waves. Water fans over the bow and drenches my rain gear. To the south, gravid clouds obscure the high peaks. Gusts beat at us, nudging us northward and filling our lungs with a scent of crystalline blue-brown. Thirty meters ahead in a solo canoe, Julian cants his rippled forehead into the wind and tears ahead like a gladiator.

We're heading to Webb Canyon for a harlequin duck survey. Tim studied these elusive ducks for his master's research and continues the project as part of his job at the park. Classified as "sea ducks," *Histrionicus histrionicus* live in clear, fast-moving mountain creeks where they feed on stoneflies, caddisflies, and mayflies. The drakes mate in the northern Rockies in the spring, then take off to spend summers in coastal areas of the Pacific Northwest. Their mates stay behind to lay and incubate eggs and raise the young to fledging.

Progress across the lake is slow. With every stroke I lean ahead and paddle hard through the water, twisting my back to its limit, throwing all my strength into the motion. As my shoulders go numb, my muscles tingle with the work. I relish every stretch. Finally I'm using my whole body, living my whole life, shooting it all.

Back east I tiptoed through life in fussy clothes and impractical shoes. Like everyone I knew, I lived with much to spare. I held back, saved it for storms. "It's too hot to ride your bike to the library," my mother would say, fanning herself with a folded newspaper. "It would tax your heart." My grandmother would nod in agreement as she reached into her pocketbook for the keys to her sky blue Ford.

But here, restraint is an alien concept. No task is off-limits, and seemingly impossible feats are made to look effortless. I watch Julian as he calmly maneuvers his canoe ahead of us through the bluster. That he and my coworkers fearlessly scurry over alpine terrain to search for bighorn sheep and rappel off cliffs to band birds fills me with wonder.

"*MB.*" Tim's voice slashes through the wind as I feel a gritty thrust under the canoe. "Snag off to the left."

A sickening grind, a lurch. Less than a hand's length from the gunwales, tree branches reach out of the water like desperate arms. I extend over the starboard side, jam the paddle into the water, and pull. The canoe rocks side-to-side like a Weeble doll before leveling. Branches rake the bottom of the boat, no doubt leaving scratches in the green fiberglass.

When I turn around, Tim's staring pop-eyed from under grizzled eyebrows. "Hew-ee," he says.

The water level in Jackson Lake varies with Idaho potato farmers' demands for irrigation water. This week the water is high and rooted trees lurk just below the surface. We came too close to flipping the canoe and dumping pricey optics and gear, along with ourselves, in the lake.

"Must have rained in Idaho last week," I say, dipping my paddle.

Cloud remnants banner around Elk Ridge and thin into fog above its slopes. Up-canyon, rock ridges undulate skyward. Dark spruces and firs litter the slopes like iron filings.

As we approach the west lakeshore, the wind fizzles and straw-colored light overlays the landscape. Funneling the canoes through an opening in the willows, Tim and I course through a vegetation-choked passageway to a clearing where Julian's already beached. I climb out and haul our canoe ashore.

"Let's have an early lunch at the cabin," Tim says.

I laugh at the ruckus that follows. At six-four, with the strength and stamina of a locomotive, Tim would sense a thirty-pound daypack as little more than a ripple in his pocket. He effortlessly straps on his footlocker-sized pack, hooks a spotting scope in the bend of his arm, and reaches back into the canoe.

Arching his gnarly eyebrows, Julian hoists on his own coffin-sized pack, then jostles Tim aside to reach the sack of bird banding gear first. "I'll get that," he says.

Their muscling and grunting as they load up remind me of chest-beating behavior in other primates. Do they realize how they unconsciously spar with one another, trying to establish alpha dominance? I find myself, though, succumbing to the thrill of the task and jumping into the fray with them. This is the kind of work I've always longed to do; mustn't allow any scent of HEF (helpless eastern female) to leak out. Strapping my sopping rain gear to my breadbox-sized pack, I heave the thing onto my back, trying to appear tough and confident.

Dewy willows ribbon over my arms as I plod through them with my waders draped around my neck like a stole. As I walk I shout, "*Hey* bears, we're *coming through* ..." But the guys just jut their chins and trudge silently.

At the far end of a jade-colored meadow, the shuttered Lower Berry patrol cabin comes into view. The narrow porch is stacked with firewood. Nearby, a plywood, pointy-roofed enclosure holds emergency and fire-fighting equipment. A litter is suspended by bungee cords from the roof overhang. I tell Tim I want to see the inside of the cabin.

"You got a key," he says.

Oh, yeah. What a *trip*, having keys to Grand Teton's backcountry cabins on my key ring! I unlock the door to a dry wood smell. Inside are a jumble of cupboards, tiny wood stove, dinged-up table with two chairs, bunks with bare mattresses. Gear dangles from the roof joists. It's a *perfect* little log cabin in the woods. Through the open door I hear breezes whispering through the spruces and warblers chortling in the willows. Until I'd experienced full silence broken only by these woodsy sounds, I hadn't realized how much I'd missed it.

After lunch on the porch we head back to the canoes. To get into Webb Canyon, we canoe across the outlet of Moose Creek and lash the boats to willows on its gravelly shore. The harlequin duck habitat begins about three miles up-canyon, so we have about an hour's hike before we need to boot up in our waders.

These quiet northern canyons—Webb, Berry, Owl—are where the grizzlies are, and the specter of confronting one is never far from my consciousness. So I carry my foolproof bear repellent: a handful of pebbles in a small V-8 juice can, the opening covered with a square of duct tape. According to the experts, a metallic clanking noise deters bears because it alerts them to a sound that doesn't occur naturally in the wild.

The guys charge ahead. Even with us all at comparable levels of fitness, I could never keep up with their long-legged strides. I assume a walking rhythm that matches my heartbeat. A song my grandmother sings plays in my mind, "In the Blue Ridge Mountains of Virginia, on the trail of the lonesome pine ..." It rolls on and on, ending only to turn back on itself and rerun in a slightly different key, a musical Möbius strip.

The sky has rinsed clear and now explodes in garish blue, with a few benign cloud rivulets to the west. Sun, sky, trees, flowers, earth, rocks. A sweet scent wafts from the willows along the creek. In the meadows: yellow mules' ears, purple larkspur, crimson Indian paintbrush, peach-colored buckwheat; bubbly rocks coated with flakes of green and orange lichen; patches of huckleberry bushes, thick with ripe berries that I pick and pop into my mouth as I pass. No animal tracks yet. As I enter a dense purpose of fir and pine, a sandhill crane croaks overhead. Looking up I spot a scrap of wing through the knitted boughs. The trail winds ahead, blurry with dust, calling me into the wilderness that I now call home.

But while I love the profusion of color, the gloss of sun, the symphony of sounds, smells, and tastes, I'm aware that the guys are out of view, out of earshot. I'm doing something we advise against in the park literature we ourselves write: hiking alone in grizzly country. Only a V-8 can and a few stones stand between me and the silvertips. I pick up my pace, rattle the can more vigorously, and yell, "Comin' through, bears! *Outta the way.*"

Moose Creek cascades over logjams, spewing spray and tan foam. Finally, where the salmon-colored pinnacles rise up near the rocky cliffs of Elk Mountain and Owl Peak, I spot the guys ahead in a clearing. Tim lies on his back with binoculars glued to his eyes; Julian leans on one elbow and peers through a spotting scope.

"Hey." I worm out of my pack and fish out my water bottle. "What're we looking for?"

"Peregrines. Bighorns." Julian inches the scope around on its tripod.

Using my pack as a pillow, I lie down and peer through my own binocs. Nubbles of grass, dirt clods, and pebbles press through my gray shirt, warming my back, their heat intensified by this pulsing, high-altitude sunlight.

After glassing the peaks for a while, we continue up the canyon until a finger of willows curves toward the trail. Tim stops and paws sweat off the bridge of his nose. "The creek starts braiding here," he says. "We can each take a section." Without warning, he strips down to his BVDs and pulls on his chest waders.

The rubber of my own waders burns hot as I bring them up over my green jeans. But when I wade into a deep pool, the heat dissipates and a cool compression massages my legs from ankles to thighs like rubber anti-embolism stockings. I head to one of the channels of the creek where the water slows and flattens.

Sloshing through my willow-choked strand of the creek is slow. I focus on every step, balancing on round cobbles. Every few steps I glass the water up and downstream, paying particular attention to streamside rocks and their shadowy overhangs. But all I see are water striders that look as big as grape leaves through the binoculars.

Eventually we all meet up on a gravel bar.

"Any luck?" I ask.

"Nup," says Julian.

"*Nada,*" Tim says, swatting at a gnat on his arm. "Let's head upstream."

We continue on, a ratty wader parade, to a fragrant stand of subalpine fir.

"Let's split up again. Julian, you get into the creek here and wait. I'll head about half a mile upstream. MB, you scan in between. Stay low. If you see any ducks, herd them downstream toward Julian." Tim ambles on up the trail, dust clinging to his waders.

I act like I know what I'm doing. Following him, I make mental calculations: If he's going a half mile, how far is that on the ground? How much time? About ten minutes? Maybe less for the stilt-man. To be on the safe side, I check my watch and go off trail after about six minutes. I plow through the willows to the creek bank and find a mica-speckled rock hidden in the shrubbery where I can sit straight-legged while scanning the creek through an opening in the branches. After a few Wheatsworth crackers and a bite of cheese, I get comfortable for the survey.

Botanists have it easy, I think, fingering a leaf of *Salix,* willow. Wildlife biology can be tedious, lonely work: long hours of sitting still and waiting for animals to come to us. Peering through binoculars with my elbows levitating at my sides, my neck muscles start to contract in rebellion, so I draw up my knees and lean on them. A twirl of the focus ring brings the creek's eddies, bubbles, and globs of spume into shattering clarity. In the middle of the creek, water sheets over a slab of stone. A soot-gray bird lands on it and does four or five knee bends before flying downstream. I recognize it as an American dipper, or ouzel, that spends its life on mountain streams like this, diving underwater for insects, larvae, and small fish.

Time elongates. Except for my peephole to the creek, I'm encased in a cocoon of willows. Before I'm aware of it, my mind is ensnared in a familiar chain of what-ifs. What if a grizzly bear decides to come down for a drink in the creek right *here?* What if, just beyond that creek bend, are a moose cow and calf? They could stampede me where I am and trample me to a bloody pulp. What if I drop my pants to pee in the bushes and a mountain lion nails me from behind, and later on the guys find me, bottoms up, again a bloody pulp?

I laugh at the fears tapping at my inner window. Undoubtedly I'm the only S&RM employee who even thinks about such things. (Some people have no imagination.)

A doughy cloud rambles across the sun and dims my willow copse. I set down the binoculars to rub my neck, then catch a breath halfway. *Hoo, what's this?* A brown motion bobbles near the opposite shore, moving downstream with the creek flow. I slowly bring up the binocs. There's a duck, the mother, dun-colored with a white disk behind her eye, followed by six similarly patterned young. Seven harlies!

As soon as my hand aims for my radio holster, the mother spots me and turns, signaling for her brood to follow. I unsnap the holster and yank out the Motorola. "*Tim!*" I rasp. "*I see some. A mom and six kids.*" I'm so shaky I have to scramble-grab the radio to keep my sweaty hands from flinging it into the creek.

"Cool. I'm on my way."

"They're headed upstream," I say.

"I'll stay in the water and herd them back down." Then, a minute later, "I see 'em. They're just chillin' under a rock overhang."

Julian's barely audible squawk is next, "I'll string up an Avi-net."

I stay hidden in the willows, my breath coming in shallow puffs. When I project ahead to what these ducks are about to endure, a grainy heat floods my ribcage. *No, no, no.* They're in their home, snug in the wilderness puzzle in this far-flung place, doing what harlequins do, living life, and we're about to ambush them and scatter all the pieces.

The ducks stream past me. Then Tim appears, a lumbering galoot, sloshing through the water behind them. I slip into the creek to join him.

"Let's put up another net," he says, "in case they turn back."

He hands me a plastic bag, and I withdraw a bundle of soft black netting. We tie off the top ends of the net to two willow trunks, one on each shore, and anchor the bottom edge underwater with stones. The ducks are now swimming between Julian's net and ours. The young can't fly yet, so they're trapped.

We shoo them downstream. My heart breaks when I round a bend and see all seven ducks flapping helplessly in Julian's net.

I watch Tim fold his hands around the mother's body, disentangle her from the net, then place her into a cloth bag Julian holds open. Using the same technique, I cup one of the ducklings in my hands and wangle it free of the net. "*Forgive us,*" I whisper. Its tiny paddle-feet quake as I release it into the bag.

One by one, we fish the ducks from the bag to weigh, sex, and band them. Tim does the sexing, holding them upside down in his lap to poke around for the recessed sex organs. "I know, I know," he says as one youngster struggles. "I wouldn't want someone turning me upside down and sticking me in the butt either. But don't worry; you'll be fine. All your siblings had to go through this, and now it's your turn. Didn't your mother warn you about us?"

While Julian takes down the nets, I hold a young harlequin duck in my hands for Tim to clip on a leg band. This baby is a bundle of squirmy brown down with a stubby bill. Straining warm against my hands, it plops a white dollop of anxiety-induced poop in my lap. I resist the urge to hold it to my chest and murmur "*There, there, baby. You'll be okay.*"

When we've finished recording the data, Tim cuddles the bag in his arms and crunches into the water with it. The ducks splash out and regroup, then paddle downstream into the shadows.

It's past sundown by the time we roll up the nets, with five and a half miles left to hike out. On the way down we get sidetracked in a huckleberry patch, dropping handfuls of berries into an empty Nalgene water bottle. Night comes, and we walk back in the tree-sifted light of a three-quarter moon. I'm especially uneasy hiking through prime grizzly habitat at night reeking of huckleberry juice, but we stay together for the remainder of the hike back to the canoes.

Through velvety water lit with silver moonlight, we paddle across the Moose Creek outlet.

Thwack! Water splashes over the gunwales. I hold my paddle in midair, whip my head side to side.

Thwack! Thwack!

All around us, beavers, annoyed at our presence, slap the water with their tails and dive under our canoes. I look behind me to share a hushed laugh with Tim, whose eyes shine through the moonlight with the same dreamy reverence that I feel.

19

Taproot

I pledge to never leave the Tetons. On Darcy's dashboard, I display animal bones I've found in the woods—the lacy skull of a vole, the chunky humerus of a deer, the fissured molar of an elk, the section of coyote tail whose slender bones are beaded together by dry strings of soft tissue—as if these timeless things could root me to this place forever.

Seeking oneness with the wild, I hike alone to creeks and lakes and dip naked into their waters. Sometimes the water is so cold my head goes pounding numb. Then I emerge and lie prone on white rocks to dry in sunlight so hot it evaporates the sheets of water from my skin without warming it. I feel so egoless that I wonder if my body has morphed into something ethereal and spiritlike. When I run my hands over my body, my skin feels cool, disembodied, pure as rain. When I stand and lean my naked body against a smooth aspen trunk I feel no separation: My toes root down into the earth, my head stretches up to the sky, and my arms from shoulders to fingertips seem to flutter with wafer-sized leaves.

My parents hang on to the notion that I'll come to my senses and return home. But Massachusetts, with its crowded shores, gridlock traffic, and lushness born of fog, has become anathema to me. The Tetons are in my blood now, and I can't even remember a time when they weren't.

I'm not alone. Everyone I know here has migrated from somewhere else; I have yet to meet a Jackson native. But unlike other resort towns with similar demographics, Jackson Hole has long attracted a different sort of person, the type who often finds himself or herself flirting with the outer edges of the cultural norms. In his hilarious book *Snow Above Town*, Donald Hough wrote in 1943 that, as American society became more complex, Jackson Hole "was captured, hands down, by the walking wounded. As queer a collection of halfwits, apostles, remittance men, social outcasts, certified public accountants, broken aristocrats, chronic drunks, [and] last-ditch women haters as ever floated into the same backwater now discovered the ramparts of the Tetons. Once started, the movement became unanimous. Each new arrival in turn took one look around, saw he was among friends, and threw down his pack." Hough, who ended up in Jackson Hole because he lost all his money gambling, and who attended his first cocktail party in the Jackson office of the US Postal Service during Prohibition, clearly met his own standards.

As a certifiable member of the "walking wounded," I prefer to identify with what Robert Betts in his 1978 book *Along the Ramparts of the Tetons* more benignly calls "rough-hewn nonconformists" and "free spirits." For me, these mountains and forests, now so close and accessible, bring previously unreachable desires into the realm of possibility. Locking my gaze is the glistening beacon of wilderness solitude. I'm enthralled by backcountry rangers and "trail dogs" who work ten days at a time doing patrols and trail maintenance in the park's most isolated areas. I wonder, could I do that? I believe I could, and love it. Like everyone else I've met here, I buy into the romance and long to up the ante and meet nature alone on her own harsh terms.

Julian, who manages to extend his field season well into December with occasional trips to Missoula for graduate committee meetings, welcomes the solitude of a Teton winter with confidence. "I always take off and spend Christmas with various friends and family," he once told me, head slanted and chin tucked, "but for once I'd like to stay here and spend the whole week totally alone."

I understand what he means. In our minds, our ability to thrive in solitude somehow proves our wilderness mettle and ultimately justifies our value as woodsmen and woodswomen, our place in the puzzle.

"There is in every American, I think," said Vice President Hubert Humphrey, "something of the old Daniel Boone—who, when he could see the smoke from another chimney, felt himself too crowded and moved further out into the wilderness."

I dream of nesting and rooting here, in a real home, with quilts on the bed and a Mason jar of wildflowers on the kitchen table. But not a Mission 66 house, like the ones in the Moose Employee Housing Area, three-bedroom ranches surrounded by other three-bedroom ranches with identical floor plans.

"For many years," wrote Teton climbing guide Jack Turner in his book *Teewinot: A Year in the Teton Range*, "I dreamt of a hermitage in the northern mountains dear to me—somewhere up in Snowshoe Canyon. I would find a well-hidden overhanging glacial boulder in a cul-de-sac with water and a view of the peaks. I would surround the overhang with rock walls just as they have done for millennia in the Himalayas. . . . Once or twice a year, I would visit and listen to the silence for weeks on end."

But hovering in the back of my mind is a different kind of shelter, the quint-essential wilderness home—a log cabin in the woods. Skis on the porch. Wild animals scratching at the door. A rustic den where I could be one with, yet pro-tected from, nature. A cozy interface between nature and civilization but on a humble scale: a morsel of civilization in a sea of nature, a welcome reversal to modern society's lopsidedness.

In American culture the allure of a log cabin in the woods holds an atavistic power, taking us back to our pioneer roots when life was uncomplicated and free of technology. It brings to mind Lincoln's modest beginnings and Thoreau's mindful solitude, without which we flounder and flop.

"We need the tonic of wildness," wrote Thoreau in *Walden*, "to wade some-times in marshes where the bittern and the meadow-hen lurk, and hear the booming of the snipe; to smell the whispering sedge where only some wilder and more solitary fowl builds her nest, and the mink crawls with its belly close to the ground. . . . We can never have enough of Nature."

We still need those things. But we also need shelter from them, a porous space that keeps us warm and dry, but still lets in the sound of the soughing wind and the smell of rain. Unlike modern buildings, designed to shut out as much of nature as possible, log cabins, built of whole boles of trees, smudge the boundary between outer and inner. While strong and protective, wood invites the outside in. Like owls in a tree snag, the cabin's inhabitants are also part of the forest ecosystem. Perhaps no cabin builder better illustrated this principle than John Muir, who diverted Yosemite Creek to run beneath the floor of the cedar and pine cabin he built. Plants grew through the floorboards; frogs chirped beneath him while he slept.

I see myself in a place like the Lower Berry patrol cabin, peering out into a blizzard, a fire crackling in the stove, passing the snowbound time by taking pen to journal, commingling outer and inner. I envision myself an erudite and discerning chronicler of nature like Annie Dillard, whose *Pilgrim at Tinker Creek* left me quaking in veneration when I first read it.

I want a place where I can burrow in and where nature and wildlife fill my days and mold my behavior. I want to tell my family, "Had to shoo a bear away when I went out this morning." I want to hear, "*How* much snow?" and "*How* many degrees below zero?" so I can square my shoulders, answer honestly, and feel I can weather any hardship.

But even John Muir, the guru of wilderness solitude, once wrote, "I find no human sympathy, and I hunger." This is where Julian and I part company.

"When people tell you they don't need anybody," Doc Whitmore once told our Counseling Techniques class, "don't believe them." He frowned and then swooped one fist. "'Cause I tell you what. They just *think* they don't need people. They really do."

My cabin will become the framework around and within which I will build and nurture my new family: these people I've met here who find solace and sustenance not only in nature, but also in each other. We'll hike and ski right out my back door, then spend evenings by the fire sharing food, stories, laughter—all those things that hone one's life to a treasured clarity.

I crave solitude, but with limits. Now, if I tire of being alone at Beaver Creek, I can walk around the loops and find people sitting around campfires or playing horseshoes, happy to welcome me for a visit. My solitude is circumscribed by ample conviviality, here for the taking whenever my ear craves another human voice. I truly believe it will always be so, and I look ahead to my next chapter with hope and excitement.

But while I may think I've cut the cord to fully fit, free and relaxed, into this new world of mine, I'm still carrying with me a daunting set of luggage.

20

Ghosts

Day 1 of Elk Classification. 5:40 a.m.

Rarefied smoke in the air from forest fires in Idaho. Grayish-red banners in the eastern sky. Eyelash of a moon over the Teton skyline. To the south are the Potholes, with their craterlike dips formed from chunks of ice dragged and left behind by receding glaciers. Forested Burned Ridge wedges into the sage flats.

I'm seated on a log, armed with binoculars, taking it all in. At dawn and dusk, elk congregate in places like this—open areas near trees. For a full week every August, biologists from the park and the National Elk Refuge observe from various posts around the valley to get a handle on the size and demographics of the Jackson Hole elk herd. I'm ready to count and classify any elk I see into age and sex categories—bull, spike (a yearling male with unbranched antlers), cow, calf of the year. On my lap is a clipboard with a worksheet, one column per category.

I'm jiggly with excitement. Part of me feels I don't deserve these momentous changes for the better in my life. I am Portuguese, after all. We don't expect good things in life. For my ancestors in the Azores, mere survival sucked every spark out of them until they were so tired they just died. Life wasn't about being successful or happy. If you happened on either of those things, it was an anomaly. In fact, Dad always topped off any personal accomplishment with the qualifier: "How's *that* for a Portuguese kid from the south end of New Bedford?" The culture's understanding is: We'll never amount to anything. Long forgotten are the big names from the Age of Discovery—Prince Henry the Navigator, Vasco Da Gama, Ferdinand Magellan. Every now and then we produce a Meredith Vieira. But most of the names you see riding the waves of success nowadays are not Lopes, Soares, Gomes, or Gonsalves.

I recall the exact moment I learned there were such things as "wildlife biologists." It was 1972, the year my dorm mates and I watched the draft lottery, the year that "Rocky Mountain High" hit the airwaves. At nineteen, I was already homing west.

"Mary! Come watch this." Dad was calling me from the den when I was home from college one weekend. I found him hunched over a TV tray with a jumble of metal plates, screws, and cords that I recognized as innards of a Skil saw. He gestured at the television with a screwdriver and a cigarette. "This lady works with *buffalo* at Yellowstone National Park. *And . . . ,*" he said proudly, "she's Irish."

Sitting on the ottoman at his feet, I cranked up the volume. On the screen, buffalo snorted and stomped by a steaming river. The camera panned to a woman surrounded by shelves of books and a busy-looking desk. Wearing a buttoned blouse, she looked more like a librarian than a woodswoman, but her poise and knowledge about the buffalo, or *bison,* as she called them, were expansive. Her name was Mary Meagher, and her title was "wildlife biologist."

"You should write to her," Dad said, aiming the screwdriver into the hodge-podge of metal and wires.

Although I'd never heard of it, I knew then and there that wildlife biology would be my ticket to the West. But other than a two-minute introduction to Mary Meagher, I had no idea what wildlife biologists did. Were they like game wardens, I wondered, carrying guns and stalking poachers? As much as I loved nature, this didn't seem like my calling. I was majoring in basic pre-med biology at college. Somehow, I realized, I had to change tracks. The University of Vermont in Burlington offered an undergraduate wildlife degree; I toyed with the idea of transferring. But my parents and I agreed that Stonehill's strong science program would give me a broader foundation, which would lead to better job opportunities in the future. To this daughter of a draftsman and a hospital-trained RN, the idea of having a job as a wildlife biologist, of getting paid to study wildlife, seemed preposterous.

What a difference twenty years can make.

Cheow. I start at the strange noise. Standing a car's length away from me is a pronghorn buck, head lowered. His spindly legs seem fragile as pencils, but his hooked black horns are aimed straight at me. My eyes balloon. Will he charge? I doubt it. He's smaller than I am. All I have to do is stand up, clap my hands, yell "Git!" But instead I stare him down. "Hey there, buddy," I say. "How ya doing today?"

I swear he frowns as if to say, "What the hell?" Then he shouts his hoarse *cheow* again, pivots on his hind hooves, and flees.

I picture Dr. Mary Meagher sitting on a log as I am now, training her binoculars on a bison herd. Tim told me that she studied under A. Starker Leopold, son of Aldo, and that she still works at Yellowstone. I'd like to meet her some day and tell her how she once influenced a confused college student in Massachusetts. I never wrote to her back then, but I did eventually get into a wildlife graduate program.

Although they didn't like that I'd left my fiancé behind in Boston, my parents were thrilled when I entered Virginia Tech. They boasted, "Mary's a graduate student in wildlife at Vuh-gin-i-a Polytechnic Institute and State University," chests puffing as they enunciated the full pompous mouthful of the school's name. "She's one of only three *gerls* out of *fawty* students in her class."

With my two female classmates and a passel of easy-riding, shaggy-haired boys, I strolled around Cheatham Hall in sturdy dungarees, plaid shirts with rolled-up sleeves, and Tyroleans, orange leather work boots with tan rubber soles. We admired our professors, two of whom were especially notable: droll Henry Mosby, known for his research on the wild turkey, or as he called it, "God's noblest game bird," and forward-thinking Bob Giles, who'd edited our *Wildlife Management Techniques* manual. We knew all about the greenhouse effect and how polluting gases trapped in the atmosphere were warming the earth. We understood that the J-curve of human population growth was unsustainable, and that our sheer numbers would soon exceed the earth's carrying capacity. We agreed that human overpopulation was the mother of all environmental problems, and professors freely advised us to be responsible stewards of the earth by using birth control and having small families. It all seemed so diamond-crystal obvious to me that I couldn't imagine there'd be anyone in the world who would disagree. *We're going to solve this problem soon,* I thought, *no doubt in my mind. Our vision and action will save the earth.*

I dove into academic challenge and arduous fieldwork. I devoured Aldo Leopold's *A Sand County Almanac,* Durward Allen's *Our Wildlife Legacy,* Edward Abbey's *Desert Solitaire.* I took courses with buzzword names: Population Dynamics, Game Management, Ornithology, Dendrology, Physiological Adaptations of Wild Animals, Forest Ecology.

Early on I discovered I had a propensity for working out problems in Population Dynamics. Dreamy blond boys from Montana and Colorado sought me out for help with assignments. With a diamond engagement ring on my finger, I worked with them to create "backward reconstructions" of deer populations:

Using hunter check station data, we calculated mortality rates per age class to reconstruct the demographics of the living population.

While I enjoyed helping out my classmates, I was gaining something from them. After working through the population calculations, we lounged in the grad offices and gabbed about the Rockies. "Why don't you come to the Grand Canyon with us over spring break?" one of the Colorado guys asked me. "We're gonna drive straight through and backpack for a few days."

An inner voice called, *Hop on board!* I was intrigued and tempted, but my path was already set, engraved in a set of principles no one here would understand: the Vila Franca do Campo tiles. Nonetheless, I knew that with my wildlife degree, I'd eventually make it to the Rockies. I just had to figure out how to play my hand so that Bill would hop on board with *me*.

How naive was *that?* Suddenly aware of the cold, I rub my gloved hands together, then take up the binoculars. No animals yet, other than my earlier pronghorn visitor ambling to the west while he nibbles on sagebrush. I listen through the clotted silence, but all I hear are my thoughts.

On a December day soon after Jimmy Carter was elected, Bill and I walked down the aisle of St. Mary's Church. This is what I was thinking: *This marriage will be different. I'll keep my maiden name and go by "Ms." I'll have my own career. My Pill-Pak will keep me free. We'll split the housework. And someday we'll move out west.*

Flitting around the reception hall, I babbled about my Virginia Tech year to anyone who'd listen. I gushed about my quirky new friends, bluegrass music on farmhouse porches, wild turkeys gobbling at dawn in forests thick with haze and mountain laurel.

Her dark eyes furrowed with concern, my great-aunt Dot took my arm and said, "It was too much, wasn't it?"

I looked at her. "*What?*"

"You shouldn't have gone to Virginia, engaged. You should have stayed home and taken the time to plan your wedding instead."

"Oh, *no*. It was the best year of my life."

She didn't get it, and I was floored that someone I loved so much could have misread me so completely. Or did she? That she might have had her own family-first agenda never occurred to me. Unlike *Tia* Mame and *Ti'* Elena, her older sisters who never left the farm, *Tia* Dot had followed her husband and his post office job to Hartford, Connecticut, two hours away, after World War II. Although she'd done some traveling, Dot couldn't comprehend a dream like mine, nor the progression of steps necessary to pursue it. To her, Virginia might well have been Timbuktu. And now Wyoming. I wonder how she'd react to this strange, wild place?

In the gluey dawn light I scan the whole view with binoculars. Oops . . . *what's that?* I swing the lenses back. Two cow elk clamber over a ridge to the southeast. They must have been grazing in the Snake River bottom and now are heading to the Potholes.

Hands shaking, I make two vertical tick marks in the "Cow" column, then swing the binocs back up. Now there are six or seven elk, with more heads popping into view behind them. Cow, Cow, Spike, Calf, Cow. . . . In the appropriate columns, I make four tick marks at a time and cross them out with the fifth. My cast makes for clumsy writing, but I keep on. Five, ten, fifteen cows. Five, ten calves. Two, three, four spikes. Animals keep appearing. *Oh, man.* It's thrilling! I can hardly keep up, heart slamming my ribs.

When elk are no longer bounding into view, I bring down the binoculars. The sun presses at the horizon. I can see the whole herd now, straggling along in a serrated line. I whip up the binocs again and count all the animals I can see.

Seventy-seven. But I don't trust it. I count them again. Seventy-four. *Damn.* The third time, I get seventy-six. Screw it. I count up my tick marks. Seventy-five. The elk are now milling around the Potholes shoulder-to-shoulder in an amoebalike blob. It's okay. This is science. I *am* allowed a margin of error. Later, I can compare my numbers with Julian who's stationed somewhere on the River Road. No doubt he'll have counted the same herd.

Noticing the drum roll in my chest, I draw in and release a lungful of cold air. My lower back goes soft.

The herd veers toward the south side of Burned Ridge where the forest swallows up groups of animals. I check my watch. Quarter past six. I yawn, rub my cramped neck. Cresting the mountains of the Gros Ventre to the east, oat-colored light pours over the flats, wringing thin shadows from the sagebrush. I squint into the sun, will it to warm my shivering body. I check my radio, make sure it's on.

With a scrabbling to my right, a metal-colored bird with white outer tail feathers descends onto a sagebrush tip. A dark-eyed junco. It nods its head in all directions, then flies off. As I track its flight with binoculars, a blur of fur appears in the outer range of my field of view, and I spin around to follow it. A coyote stops trotting and sits on its haunches, facing me, tawny eyes peering over its nose. I imagine how it's taking me in. *When a feather drops in the forest, the eagle sees it, the coyote hears it, the bear smells it.* Does this coyote hear the soft swoosh of fleece as my arms slide along my torso? Does it hear my breath? My heartbeat? My thoughts?

I imagine my father sitting beside me on this Teton morning, as spellbound as I am by the wildlife. I so want him to release the hard-husked seed of anger he holds in his heart and feel happy for me, that I got to live the lifestyle he once dreamed of.

But more than that, I want my family to understand why I left, and to forgive me for it. When I informed my parents I'd joined my Virginia Tech classmates and become a vegetarian because producing meat is ecologically wasteful, my father had said, "*Jeez,* you send your kids away to college and look what happens to them."

But vegetarianism is a far cry from a broken marriage. My divorce and move to Wyoming ripped the family fabric in a way that seems forever unmendable. Along with Bill, my parents thought I'd eventually "get this out of my system" and be eager to return to the clogged inertia and morbid predictability of my past life. The way they see it, my wanting to stay here alienates me from their values and all that's important to them.

My counselor friend Jan once told me she envied me because I had this dream of being a Rocky Mountain woodswoman. She'd never had such a dream and couldn't understand feeling so passionate about anything in her life. Part of me envied her, but another part felt pity. I couldn't imagine my life without this drive, this intense longing, although things would have been much easier without it.

There are many ways to live a life. I could have squelched my angst-ridden dream, stayed, and had a perfectly acceptable life as the good wife/daughter/sister/niece in my family nest—frizzy-haired and smooth-skinned from seaside humidity, fat on clams and scrod, barbecued *carne d'espeto* and sugar-dipped *malassadas,* my free time spent in shopping malls.

Of course I couldn't.

The coyote trots away when Julian calls on the radio. "Ready to head out?"

Before I can answer, I hear his truck on the RKO Road. "I'm on my way."

One day Bill will tell me, "I gotta say, Mary, we had trouble for years, but you were the one who had the guts to do something about it." Eventually *Ti'* Elena will tell my mother, "If they weren't happy together, then it's good that they split up." The rest of my family will be wowed by my new life, and of course they'll understand why I left, who wouldn't?

But now, as I sweep through the sagebrush, pack slung over one shoulder, part of me is prancing, but there's a heaviness inside.

21

Short Timing

A day comes in mid-August when the light changes. In the morning, before I even raise the window shades, I see that summer's subdued light is gone, replaced by the vivid, searing light of fall. Mornings lag behind drawn-out nights, temperatures dipping. We turn on the furnace in the trailer; it groans and clucks like a brood hen.

The salvo of tourists winds down as schools open. Bear activity ramps up as they seek out high-calorie foods to fatten themselves up and carry them through their winter sleeps. Berries ripen and drop. Once hardy wildflowers wither into dry spindles.

Grand Teton's seasonal work force begins to move on. Up the road the Highlands employee housing compound clears out, and a few later-working seasonals move from cabins there to the barracks houses and trailers being vacated at Beaver Creek.

To my delight I arrive home on a Friday after having my cast removed at the clinic to find Brenda armpit-deep in cartons, her warehouse of small appliances and dishes strewn on the counters. By Sunday evening I have, at last, a home of my own. I move to the back bedroom, with its double bed, spacious closet, and full-length mirror cracked across the middle like a Wyoming windshield. It's still Beaver Creek 447, a leaky, mouse-infested trailer. But it's my place—*my own home*—for two months anyway.

I lie on my new big bed and compare my two hands, glad to have them both functioning again. Although thin and atrophied, my right hand is healed and needs no further medical attention. What a blessing that the body heals so well. The spirit? *Ah,* that's another journey with its own set of rules.

My job ends October 30, and with it goes this trailer. My original plan was to work a summer at Grand Teton, then move to Salt Lake City. I have friends there—a counselor friend from Massachusetts and her partner. I expected I'd find a counseling job and a nice apartment, and that I'd survive city life with frequent forays into the Wasatch National Forest and the Uinta Mountains to keep me sane.

But as the Teton lifestyle mainlines into my veins, that plan evaporates. I ask around—how can I stay here year-round? Jackson winter jobs are menial and housing options few and expensive, but there are ways to stay. Friends rally.

"You won't have any trouble finding work. The Jackson businesses always need people for the ski season."

"Find someone who needs a roommate. No one can afford Jackson rents on their own."

"You could house-sit or caretake somebody's vacation home."

"If they'll let you volunteer at the park, you can stay in your government housing all winter."

None of these options appeals to me.

I overhear Glen telling 3-1-1, "Seasonal life sucks. I gotta get on permanent."

"We're doing what we can," 3-1-1 says, chin whiskers bristling as his jaw clamps.

The PGJ, Permanent Government Job, is the seasonal employee's Holy Grail. For seasonals who as a whole seem to abhor security, the desire for a PGJ seems incongruous. Last month Elaine, who has two master's degrees, was overjoyed to land a permanent job as a secretary in the Maintenance Division. "And we get a house!" she'd cried. But now she says, "Security isn't all it's cracked up to be. It can trap you."

How well I know *that*. An old friend worked several decades at New Bedford's Continental Screw Company where, for forty hours a week, he operated a device that cut the slots in the heads of screws. In New Bedford multiple generations of European immigrants pool their earnings from similarly repetitive but benefitted jobs to buy three-story tenement houses where they live forever, the tenements passing from deceased grandparents to newly married grandchildren.

"Be a free spirit for a while," Elaine tells me. "Live in the moment. Have some fun."

I so want to do that. But the words "free" and "spirit" have never been aligned in my particular star chart.

"Impermanence," the Buddhists say, "is a fact of life. Embrace it." But how?

As summer wanes my work becomes more solitary. Tim has Chris and Robert spend their last work days on an office face lift, clearing out old files and moving furniture and books, while Glen or Julian snatches up lithe, winsome

Rachel to help with wildlife surveys. After a day in the field soaking up Rachel's bountiful charms, the guys return limp-eyed and grinning like goons.

I continue to check my swans and amphibians, and spend entire days by myself surveying weeds along roadsides. But while I love being out in the park, I feel stagnant doing these repetitive tasks alone, and these are the times the Creature scratches at my heart-door.

Tim sends me up Steamboat Mountain one day to check on some cygnets that Wyoming Game & Fish biologists spotted from a plane. On a park map he shows me the route to a rock outcrop that overlooks the nest. "It's easy to find," he says, pointing with long, knobby fingers. "But keep an eye out. Could be grizzlies up there. Make a lot of noise."

Well, map in hand does not a woodswoman make. I consult it religiously and still find myself blundering back and forth on the wide-summited peak checkered with stands of lodgepole and limber pine, thorny gooseberry thickets, and blowdowns, with no views to the river below. Rock outcrop? Where? I never find it, and later return meek and red-faced to the office.

Weekends become harder to fill. Rachel usually hikes or backpacks with various men who shamelessly call the office during the week looking for her. Elaine and Jack and Katy and Patrick usually have other plans. To top things off, Bill calls one night to say he and Leah are really hitting it off, and how adorable her kids are. *Big whoop.* Just what I need to hear, *thankyouverymuch.*

The spur-of-the-moment living that I so effortlessly fell into earlier in the summer has morphed into an anchorless existence that I find trying. It's light years away from my past life, where my work days buzzed with the cacophony of troubled people and my home life bustled with family attention, wanted or not. Now my days are filled with the unstructured, solitary silence of wilderness. Be careful what you wish for. . . . While there's so much I love about it, this milieu hasn't turned out to be the healing panacea I'd hoped for. Long periods accompanied by nothing but my tortured thoughts are rendering me as thin, sheer, and useless as over-pulled taffy.

As much as I try to live in the moment, my mind keeps projecting. *What will I do this winter? Will I find a job? Where will I live? Will I be able to afford it?* And always that nagging question—*Can I be happy living alone without a partner?*

The benefits of a permanent job—steady income, health insurance, pension plan—start to lure me. With these things, I taunt myself, I won't need a partner.

My feminist tendencies resurface and play along: Do whatever you must to support yourself, so you won't have to depend on a man.

This craving for stability translates to a yearning for a new family, for belonging. Maybe I can find what I need if I'm a full-fledged member of the Park Service family.

I consult the Personnel Office to educate myself on the ins and outs of landing a PGJ. Most permanent job openings, I learn, are only open to current federal employees or those with "permanent status." In a classic Catch-22, the only way to achieve the elusive "status" is by working in a permanent job. Occasionally jobs are announced as "Open To All Sources." This means the average Jane can apply.

A few people, like Tim and 3-1-1, had the outrageous luck to land permanent jobs after working only a season or two. Far more numerous are those conscientious people who worked years as seasonal employees before they became permanent. The winner is a woman at Yellowstone who worked twenty seasons before she finally was hired as a permanent botanist.

With the big 4-0 looming, I don't have that kind of time. I hear about a frowned-upon but totally legal shortcut, a way to increase your chances: If you can land *any* permanent government job *anywhere,* even if it's a janitor position in a Washington, DC, post office, you only need to work *one day* and you'd automatically have three years of status.

I pore over the "pink sheets," the federal job announcements tacked on the bulletin board outside the Personnel Office and watch for "Open To All Sources" jobs. For these, I'd still have to compete with the recent barrage of new veterans from Desert Storm, but a tiny chance is better than none.

Glen tells me about an open announcement for several biotech positions with the US Fish and Wildlife Service in Commerce City, Colorado, just north of Denver, at a place with an ominous-sounding name: the Rocky Mountain Arsenal.

"You going to apply?" I ask.

"Hell, no," he says. "*I* don't want to live in Denver."

"Well, neither do I, but they *are* permanent jobs."

I mention them to Tim who says, "They're probably wired for certain people, but call and ask them."

I phone one of the Arsenal biologists who explains that the Arsenal's twenty-seven square miles of prairie are home to a variety of wildlife, including bald eagles, whitetail deer, jackrabbits, prairie dogs, and burrowing owls. They recently opened up the biotech jobs with the intention of moving their own seasonals into them. She urges me to apply, but not to get my hopes up.

Just as Tim said, the jobs are "wired."

"Waste of time," I tell myself as I drop the application in the mail.

A few days later 3-1-1 brings news that Glen has inched closer to his longed-for PGJ at Grand Teton. The superintendent has approved a four-year limited "term" position for him, a hybrid position between seasonal and permanent. Term appointments are year-round jobs, with a month or two of furlough. They come with some benefits, like park housing and health insurance, but not the coveted government status. They also don't accrue seniority or time toward retirement, and, of course, they end in four years.

"Congratulations, Glen," I say, "on your new job."

"Hmph," he says, the edge of his mouth turned in disgust. "It's still not *permanent*. And no raise."

"Like people tell me, we get paid in scenery."

"And at least I get to stay in my house."

"That's *great*."

Inverting his arms over his head, he drops his head back. "Grand Teton employees are short-sighted," he says. "A guaranteed four-year job here is comparable to a lifetime of job security anywhere else."

I agree with him.

22

Transition

I'm walking through Beaver Creek after a hike around Taggart Lake when the door of one of the barracks buildings opens. Julian waves from the doorway. He can't be trying to connect with me, I'm thinking, so I won't embarrass myself by stopping. I wave and keep walking.

"Mary *Beth*," he calls.

I wheel around.

"Hey, I'm cooking extra for dinner. Would you like to join me?"

What?

Standing there is someone I've never seen before. One sinewy arm holds open the rickety door, and I hardly recognize this warm and inviting countenance as Julian Stewart, Montana mountain man. He's transformed from self-absorbed scientist with a shadowy chasm between his eyebrows to friendly neighbor with an alluring smile. Something shifts deep inside me like an animal stirring after a long hibernation.

"Thanks, Julian," I say. "I'd love to. Let me shower and change first."

"Sure."

In the shower I sing "Great Balls of Fire" and pound imaginary piano keys like Jerry Lee Lewis. Butterflies pulse through my ribcage. I've been melancholy for so long that this joy I feel is novel. I dare to speculate, is this a *date?*

Oh, don't be ridiculous. What would this painfully cool Teton dude see in *me*, with my anthill boobs and spiderweb hair? Besides, we *work* together. We're just getting together for dinner as friends. *Friends.* I need to learn how to be on platonic terms with men before I get back into a romantic relationship. This is ideal.

I blow dry my hair, smooth it over a brush, scoop it behind both ears. What to wear? I decide on jeans, a yellow T-shirt printed with wildflowers, ribbed gray socks, and Birkenstocks. Digging through my jewelry case, I choose silver loop earrings. They give me a freewheeling hippie look, not typical for me, but I like it. This is the new me. I so *need* a new me. I throw on a gray fleece vest and look in the mirror, hands in my pockets. No more counselor costumes for me. I'm a hippie woodswoman now.

"Come on in," Julian calls through the open door as I walk up the steps. Absentmindedly scraping my feet on the mat, I check out the stuff in his foyer. Skis, boots, poles. Rock climbing gear—pitons, carabiners, nylon ropes. Two backpacks. Leather rifle case. Tools of the mountain man trades—skiing, mountaineering, backpacking, hunting—arcane wilderness paraphernalia that enthralls me. And something I've seen in every house I've visited in Moose: stacked blue plastic bins labeled NEWSPAPER, CANS, GLASS. Although my trailer has no foyer, a corner of my bedroom holds my own mountain woman accoutrements: skis, packs, camping gear, hiking boots. And while I haven't invested in plastic bins, I've placed a carton in the kitchen for recyclables that I haul to the Jackson Recycling Center now and then. Back east I was always justifying my gear collection and environmentalism to skeptics, but not here. Something inside me smiles.

Wielding a wooden spoon, Julian peeks around the kitchen partition and waves me in. The living room is furnished with the same wood and Naugahyde furniture I have in my trailer, and there's a rodent trap line against one wall. Half of a duplex, the apartment consists of a tiny kitchen and modest living/dining area, with a bedroom and bathroom in the back. I recognize the New Deal–era construction.

"A CCC barracks," I say.

"How'd you know?"

"Because I spent some time in one just like this while I was doing my master's research at Shenandoah."

"Shenandoah? What were you studying?"

"Human-bear interaction." I puff up with pride. "I interviewed park visitors about their perceptions of bear problems, then came up with some suggestions for how the park could prevent conflicts between people and bears."

"Cool," Julian says, stirring tomato sauce in an enamel pot.

When I sniff the sauce, my mouth waters with the scent of some kind of meat, thick with earth and woods. It's like no spaghetti sauce I've ever smelled before.

"Mmm-m-m. What kind of meat is this?" My eyes, I can tell, are full-moon round.

"Moose." He sweeps slivers of fresh basil from a cutting board into the pot. "I won a license in the lottery last fall. You like moose meat?"

I've never tasted it, but if it tastes as heavenly as it smells, I'm in. "Love it," I say.

As he dips a spoon into the sauce and tastes it, the setting sun streams through the picture window and catches the gold tints in his hair. No comma-ponytail today; instead, rusty frizz flirts around the collar of his faded chambray shirt. He has that classic redhead look: milky, freckled skin and a barely notice-able lengthening of the forehead.

"What can I do?"

"The sauce could use a little more garlic," he says, setting a clove and a knife on a cutting board.

I fumble with peeling the clove, since I'm the type who normally pours garlic powder from a plastic container.

"Here," he says. "This works best." He slices off both ends of the clove and the skin slips off.

Man. The guy's amazing.

He sets a salad on the table, then dumps a saucepan of spaghetti into a col-ander in the sink, disappearing briefly into the cloud of steam. From the oven he draws out a foil roll and opens it to reveal slabs of buttery garlic bread.

I'm impressed. Julian, a man, is cooking dinner and waiting on me, a woman. This has never happened before in my whole life, and possibly in human history. At least in my history, my family history, going back generations. (Oh, I'm wrong. Bill once heated up a can of soup for me when I had the flu.)

I ask the usual Teton First Question: "Where are you from, Julian?"

"Texas. My mother still lives there on the family ranch." He points at the sauce. "This is her sauce recipe, from some Italian woman she knew years ago."

I'm thinking of the jar of Ragu in my cupboard. He also gets points for say-ing "woman" and not "lady."

As we fill our plates and sit down at the table by the window, a rosy blush saturates the western sky.

He rips off a chunk of bread. "So you worked as . . . a counselor, right?" He looks down at his plate because he already knows the answer, and he knows I know he knows.

I nod, twirling spaghetti around my fork. "Before I got into it, I had a Woody Allen concept of therapy."

"Oh?" His beard parts as he smiles. (Have I mentioned I *love* beards—that rugged, untamed look?)

"You know, a nice office in muted colors with plants and big windows. And smart, insightful clients eager to talk about their problems and motivated to work on them. *Hah.*" I pause to lick sauce off my fork. "I had an institutional green office with hissing radiators and asbestos-wrapped pipes. And my clients were pissed-off teenagers who wouldn't say a word, court-ordered drunk drivers, couples on their way to divorce, depressed people talking suicide."

"*Jeesh.*"

"So this is a big switch for me, getting back into wildlife work."

He smiles humbly, attentive to my every word. I'm liking him more and more. I was wrong—so wrong. He's not at all the self-absorbed prick I'd pegged him as. For once I'm thoroughly enjoying being wrong.

"Counseling must be pretty stressful," he says, tilting his bottle of Heineken to his lips.

"Tension headaches every day. Of course, my marriage could have been a contributing factor to that."

We keep eating, admiring the sunset and the Teton skyline, making small talk about the natural beauty and our undying love of these mountains.

"The only problem with this place?" he says. "I can never find climbing partners."

"Why not?"

"The only other climbers I'd want to go with are the Jenny Lake climbing rangers," he says with a sniff, "and they don't get weekends off."

If the Jenny Lake rangers are Julian's climbing equals, I'm mightily impressed. They are, from what I've heard, the super-elite, the best in the country. They run complicated routes all over the peaks and make hair-raising rescues.

When we finish our meal, Julian brings out a quart of vanilla ice cream and a squirt bottle of Hershey's chocolate sauce. "Sundaes for dessert."

"*Wow.* This is *great.*" Okay, maybe I do sound a bit over-the-top.

"So you're divorced?" he asks, plunking down bowls and spoons.

I scoop out a mound of ice cream. "Worst experience of my life. I don't wish it on anybody."

"*Hoo.* I hear ya. I'm in a similar situation."

I look at him sideways. "You're divorced too?"

"We weren't married, but we split up a few months ago, and she moved back to Dallas."

I pause to enjoy a thick, cool slide down my throat. "Long relationship?"

"Four or five years. But she just dropped a bomb on me."

"What's that?"

"She's pregnant."

"*Holy shit.*" I peer into his walnut-colored eyes, trying to read them, but they look away. "Is it yours?"

"It's mine." He squirts chocolate syrup into his bowl.

"How do you feel about it?" Okay, I shouldn't be counseling him. But I have to admit I'm flattered that he's confiding in me. He doesn't seem the type to share confidences.

"I'm *pissed.* I don't want a kid." He sets his spoon down and clamps his arms over his chest.

Uh–oh.

"And we used condoms, too."

"So you're in the five percent minority."

"Of all the luck, huh?" He slams one fist into the other. "*Damn.* Had the vasectomy just a few weeks too late. All I know is, she and I are over."

"Does she know that?"

"We're totally incompatible."

"That's not what I asked you."

He wiggles in his chair. "She knows."

"You realize you're still going to have to pay child support?"

He winces. "There's no way. On my measly graduate stipend? How *can* I? Besides, I didn't *want* the kid."

"That's not how the law sees it." I pile up the dishes. "I'll help you wash these."

"Nah, I'll do them. Thanks for listening."

I press my lips into a thin line. "I'm so sorry to hear about all this, Julian. It's a tough situation to be in. I suppose . . ." I'm ready to start listing the feelings he might be having, but I check myself. *No counseling!* We're *friends.* That means it goes both ways. "If it's any consolation," I say, "I didn't want kids either and was married to someone who did. Major sore spot."

"So you didn't have any?"

"*No.*" I shake my head. "Thank *goodness.*"

"Why do you say that?"

"I just don't have the mothering gene. Except, of course, for animals." I wink.

"Ah—one of *those.*"

"I suppose so, whatever 'those' are," I say, checking my watch.

"Hey, look." He points at his watch. "What does *this* say about our personalities? You have an analog watch that shows the phases of the moon. Mine's digital with a built-in stopwatch."

It says a lot, I think. "I'd better go."

As I turn to head out, he says, "Hey—I was thinking of going to town tomorrow for dinner and a movie, *Prelude to a Kiss.* You interested?"

I don't hesitate. "Sure," I say.

23

Kissing Toads

Just friends.

I keep saying these words to myself as, all at once, I awaken from a tedious, monochromatic sleep and my life blooms in Technicolor. Sunrises and sunsets explode in rainbow prisms. Never before has sunlight seemed so liquid. The subalpine fir, my favorite conifer, booms with unprecedented clarity and texture, scents the air with heady perfume, and penetrates the gaudy skies. And the *mountains.* What can I say? Screaming crystal, every day, in every weather. By night, they splash across my psyche like brazen, uninhibited thoughts.

Against this backdrop Julian and I cook, share meals, shop for groceries, and have the most intimate conversations either of us has ever had with anyone. He pours every aspect of his current life crisis on me; I willingly take it on, offer my perspectives, hope for the best for him. At the same time I dump on him my whole pathetic divorce story. His range of understanding, expression, and empathy surprises and strengthens me. For the first time, I feel I will emerge whole from this wreck of a life of mine. *Friends will get me through this:* I've sensed it all along; now I know it.

I press him with questions I've always wanted to ask a man outside of a counseling session. "Tell me about your first girlfriend." "What was your first kiss like?" "How did it feel when you fell in love?"

Preparing to answer, he leans back and strokes his beard. His eyes gleam and his lips quiver as he searches for honest answers and haltingly expresses them. I make him squirm, and he loves it. Why not? I've got nothing to lose. After all, we're *just friends.*

I'm careful. I don't want to get tied down to a man right now. It's too soon. I recite to myself all the hallowed mantras of counseling: I need time on my own, in my own space, to get closure. I'm not over the divorce yet. Have to get through the lingering depression before I dive into another relationship. If I get involved with someone too soon, what Doc calls "short-circuiting the grief process," the Creature will haunt me forever.

Besides, I'm still fuzzy about his relationship with the ex, Pam. He says it's over, but they seem to talk on the phone a lot. He talks about their relationship constantly, asks for my input. The fact remains that he entered my personal life soon after he found out I'd been a counselor for many years, but I put that out of my head. He's got problems; who doesn't? Besides, he's unexpectedly become somewhat of a counselor to me, too. I'm feeling stronger, coping better through this transition period.

At work we maintain fastidious distance, and I'm fascinated by his ability to dissociate. In the office he still sports his stern, intellectual scientist mask. But outside the office the mask falls away and I glimpse another side of him.

On a dreary Saturday we canoe the Snake River from Pacific Creek. As we approach the open shoals and steep cuts near Deadman's Bar, he backpaddles us through an eddy to a calm spot of water behind a willow break. "We're in no hurry," he says. "Let's just talk for a while."

Setting my paddle down, I lounge back against the bow, lay my rain gear–clad legs over the seat, and close my eyes. Mist settles onto my eyelids; cold from the canoe floor seeps into my backside.

He figure-eights his paddle through the water. Pouching out his upper lip with his tongue, he smiles and asks, "So what qualities would you want in your ideal guy?"

"Hm-m-m." I dip my fingers into the cold water. "Outdoorsy, handsome, smart, resourceful. A little on the scruffy side. Likes to dance and have long talks." I tip my head, inch out on a limb. "And he'd have to be a good snuggler and enjoy making love in the woods."

I peer at him through one eye as his mouth stretches into a reserved smile.

"And your ideal woman?" I ask.

"Outdoorsy and smart, attractive of course." He scoops up a sheet of water with the paddle and pours it into the river. "Affectionate." He nods. "And sexy. I *love* a woman's touch."

Something that breathes scurries over my heart when he says that.

⌒～⌒

The first night we sleep together I hear an elk bugle, and the sound imprints forever in my heart as a bifurcated seed ripe with the twin emotions of desire and loss. The bugle starts with a low rumble, then accelerates, fluting upward in pitch to a piercing scream, then ends with a series of guffaws. Olaus Murie described the sound in his 1951 book, *The Elk of North America:* "*A-a-a-a-ai-e-eeeeeee-ough! e-uh! e-uh!*" It's the quintessential call of the wild, and I can't get enough of it.

I freefall into this new dimension, into a primal exuberance and youthful recklessness. As a wildlife biologist, I now have a whole new view of sex. While I claimed an open mind when I was married, my views were tainted with an impatient, yet envious disdain for single lovers. Now I see sex as the most natural thing in the universe. Evidence abounds around me. Some animals, like trumpeter swans, are monogamous for life, while others, like deer and moose, will couple with many mates over their lifetimes. Bears, too, are promiscuous. In fact, bears can exhibit multiple paternity, that is, females can carry cubs sired by different fathers *in the same litter.*

Julian and I dart between one another's houses only under cover of darkness. The unspoken rule is no one will know about our trysts. We sleep together only a few nights a week, and are always back in our own places before dawn.

Rachel says, "I stopped by your house last night."

"Oh," I say, "I must have been out . . . walking."

❧

Six a.m. on our third Saturday together, and dawn seems more assured than real. After a night apart, Julian and I sit with spiraled torsos, elbows bent over the back of my sofa, peering out the window into a spectral fog. Black tree trunks stand out like lean soldiers. We're dressed for the weather—long underwear and rain pants, layers of polypropylene and fleece. Hats, gloves, and boots lie in a pile on the floor by the door.

Oatmeal rolls undigested like grit in my stomach. He hasn't said two words since he arrived ten minutes ago to collect me to go wildlife watching. Even in the low light I can see the angled crack between his eyebrows. With a droopy jaw and drawstring lips, he looks like he's trying to keep an egg from popping out of his mouth.

I tap his wrist. "You okay, Julian?"

"*Eeh-oh.*" His reply is as terse as the wrap-up of an elk bugle.

"Think we'll be able to see anything this morning?"

"Dunno." Then comes a huge sigh, gaining momentum and bearing down like a tidal wave.

I can't stand this. Pulling myself up from the sofa, I plant my hands on my hips. "Julian. It's obvious something's going on. Would you please let me in on this?"

Another tsunami sigh. "Just overtired, that's all."

"Didn't sleep well?"

"*Phee-ew.*" His lip crimps in exasperation. "Spent most of the night on the phone."

The Portuguese have a proverb: *A verdade é como o azeite; mais cedo ou mais tarde vem à tona.* "The truth is like oil; sooner or later, it rises to the surface." A rancid taste tickles my throat. Teeth clenched, I bury one hand in the other. "Pam."

"She called at eleven, then at two, then at three-thirty. Finally I just got up at four."

"What the *hell's* going on?" I'm spitting fire.

"She can't take 'no' for an answer."

"What's that supposed to mean?"

"She wants to get back together."

"Do you?"

"I don't know what I want."

This is the exact moment I start kicking myself. I should throw his boots at him and show him the door, brush my hands of this whole sorry mess, and take my life back. But instead I pull into self-protection mode. "Maybe you should just get a new phone number. She's in Texas, you're in Wyoming. It's not like you can't remove yourself from the situation."

Arms twined around my waist, I pace over the carpet, my wool-socked heels pounding out a march rhythm: *thump-thump-thump-thump,* turn around and back again, back again, back again. I want to say, *Don't be such a wimp. Show some gumption. Stand up for what you believe.* But I hold my tongue. Because I know he doesn't know what he believes.

When my heels start to ache, I collapse beside him on my knees. Stacking my arms and chin on the sofa back, I peer out the window. No further words pass between us until a moldy light bleeds through the kitchen window and the fog thins to a slurry.

He takes my hand. "How about we head downtown to Jed's for breakfast?"

And so begins this on/off scalding/tepid relationship of ours, as I decide I'd rather be his counselor than let him go. But the problem is this: I'm not a detached counselor. I feel used, betrayed, and royally pissed off. But I agree to go with him to Jedediah's, where we gobble sourdough biscuits and eggs, drink tea, and gab, gab, gab.

"I think she stuck holes in the condoms."

"Oh, come *on*," I say, laying down my fork with an all-knowing, motherly chuckle.

"I'm *serious*."

I thin-line my lips, roll my eyes, and vibrate my head like I'm dealing with a twelve-year-old. "So you're saying if she hadn't gotten pregnant, everything between you two would be hunky-dory?"

"*No.* I'm not saying that at all. We were doomed."

"Why?"

Cheek pouching with eggs, he leans back, then swallows. "'Cause she wants kids, and I don't." He frowns into his cup. "My life is so fucked," he says.

"Yep," I say, reaching for my napkin. "It is."

Our waitress appears, a stick-thin woman with toast-colored bangs riding on her eyelashes. "Is there anything else I can get for you?"

"Yep," Julian says. "There is. The check."

She reaches into her apron pocket and sets the green and white paper slip on the table. "You can pay at the register."

Julian peels off his wire-rims and seals the heels of his hands over his eyes. "I don't know what the hell to do," he whispers.

A tough, confident mountain man unsure of what to do? So many surprises.

Taking a five from my wallet, I drop it on the table. I don't expect him to treat, but I'll let him look good. Standing, I slide into my jacket, then lean my knuckles into the table and get in his face. "Here's what the hell you should do," I say. "Pay at the register and meet me outside."

He joins me at his truck, parked on the town square. As he unlocks my door, he asks, "How about a drive up Pacific Creek?"

"No. Drop me off at home."

Just friends.

⌁

In a book I will love forever, *Emily of New Moon* by Lucy Maud Montgomery, Emily's father says of her, "She will love deeply, she will suffer terribly, she will have glorious moments to compensate." These words sum up my life.

I spend the rest of the day stewing while I defrost my refrigerator. Mid-afternoon, I realize what I need is yoga. But, thoughts-a-leaping, I drop into Trikonasana, the Triangle pose, and pull a hamstring. Okay, it's time to let someone else in on this. I limp over to Rachel's trailer. In a worn sweatshirt and jeans, she sits cross-legged on the living room floor, tufts of hair escaping her French braid. Noticing that she's packing moving boxes pushes me over the edge, and I start sniveling. She leaps up and hugs me, and I dump the whole story on her.

She clasps her hands and presses her thumbs to her lips. "I'm so sorry." She invites me to dinner. Pooling our food, we concoct a feast of lemon-pepper chicken, carrots, rice, and salad. But to me the food is little more than texture. My tastebuds seem sealed and unavailable for duty.

"You know," I say, "there was always *something* about him. I could never quite put my finger on it, almost like he was trying too hard to impress me. Like maybe he was hiding something? I don't know. He just didn't seem quite *genuine*."

"You had a *hunch*."

"Woman's intuition, eh? But I ignored it."

Rachel rolls her eyes. "We never pay attention to it, do we? Could have saved yourself a lot of heartache."

I nod and cup my chin in my hand. But *no*, I'm thinking. "*NO*." I say it so emphatically that Rachel recoils. "I wouldn't have changed a thing. I'd still have done it, because it was so beautiful, so romantic, at the time."

"'Love like it's never going to hurt,' they say."

After we eat, she reaches into a cupboard. "You need chocolate," she says, setting a Duncan Hines devil's food cake mix on the counter, "and I don't want to carry this home."

Listening to James Brown on her cassette player, we spoon-mix batter and sway to the music. While the cake bakes, we talk and talk. She packs dishes. I fold a load of her clean clothes, moving them from laundry basket to moving box. Doing this humble favor for her lifts my mood. Her easy chatter and laughter chase away the pain I feel over this next loss in my life.

"Men can be such assholes," she says.

The next day she and I hike to Bradley Lake, each of us with two mousetraps strapped to our packs. We stop at a clearing near the lake.

"Okay, sweetie peas," I say, "you're on your own now."

"Yeah," Rachel says with a laugh. "No more peanut butter and oatmeal."

We hinge open the trap doors and shake out four trembling *Peromyscus*. They dodge and bump into one another, then take off in various directions, parting the papery, lifeless plants.

It's a cliché, I know, but nature and friendship do heal. I try not to think of the inevitable—that by nightfall these little mice will be gobbled up by predators, that this dear friend and confidante of mine will be gone from my life in a few days.

⌒⌒

On Rachel's last day, a paradox of lacy, warm-weather clouds and an ominous, chilly breeze, Tim sends us to Colter Bay to catalog weed infestations. "If you get a chance later on this afternoon," he told us as we were leaving, "take a trip out to Halfmoon Lake." He pointed it out on the office map. "The Game and Fish guys saw a swan there, but it might have been just passing through."

Summer crowds have dwindled, but a few tour buses are parked at Colter Bay. Foam-haired women in spanking-white Reeboks shoulder giant handbags and head for the visitor center and Indian Museum. Rachel and I separate to cover more ground.

I plod around, noting stands of musk thistle, knapweed, mullein. I can't get into it. The Creature is back, polishing a kernel in my heart until it grows hard and impenetrable. I've been dragging myself through these end-of-season days bitter, closed, and consumed by my endless ruminations. Now, to add to it, I saw a young woman leave Julian's barracks this morning as I walked to work early to input some data.

After surveying the areas around the horse concession, cabins, and tent village, Rachel and I meet at the picnic area to share lunch. A raven croaks from a light pole. Across Jackson Lake, Mount Moran is sugared with new snow, and the Skillet Glacier glows in the midst of it. With the smell of dry pine in the air, we spread our sandwiches, celery sticks, and apples on a weathered picnic table.

I take a bite of my sandwich, but my stomach goes queasy-bloated. Stalling, I say, "My *God*, Rachel, look at this. It must be paradise in the winter."

"Awesome," she says.

Get to it. "Rachel, do you know Anita Fletcher? The seasonal ranger."

"The cute one with short hair? Just moved to Beaver Creek from the Highlands?"

"I saw her coming out of Julian's place this morning."

"Oh no." She sets down her sandwich to nibble at a scrap of skin on her thumb.

"For all I know, she may have been borrowing toothpaste or something. Tell me she was just borrowing toothpaste, Rachel."

She sighs. "I saw him with her at Dornan's yesterday."

"The Beaver Creek Stud. Hanging on to his ex, screwing me, and now there's *another* one."

Rachel sighs. "*God.*"

We finish the weed survey, then drive to the east park boundary and hike to Halfmoon Lake. The sun is strong, warming the air to T-shirt temperature. We wade through scratchy sagebrush. As we approach the expanse of dry, cracked mud encircling the lake, I grab Rachel's arm and point. "Look at *that!*"

The ground ahead undulates and writhes with hopping dark spots. Locusts? Mormon crickets? We creep closer.

Covering the ground are hundreds of baby boreal toads, so many that we have to sweep them aside before we step to avoid squishing them with our boots as we walk.

"I don't know what it is about fecundity that so appalls," wrote Annie Dillard in *Pilgrim at Tinker Creek.* "I suppose it is the teeming evidence that birth and growth, which we value, are ubiquitous and blind, that life itself is so astonishingly cheap, that nature is as careless as it is bountiful, and that with extravagance goes a crushing waste that will one day include our own cheap lives, Henle's loops and all."

But far from being appalled, Rachel and I are awestruck as we stand breathless in the midst of this poppling carpet. Succumbing to the universal human need to claim some wild, sweet treasure as ours for a time, we each squat and grab a toad.

My hands close around it in a lopsided prayer position. Holding this warty, throbbing bit of flesh, barely bigger than a cranberry, I relish the cool *screel* of its splayed toes on my fingers. Slowly I lift the roof of my bent fingers and peer at the toad in the dark cavern of my hand. I feel the need to keep it shaded, fearful that it might perish in the light while it's in my care. It sits on my palm, motionless, drab-eyed, its mouth a cartoonish, downward-curved slit.

When I was a little girl, my father, returning from a country drive, said he'd held an injured baby rabbit in his hands for a few minutes before setting it back down on the ground where it would surely die.

Horrified, I asked, "Why didn't you bring it home so we could take care of it?"

"Mary," he said softly, "that bunny was too sick. You couldn't have made it better."

I launched into a hissy-fit, pounding my fists on my thighs. "Then why did you pick it up?"

He sighed. "I don't know. It was so cute that I just wanted to hold it for a little while."

It's called *love*. I know that now, and I'm humbled.

I touch my fist to my chest, then kneel down to release the toad. It bounces away. I think of all the elk, moose, bison, and deer with their offspring that I've seen this summer, and of my treasured swans. At a time when I've been wondering if I might ever experience love again, I realize that's exactly what this achy-yearning feeling is that courses through my heart.

Her car bloated with boxes and a bike hanging off the hatchback, Rachel zips out of Beaver Creek the next morning leaving me thick-throated and blurry-eyed. In my flannel nightshirt, sweater, and Birkenstocks, I stand in the street and wave until she turns out of the housing area.

I arrive at work ten minutes late. Growing up, I was taught to greet anyone in a room when I enter. But to the guys I work with, courtesies like these are unnecessary distractions. Playing the SAPs' game, I sit down at my desk beside Julian without saying a word. This really goes against my grain; I have to pin my tongue against my teeth to avoid saying, "Mornin', Julian," like I have every other morning this season.

We ignore each other and peck away on our keyboards, separated by three feet. A drop of fire kindles just behind my sternum, then damps to a steady smolder. When, after a couple of hours, he turns to me and asks, "Is there some reason you're ignoring me?" I lose it.

"How can you ask such a thing?" I snarl. "Pouring all your problems out to me, sleeping with me, hanging on to Pam, and now there's a new one?"

He wheels backward in his chair, holds up his hands like it's a stickup. "*Hey.* I figured you and me were over."

"Over? *Over?* In *four days?* Do you get over relationships that quickly?"

"You and I—we were always having these heavy, deep conversations. I don't need that right now. Things with her are light and fun."

"Light and fun. Terrific."

"And temporary. She's leaving in a week."

"I can't believe what I'm hearing." I stomp out of the office and take comp time for the rest of the day. I load up the pack with food and water and hike to Amphitheater Lake—five relentless uphill miles—and back down, quads burning all the way. Seeing a black bear scrounging for ants and grubs on a log makes my day.

Eager for diversion I resurrect a dormant interest of mine—choral music—and attend the year's first rehearsal of the Jackson Hole Chorale in the junior high school music room. Open-faced people in their forties, fifties, and beyond swarm around me, ask what I do, tell me how glad they are to have new singers. At the front of the room, surrounded by chattering women passing out sheet music, stands a portly man in polyester pants, bolo tie, and cowboy boots and hat. He strides over to me with a rigid gait, a souvenir of a long-ago battle with polio. Pumping my hand in both of his, he bellows, "Welcome, Mary Beth. I'm Bob Partridge." Strands of thin white hair stick to his shirt collar. "Welcome to the Jackson Hole Chorale!"

I find a seat in the soprano section. Beside me a woman with a silk peony pinned in her silver hair taps my forearm. "I'm Betty," she says. "We're so glad to have you sing with us."

"Let's warm up." Bob gestures to the accompanist. "No piano on this one; we'll sing south of the border—Acapulco. Ready?"

> Oh, the cow kicked Nelly in the belly in the barn,
>   The cow kicked Nelly in the belly in the barn,
>   The cow kicked Nelly in the belly in the barn,
>   But the old folks said it wouldn't do her any harm.

He snaps his fingers, sways his fleshy hips. "Second / verse / same as / the first. A little bit louder and a little bit worse."

We sing and roar in laughter. My smile is wide and my larynx is elastic when we turn to *The Messiah*. Soaring into first soprano range, I belt out familiar melodies: "For Unto Us," "Glory to God," "Hallelujah Chorus." For a few hours I bask in a light, soothing place far from impending unemployment and homelessness, departing friends, and duplicitous boyfriends.

24

Turning Point

A phone call comes at 6:45 in the morning. It's Bill.

"I'm just calling to tell you something," he says, his voice low and squeezed, as if his head were kinked forward. "I'm getting married."

Married?

Outside the trailer window on a lodgepole branch, a robin occupies itself with a niblet of some kind between its toes.

"Are you there?" he asks. "Did you hear me?"

"You're getting *married?* Is that what you said?"

"Yeah. In October."

This isn't registering. Our divorce just became final in April. How could he be getting married six months later?

"Already?" My whiny tone hints of an impending meltdown. I hate that.

"Leah and I have really hit it off, and I love her kids. Kristen's ten, Brianne's eight. What about you? You dating anyone?"

Inevitably he has to show his concern for me. I hate that, too. I want to reach right through the phone and smack his orthodontically perfected smile. What can I say? "Umm-m." That buys a few milliseconds of time. "No. Not right now. But I have lots of friends. And work is great. We trapped a problem bear a while back."

"Right up your alley." He takes a sharp breath and his voice tone and cadence rise. "Mary, you would *love* the girls."

The name *Mary* sounds thin, incomplete.

"They love to hike and read. They love animals. And Kristen's writing a book."

Thanks, Bill, I think. *Rub it in.* I want to ask, *How can you be over me already?* but instead I say, "That's great. Well, I need to get to work. Congratulations."

The phone receiver seems to float itself back to its cradle. My arms go numb as I descend into a blue-black rage. When I open my mouth, out croaks something unintelligible and catlike. I stomp laps around the room and pummel my knees with both fists.

But I'm meeting Julian at seven to work in the backcountry. I throw together a lunch and stuff it into my pack. Wedging a box of Kleenex under my arm, I head out the door with the Creature yipping and snapping at my heels like a Chihuahua on speed.

Under a scrim of clouds, Julian's already hauling gear out to the Bronco—tree-climbing spurs, tools, rolls of wire, a 12-volt battery, an elk hindquarter. He's wrapped the thigh of the hindquarter with plastic and strapping tape, leaving the lower leg and hoof exposed.

We're heading into the park's northernmost canyon, Berry Canyon, to set up a grizzly bear photography station. Trying to get a handle on how many grizzlies we have roaming the park, Julian's setting up cameras and bait in three backcountry canyons to try to lure bears in and photograph them.

Thank goodness for this job, I think. *If I had to wear a skirt today and act reasonable with people, I'd implode.*

"You have to drive," I say, climbing into the passenger seat and securing the Kleenex box at my side. Hot tears scorch my face. I almost say, *If you start talking about Pam and your fucked-up life, I'll go postal and smack you,* but think better of it and hush up.

Julian shoots me a sideways look, eyebrows tensed. "No problem," he says, starting the truck and nosing out of the lot.

Used tissues pile up on the dashboard as we head north.

Julian drives silently, sneaking occasional glances my way. Finally he asks, "Are you gonna tell me what's going on?"

I honk a mighty noseful into a tissue. "Bill just called. He's getting married next month."

"Oh, *jeez.*" He exhales through pursed lips as the fissure between his brows deepens.

I relate the phone conversation, adding my reactions and interpretations. He responds to each of my statements with a moan, grunt, or chop of his hand.

We roll along. I sputter and spout like Moby Dick facing Ahab. "How can he be healed already?"

Julian says, "I don't know what to say to make you feel better."

"You can't fix it." I bend forward and feign interest in my boots to avoid waving at two park maintenance workers pulling out of Lupine Meadows.

"And *I've* made things even worse for you," he says.

I glare at him. "Yes, you have. But today, Julian, it's not about you."

He makes small talk as we ride up the newly rerouted Inside Park Road, the previous Grand Teton superintendent's "monument." I've since learned that despite the NPS mission to preserve and protect natural resources, park superintendents seem driven to instigate some big construction project on their watch.

Until Julian points it out, I don't notice how the morning light has turned the Otter Body Snowfield on the Grand into a luminous mat, fiery-charged against the stark rock. We continue north past Signal Mountain, over the dam, past Jackson Lake Lodge.

"He's jumping back into *marriage* six months after our divorce. He's crazy," I say. I straighten as I realize the M-word no longer packs the same punch it did earlier this morning.

We park at the Colter Bay Marina, where our office's Boston Whaler is docked. I slide from the truck into a cold quiet punctuated by chipmunk chatter. Wood smoke from the nearby housing area tendrils through the air, softening the sharp forest smells. When I notice the brooding stillness of the lodgepole pines against the transparent morning sky, a cinder ignites in me. I exhale forcefully to clear my lungs, then inhale deeply to fill the void. *My new life,* I think, swelling.

I stow the Kleenex box under the seat, ball up the pile of wet tissues, and drop it in a trashcan. Sheer blue clouds drape Mt. Moran as we clomp down the ramp to the boat dock. A herring gull caws from the mast of the lone sailboat still moored in the harbor.

Julian skims us across the lake. Fog wisps speck the northern canyons, their meadows now draped in burnt-yellow. An osprey, talons clasped around a fish, flies overhead.

I'm about to accompany this long-legged buffoon into the Grand Teton backcountry with a heavy pack on my back. An image of the Vila Franca do Campo tiles comes to mind. It's all the same, you know—you carry your load uphill, climb over hurdles, help out your friends, hope for memorable scenery. All at once, I see the sinuous path of my life and where it has brought me, and I find myself smiling, not with my lips, but somewhere deeper and more entrenched.

We haul the boat ashore near the Lower Berry patrol cabin, spread out the gear, and divide the load. Julian takes the lead-dense four-foot-long elk leg, tools, wire, and spurs. I volunteer for the binoculars and the battery, the same size and heft as the one in my Toyota. I nest it among my rain gear and fleece jacket at the bottom of my pack. Food and water go in last with the binoculars.

Julian steadies the pack for me as I hoist it on my back. I stagger one way, then another, cross my eyes, tighten the hip strap. "*Holy shit,*" I say through clamped teeth.

"The station's three miles in," he says. "You gonna make it?"

I look at him then, and I just laugh. I roar and hoot and crow. He's lashed the elk leg to the top of his pack at such an angle that the hoof appears to point out catty-wompus from his NPS ball cap. Snapping his wrist to dismiss my hysteria, he turns to secure the boat line to a willow. A hand-sewn patch adorns one cheek of his Carhartt work pants. *The Beaver Creek Stud is looking really sexy now,* I think, giggling, but all I say is, "You're outta uniform, Julian."

Half of his face bunches up.

I think of myself lugging a car battery on my scrawny back. If I return to the boat tonight without a series of spinal compression fractures, I should buy an Idaho state lottery ticket. If we both survive hauling elk meat through Berry Canyon's grizzly habitat, we should head to Vegas with our next measly NPS paychecks.

Julian knots a bandanna around his sternum strap, then holds up one hand. "Pam called four times last night— ten, twelve-thirty, three, five." His thumb taps an hour on each finger.

Oh, great. So this work excursion will be a therapy session for both of us. I already know I'll ask him to massage my aching neck muscles when we get to the station, and that he'll willingly oblige.

I roll my shoulders, cinch up the straps, and clasp both hands behind my back to help support the load from underneath. I lean forward and start walking beside him. Together we climb into the canyon, one step at a time.

25

Altitude Adjustment

In swagger Tim and 3-1-1 to our office one rainy day, 3-1-1 leading, both in salute formation. I call it the Cool Dude Salute: the neck-bent-like-a-boomerang, hands-stuffed-in-pockets stance so favored by introverted scientists. Mark and Glen follow.

Julian, fingers ticking over his keyboard, ignores the intrusion.

Pencil poised, I look up from the topo map on my desk where two bait hamsters scuttle about. If it weren't for my doting on them, the only attention they'd get would be when one of the guys sticks safety pins through their napes and clips them to a tether attached to a raptor trap. The trap is arranged so the bird can't kill the hamsters, but it does scare the bejesus out of them. Already the little champs have valiantly pulled in several hawks and lived through the terror. I've vowed to bring some peace into their sorry little lives.

"Thought we should talk about the sheep survey," 3-1-1 says, his gaze going oblique.

I'm fizzing. I've heard the guys talk about sheep surveys, multiday excursions into the high country to look for bighorn sheep. This is the big-time wildlife biology I've been dying to do.

"Hey!" Julian lunges and grabs his coffee cup as a hamster scrabbles up the side and prepares to dive in.

I nab both critters under the armpits and drop them into their digs—a cracked aquarium lined with shredded newspapers. One stuffs food pellets into his cheeks while the other waddles to the plastic wheel and runs laps, *screep-screep-screep*.

"It'll be next week, Monday through Friday," says 3-1-1, leaning against the doorjamb. "Mark will be in Salt Lake for the raptor conference, right?"

Mark scratches his head through his fine hair. "I hate missing a sheep survey. But I gotta present that paper. I won't be back till the 24th."

"So Julian'll do Moose Basin up north. That leaves Mary Beth, Glen, Tim, and me for the south." He smoothes his goatee with his fingers. "I couldn't decide how to pair people up. So I flipped a coin, and I got Mary Beth. So she and I will cover the Mount Hunt–Prospectors area and Fox Creek Pass."

My stomach sours at the thought of prying words out of a turnip for five days. Besides, I've never spent a night outdoors with a man before, other than Bill when I dragged him on rare camping trips. I wonder how this will play out. We'll have separate tents, of course.

"So that leaves Glen and me for Static," Tim says.

"Right. I'm hoping you can make it to Hurricane Pass too. A few years ago we had some activity around there."

"Sure."

"Let's plan to join up at the Death Canyon Cabin for the last night. Mark volunteered to grunt up some real food for us."

Mark, Glen, and Tim file out as 3-1-1 turns to me. "We'll backpack three nights. We can each take a dinner, then we'll both chip in for the third night. Breakfasts and lunches on our own."

"What about a stove?" I ask.

"I'll bring my Peak 1. You got a fuel bottle?"

"I can borrow one."

"Good." He wheels on his heels to leave, then turns back. "Oh, and since we'll have to take so much heavy stuff—the Questar scope and binoculars and stuff—we'll take my tent. It's a light two-man." And he's out the door.

My jaw drops. My first thought is: *Thank God I'm divorced or I'd be fighting World War III to go on this little foray.* And my second: *What about his wife, Janet? How will she feel about this arrangement?*

I thought I'd have time to relax and rest up the day before the trip, but no way. I'm buzzing with energy. I wash and wax my car, clean the trailer, pack, unpack, repack. I can't seem to get the backpack under forty-two pounds, and this is without water, binoculars, and tent poles. I've even torn the cardboard tube from a half-gone roll of toilet paper. Bacause I only weigh 118 pounds, I'm already over a third of my body weight. Thank goodness 3-1-1 will take the stove and the Questar.

The script is already rolling in my head: What if I can't make it? What if I fall and break something? What if the rangers have to drag me out of the backcountry on a stretcher? I can imagine the headlines: GRAND TETON WILDLIFE RESEARCHER FLATTENED IN SWAN DIVE OFF ROCK OVERHANG.

I miss having a husband. You know—a guy who'd support me in everything I wanted to do, then listen to my fears without trying to steer me in a more benign direction. A husband who'd understand, give me a hug, and reassure me that I'm a competent biologist and everything will be all right. I didn't have that kind of husband, but I still miss my mental fabrication of one.

So I'm already tense and blue when my sister, Nancy, calls to tell me her husband, Fred, drew a bath for her Saturday night, turned on some New Age jazz, and fed her shrimp while she basked in the bubbles. "Oh," she says, "I almost forgot to tell you. We saw Bill with his new babe at Freestone's last week. She's *gorgeous.*"

After the call I glance out my window just as nubile Anita Fletcher, looking flush-faced and satisfied, skips out of Julian's barracks.

The potency of loneliness still surprises me. It punches me in the gut much harder than anger does. More potent than happiness? Ask me when I'm feeling happy. That night I flail and whimper and moan, go through about six hankies, and have a whale of a time on the old pity pot. At two I get up and drink a cup of Sleepytime tea. At four I'm up to pee.

But adrenaline's always been "beddy beddy good" to me. That I'm even conscious at seven when 3-1-1 drives up in the Jeep Cherokee with Tim and Glen in the back seat is a testament to its magic.

At the Death Canyon Trailhead, Tim galumphs out of the back seat. This is when I first notice he's wearing red-and-white-striped long johns under baggy green shorts. Punch-drunk with sleep deprivation, I'm laughing so hard that I can't swing my pack onto my back for several minutes. So the three of them, ready to go, just stand there poker-faced and wait for me to compose myself. Big time embarrassing because now I have an audience for saddling up the pack, which by now has chunked up to forty-five pounds. *Credo misericordia,* as my Nan says, which I think is a Vatican-sanctioned Portuguese version of *holy shit.* Finally Tim helps me hoist it onto my scrawny frame, and we head out.

It's mid-September. Fall is at its cusp and leaning, just poised to topple into winter. In the valley, breezes curdle the lemon-gold splash of cottonwood and aspen leaves. The air smells of dry vegetation. Frosts come every night. Thin snow dusts the mountains. Brisk mornings defer to eye-popping days with temperatures hovering around seventy. In the evenings and early mornings, elk bugle from the forest edges. *Sex is in the air,* they're telling us, *and don't you forget it.*

I'm so happy I'm prancing, even schlepping what feels like a recently expired corpse on my back. I'm dying to talk, sing, commune with my coworkers on this stellar day. But these guys are like Zen monks when they hike. Not a word passes their lips. Their expressions are morose and intensely focused. They walk at a hurried pace, clustered ahead of me on the trail. I so want to engage them. I think of spouting my family's repertoire of Portuguese jokes: *Ya hear about the famous Portuguese sculpture, Venus DeMello? Or the Portuguese actor, Kevin Costa?* But only someone from New Bedford would get them, so I don't waste my breath. Instead I smile at the thought of my parents as we run from joke to joke. Dad always invents new ones: *How about the three-legged Portagee, Moniz? Or the Portuguese candy bar, Almond João?* I would give anything to have them here with me now, running down the list, all of us falling together into raucous laughter.

I develop a walking rhythm with my breathing, and a song pops into my head to match it—a song from the old family gatherings when Dad strummed the chords on his guitar and everyone sang—"Yankee Doodle Dandy." I inhale to four steps, exhale to four more, as the song cycles over and over in my brain.

At the junction of the Death Canyon and Valley Trails, Tim and Glen veer west toward Death. 3-1-1 and I head south to the Open Canyon Trail. Just as we build up momentum, 3-1-1 turns to me and says, "So, Mary Beth, was Rachel dating Chris?"

My head whiplashes into the top of my backpack. 3-1-1 fishing for gossip? "What did you say?"

Removing his sunglasses, he repeats the question and wipes his brow with the back of his hand. For the first time I notice the color of his eyes: clear, drops-of-sky blue. They are eager and childlike, his smile open and without guile.

"Well, uh," I say, "you'll have to ask her."

"Just wondering."

Wow. Maybe I misjudged him. *Jace.* He's human, after all.

I grunt and pant, heating up as the sun climbs. Sweat soaks my T-shirt. We stop for a break; I wander into the woods to pee and remove my long underwear from under my shorts. When I take off my ball cap, my bangs are pasted together in slimy strings. We sip water, slather on sunscreen, and continue up the trail.

Jace stops and waits for me at a rounded rock, just before the trail turns south to the Mount Hunt Divide. "Here's a good lunch spot," he says, dumping his pack on the ground.

Relieved for the break, I sit beside him at the base of a steep, grassy slope littered with boulders. I devour a pita and cheese sandwich and a handful of trail mix before we pack up again to continue.

Jace asks, "Have you done much off-trail hiking, Mary Beth?"

"Very little."

"Then this will be good for you." With a reserved smile he nods up the precipitous, rock-strewn slope above us.

Holy crap.

He continues. "This is one of the perks of working in S&RM. We get to go off-trail and camp where nobody else can."

Lucky us. I'm not keen on off-trail hiking. I recall looking for the outcrop on Steamboat Mountain, when I was carrying only a daypack. The hike involved constant tripping over deadfall and pincushion encounters with gooseberry. I got very pissy.

We step off the cushy trail and head uphill. One step after the other, up and up, like climbing an endless staircase. We pass massive, leaning boulders and constellations of fir and pine. My heart hammers. Now and then we pause to glass the northern slopes of Mount Hunt for sheep.

Jace explains that the Grand Teton bighorn sheep population is shrinking. They estimate the herd at about a hundred animals, a relict population, with only a fifty-fifty chance of long-term survival. The problem is low heterozygosity, that is, not enough influx of new genetic material. Rather than intermingling with other herds like they did in the past, small, fragmented groups of animals stay in the secluded high country all winter. They can't get past all the human activity. As a result the same old genes keep tumbling around like a washing machine stuck on "agitate."

I remember hearing some young punks in town boast about skipping the boundaries in the high country of the Jackson Hole Ski Resort. Squeezing words out between heart-thunks, I ask, "Does out-of-bounds . . . skiing . . . have anything . . . to do with this?"

"Probably. With more skiers up there, the sheep have to move higher and higher to avoid them."

"And there's less room the higher they go." I bring up my binoculars and sweep the northern slopes of Mount Hunt. "So the inbreeding means their health declines over generations."

"Right." He tightens his hip strap.

I stand facing uphill, feet flexed like I've just launched off a ski jump, Achilles tendons stretched to the max. I waver to balance the pack, start climbing again. Jace zips on ahead, neon pink cap against tarry black hair. I'm now plugging to "Somewhere Over the Rainbow." Inhale, two steps. Exhale, two steps.

Then the tilt increases. It's no longer like stairs; it's a near-vertical wall. It's a marvel that plants can grow at this angle, that rocks don't just roll away. I tug on my shoulder straps, settling the pack closer to my upper back to stay balanced.

"Trust your boots!" Jace calls back as we head up a slant of lichen-crusted rock. No more songs.

Somewhere out there, Bill Clinton, George H. W. Bush, and H. Ross Perot are waging a presidential campaign, but for me right now, every neuron engages my two feet. Breathe in, step. Breathe out, step. I feel grateful for the strength in my calves. I notice how the load pulls me backward, and how I naturally compensate by leaning forward. Stopping to scan for the least onerous route, I remember that I've always been a good dancer. For some reason this thought encourages me.

Finally we crest a lip of rock to behold Coyote Lakes, two turquoise tarns at the base of a glacial cirque. According to the topo map, we're at 10,200 feet. High alpine. Sheep country. At first glance, barren and desolate, but gold grasses cover the lakeshores. The rubbly, scarred sides of the cirque swoop upward into bands of vertical cliffs. The only trees are victims of the harsh climate: twisted krummholz spruce and fir—deformed, miniature renditions of their lower-elevation sisters. About a head taller than I am, the trees are spicy-fragrant and the richest green I've ever seen.

While Jace sets up the tent by the smaller lake, I run up to the bigger one for what I hope will become my daily ablutions. I dunk and wring out a washcloth and rub it all over my body, poking it in and out of openings in clothes. There's no privacy here to strip and dip, the way I'd like to. But nonetheless, the mere washing away of salty sweat leaves me feeling fiery and robust.

A shivery wind skates down the cliffs, but a dinner of canned shrimp, carrots, and noodles warms us. After washing the dishes, we laughingly hang our food six feet up in a tiny spruce, the tallest tree around.

"So much for counterbalancing," Jace says, referring to the technique biologists recommend for hanging food high up in trees to keep it from bears.

Afterward I feel light as a snowflake. We walk up the hill east of the lakes and scan Mount Hunt. Just as the final rays of sunlight fade away, the silhouettes of five sheep appear on the mountain's skyline. They're too far away to classify, that is, to determine sex and age by the curls of their horns. But there they are, wild and sure-footed, and we're delighted to see them.

The temperature drops and dusk thickens as we falter down between the rocks and bonsai trees. Back at camp Jace assumes the Cool Dude Salute, kicking at pebbles and cranking his neck, pretending to be absorbed in our darkening surroundings. I can tell he's uncomfortable and doesn't know what to do or say. It's too early to try to sleep. I muster up my skill at putting people at ease, fish an emergency tarp from my pack, and spread it on the ground. "Let's watch the stars come out."

He seems relieved. After donning long underwear, fleece jackets, hats, and mittens, we lie on our backs, knees bent, arms V-ed over our chests to keep warm.

"*Look.*" He points. "A shooting star."

"Ooh! Another one—there! And there!" I thump the heels of my hands together. "*Hot damn!*"

Jace is laugh-challenged. The biggest laugh I've ever witnessed from him involves a puckering of one side of his mouth and a whistle through his nose. But tonight I hear a vibration in his throat. First I fear he's regurgitated a chunk of shrimp, but then I realize it's a genuine chuckle.

As the sky darkens a carpet of stars sharpens into focus like a developing photograph. I look for the northern circumpolar constellations—Cassiopeia, Cepheus, Draco the Dragon, the Big and Little Dippers—but they're indistinguishable in the clutter.

"Isn't this the coolest thing?" I say. "No extraneous light. Just us and the cosmos."

"*Look* out there," he says. "How can we be the only life forms in the universe? And where does it *end?*"

"It doesn't," I reply, pertly. "Spacetime curves around on itself. Just imagine: If you left your identical twin on earth and flew out in a spaceship at nearly the speed of light, when you returned you'd be years younger than him."

Jace rolls over on his belly and perches on his forearms. "That Einstein. What a brain, huh?"

"And what about black holes?"

"And quasars?"

We banter back and forth, flexing our cosmological muscle. Having rarely met anyone outside of a physics class who has any interest in this stuff, I've attained nirvana. I was, after all, *the* dorkiest girl ever to graduate from Dartmouth High, whose most rewarding extracurricular activity was Astronomy Club. But I don't mention this fact to Jace. Lying beside him on the tarp, enraptured by the shimmering sky, my mind soars, clear and unfettered. Our interaction is facile, our conversation free of angst. I know Jace will go home and boast about this "platonic" encounter to his wife, hoping she'll believe that I'm just one of the guys. But I also know that in no way does his being happily married nullify the sexual tension between us. I was once appalled when a male grad school class-mate said, "There's no such thing as a platonic relationship between opposite-sex heteros. There's *always* a sexual component." We argued till we turned mauve, but he didn't back down. Now I know he was right. I look forward to sleeping in a small tent beside Jace. Although the buzz between us is invigorating and tanta-lizing, we trust each other to operate within respectful constraints. But we'll frolic close to the edge of the pool, maybe dip our toes in and chase each other around the shore. It's sizzlingly fun, and I know he welcomes it as I do.

Jace rolls onto his side and brushes some twigs off the tarp between us. Then, picking words carefully, he asks, "Do you ever . . . get the feeling you've . . . lived before?"

What? I turn my face toward him, but I can barely make out his silhouette in the darkness. Extraterrestrial life was a stretch, but now Jace Callaway, supreme scientist extraordinaire, is asking me about *reincarnation?* I probe him further. "Do *you* feel you've lived other lives?"

"Matter and energy are constant in the universe. That means you and I have atoms in our bodies that must have been in King Tut's and Mozart's bodies, and in a gazillion others."

He didn't answer my question. "I don't think of reincarnation in that *scientific* sense. I feel it on a more personal level."

"What do you mean?"

I sit up and face him. "From what I've read about reincarnation, you can get clues to past lives by your strongest feelings. Your deepest fears and longings." Not surprisingly, the air around him seems to prickle with this steering of the subject into the realm of emotion.

"Oh? So what have you figured out?"

"For as long as I can remember I've felt this irresistible draw to the Rocky Mountains. And I've had this aversion to being pregnant." I swallow. "I wonder if I could have been a pioneer woman who died in childbirth, before she got to live her life in the place she'd always dreamed about. I think there's no other explana-tion for the power of the connection I felt to the West."

"Interesting, but unprovable."

"Must everything be provable?"

"It helps, don't you think?"

After a while we retire to the tent and change clothes side by side in the dark, bumping elbows. We drift off to sleep, nose to nose.

⌐⌐

The next morning we wake up freezing, and I have a raging sore throat. We have to pee so bad it feels like our molars are submerged. But we stay in our sleeping bags until the sun peeks over the top of the cirque and begins its warming creep down the walls.

After oatmeal, raisins, and walnuts by the smaller lake, we rinse the dishes and pack up. I'm eyeing the treacherous slope we have to negotiate to clear the cirque and head toward Prospectors Mountain. According to the map we have to skirt a nameless 10,988-foot peak and traverse an ice field on a slope whose contour lines are so close they resemble fingerprints. I'm feeling none too peppy, but I keep my mouth shut and begin climbing.

I plant one foot after the other. For the first hundred feet or so the going is easy, but after that a sack-of-flour weight starts pressing against my chest. A rasp drags across my throat every time I swallow. I pant shallow breaths.

Soon the script starts: *I'm not cut out for this . . . I can't handle this macho stuff . . .*

Heels to hamstrings, ribbons of fire flare up the backs of my legs.

This is the last sheep survey I'll ever do . . .

A toothache pain zaps the space between my shoulder blades.

But it won't matter because I'll probably die out here anyway . . .

A sensation of nails pricks the soles of my feet. Higher . . . higher . . .

What the hell was I thinking . . . ?

Jace is far ahead. Finally I come around a bend at the base of the rocks that encircle 10,988 and get my first view to the north. Before me is the back side of the Grand, a leaning, snow-swept nubbin, jutting into this racy-crisp sky, and—*Oh, man!*—I'm transfixed, and I can't wait to do this again next year.

We eat lunch on precarious rock slabs overlooking the talus slopes we must cross. Jace rattles something out of his pack. "Vitamin I?" He offers me the white bottle.

I read the label: ibuprofen. "No thanks." He downs a couple of tablets with a gulp of water. Snugging on our packs, we press on.

Loose scree rolls away to my right. Beyond it, Prospectors Mountain. Between here and there—a black ravine. I brace my legs and peer out, but I can't see the bottom; it's lost in a scraggle of vegetation and shadows.

If my right leg were nine inches longer than my left, this would be easy. The rocks, roughly a foot in diameter, are unanchored, barely held in place by the angle of repose. Each one I step on loosens and slips downward, taking me with it, and comes to rest about a stride's length from where I've originally stepped. Which one, instead of catching mercifully, will catapult down the chute and hurtle me headlong into the chasm below? Mountaineers have died this way. Why not me?

I assume a slug's pace, blindly focused on each step. So intent am I on staying upright and choosing where I'll set down each foot that I forget the forty-some pounds of dead weight on my back.

"Good news, Mary Beth." About fifty yards ahead, Jace faces me.

I stop, pump my arms to steady myself, look up.

"No ice field. Too dry this summer."

"That *is* good news."

"It gets better up ahead," he says.

"I sure hope so." Panic saturates my voice. "'Cause this is freaking me out."

But as the Portuguese say, *Água mole em pedra dura, tanto bate até que fura.* Rough translation: "Water dripping day by day wears the hardest rock away." I forge on, and finally we reach a saddle overlooking Forget-me-not Lakes, a larger lake with an orbit of smaller ones, afterthoughts. Below is Death Canyon, with its shelf above it.

When I catch up with Jace I throw off my pack, dance a clumsy pirouette, and shriek, "*Yee-hah!* I made it! I *made it!*" I leap up and down on this reassuring flat ground, scissoring my arms. Endorphins simmer and spark. "I *love* Wyoming!"

That's when I witness the heretofore unimaginable: Jace throws back his head and issues forth a guffaw the size of Alaska. "You did *great*," he says, patting my shoulder as he would a dog. He grins at me, leathery skin webbing around his eyes. I notice his teeth aren't perfectly aligned. Some of his lower incisors are twisted to accommodate one another in a crowded arch.

We zip into Gore-Tex in the screaming wind. I guzzle water, munch dried apricots and salted peanuts. Jace tries to reach Tim or Glen on the radio, but there's no answer. He then hands me the Questar and continues east toward Prospectors to glass for sheep, while I head down to the lakes. In a golden meadow I set up the scope and aim it toward the Death Canyon Shelf and the mountains to the northwest: Fossil, Bannon, Jedediah Smith.

When Jace returns, we decide to camp by Forget-me-not Lakes instead of continuing on to the shelf. I'm doubly relieved. Not only could I not face another brush with death on a scree slope today, but the area is too lovely to leave yet. An ideal tent spot appears, sheltered by a ring of Engelmann spruce and white boulders. I head to one of the outer lakes where, protected by whitebark pines, I stand naked in unfiltered sunlight and sponge off with icy water.

Jace's dinner of noodles, tuna, and pesto satisfies completely. As vermilion streamers dance over the mountaintops, we bundle up in layers, sip mint tea, and munch vanilla wafers.

"You could bring some people out here and they wouldn't care a bit about this," Jace says, sweeping his arm. "But others like you go nuts over it. It's great."

It feels like a special blessing. I grin.

After dishes we find a taller tree where we can hang and counterbalance our food in the way we biologists recommend for the rest of humanity. Tonight again we lie on the tarp as the stars unfold. Resting our heads on our bent arms, the dialogue takes a cozier turn.

"Do you ever hear from your ex?" Jace asks warmly.

"*Shit.*" I flap my mittened hand through the air. "He's getting married next month."

"*Already? Jeez.* So this other woman must've been in the picture before you guys split up."

"*No.* They just started dating a few months ago."

"*Wow,* he moves fast."

"I'll say. I can't wait to hear what my folks have to say about it."

"Why?"

I tell him about my parents' reaction to the divorce. "I guess I should have expected it, knowing how traditional they are, but I was still shocked, you know? You never dream your parents might turn against you in a crisis. I was a basket-case. Still am."

"I'm sorry to hear that," he says with a sigh. "My parents have always supported me in anything I wanted to do. I can't imagine anything different."

"My folks are old school, traditional, Catholic. Besides, they always thought Bill walked on water."

"And they probably were hoping for grandkids."

"Oh, sure. But, believe me, if I'd had kids with Bill, I would've had a psychotic break."

"Oh, come *on* . . . "

"I mean it. I'd be living in a hospital somewhere, training pea tendrils on trellises."

He croaks some sound in the nether world between a choke and a gurgle, then rolls to his back. "Well, I think it's great you had the guts to get out of a bad situation and make a new life for yourself."

"Thanks for saying that, Jace." When I swallow, I notice my throat feels clear and slick again.

We lie in silence for a long time, watching stars.

Wednesday's hike justifies my divorcing the Messiah, becoming the family pariah, and moving across the country. I feel agile and strong as we head gently uphill toward Fox Creek Pass, then descend through stunning alpine terrain to Pass Lake.

After lunch, with clouds heaping up on the horizon, we set up camp just over the park boundary in the Targhee National Forest. About a hundred yards from camp we find a bear tree, a tall spruce with wide branches, and pitch the rope into it so it'll be ready when we finish dinner. Then we separate. Jace heads up to the Death Canyon Shelf with the Questar to check the northern slopes of Mount Hunt and Prospectors. I head south over the layered rock tables below Spearhead Peak to Indian Lake.

Heart dancing, I climb on spume-white slabs up the gentle slope. Minus tent poles, extra clothes, and sleeping gear, my pack is light. Boots on rocks, head held high, lungs rinsed clean in the pure, cool air, I pass patches of leftover snow, colored like watermelon thanks to *Chlamydomonas nivalis,* a species of unicellular green algae with a secondary red pigment. No worries about getting lost; I can see where I'm going. The song in my head is inspirational: "Climb Every Mountain." Never have I felt so full, so complete, so nourished. After a short clamber over talus rock, I crest the cirque above Indian Lake and peer down to the seldom-seen, elongated tarn two hundred feet below. Breezes puff over its surface, refracting sunlight into a net of diamonds.

I'm smitten, besotted, drunk on life, as I grasp the truth of a premise I've always believed: *Place clarifies essence.* I sprawl on a rock, binoculars at my eyes. After an hour of surveying I spot two sheep, a ewe and a yearling female, grazing alongside two mule deer bucks. I'm all a-flutter and can't wait to get back to camp to tell Jace.

Later, while we're eating our chicken and rice flavored with asparagus soup mix, raindrops spatter the forest floor. We rush through dinner and dish washing and hang the food sacks. With the sky darkening and clouds cracking open, we dive into the tent. I set my Mini-Mag flashlight in the gear loft overhead, and we lie in our sleeping bags for our nightly chat.

"So what's it like, Mary Beth, being newly single again at thirty-nine?"

I look at him, surprised that he's brought this up. "Scares the hell out of me."

"Why?"

"AIDS."

"Mm-m. Pretty bad."

I think of two of my counseling clients, gentle men in their early thirties. "I know two guys who've died of AIDS. It's horrible. And it's starting to enter the straight population."

"AIDS and herpes have tainted the purity of sex." Jace swipes the air and squashes a mosquito in his fingers.

I can't believe I'm having a conversation with my boss about sex.

He continues. "Sex shouldn't have anything ugly attached to it."

"It shouldn't. You're right." Embarrassed, I take shelter in non-versation.

"And *condoms*. I *hate* 'em. Wearing a condom is like wearing a blindfold to a movie."

I giggle as thunder grumbles in the distance. I want to know about his love life. Dare I? I do. "How did you and Janet get together?"

"It had kind of an odd start," he says. "But it's worked out great. I first dated her sister, Sally. She was a musician—a violinist, and eventually she left for New York. Wouldn't have worked out anyway. But Janet started hanging around, and I thought, gee, she's kind of cute."

I'm astonished he's telling me all this.

"So we went out a few times. Then I moved to Seattle for grad school and I thought it would just end. But she started sending me letters, and for a while I got a letter every day from her."

"*Yowza.* She had it bad, huh?" I brush at a bug making headway between our Thermarest pads.

"I s'pose."

"It didn't put you off? You didn't think she was too pushy?"

"Hell, no. I *loved* it."

The tent sides swell and deflate in the wind; rain pecks on the nylon. The sound chills me. Muffling my sleeping bag around my neck, I ask, "So what happened next?"

"I invited her out to Seattle. She moved in. We got engaged a year later. The rest is history."

"That's *so* sweet."

"Yeah," he says, his eyes arcing up to the tent ceiling. "It is."

I clam up. Could I go after a man? It's something I can't imagine doing.

He reads my mind. "Trust me, Mary Beth, men *love* to be pursued by women."

"Really?"

"I've only pursued two women in my life," he says with a smug smile as he rolls belly-up. "All the others have come after me."

Is he gloating? No, it doesn't seem so. But I do wonder what that says about him. Was he too shy to approach women? Or just not interested, too much of a scientist? I suspect the former.

I press him further. "Do you and Janet plan to have more kids?"

"*Nope.*" The decisiveness of his answer impresses me. "We're doing our part for the planet," he says.

"Thanks, Jace. Thanks for caring *that much.*"

Warm and satisfied, we lie quietly for a few minutes, listening to the rain and basking in our thin, puffing shelter. Then he rolls onto his side and faces me, cheek resting on his fist. "So what happened with Julian?"

Right then a slice of lightning lights up our yellow cocoon. I jerk.

"I knew you guys had a thing going not long ago."

I don't want to get into this with him, but he presses. "I imagine it's been hard for you, with Pam and the others."

How does he know all this? I reach up and turn off the Mini-Mag light. "Let's just say I'm missing a friend." With that I zip into my bag. I won't get into this with him. Conversation over. "Good night," I say.

For hours I mull.

November sunrise on the Tetons

Tools of the trade: Bighorn sheep survey above Moose Basin, with the Grand and Mt. Moran in the distance.

Bear #17 (Cream Puff) re-enters the world.

Beaver Creek #56, a CCC barracks

The snow! The Grand from my bedroom window

Science & Resource Management Office at Beaver Creek

Bradley Lake Trail with arrowleaf balsamroot

Jackson Lake with Mt. Moran in the distance

Schwabacher Pond

Baiting the bear trap

With a sedated black bear
SHIRLEY CRAIGHEAD

The Row Fire, August 1994

Hunter Barn after the Row Fire

On a sheep survey: Moose Basin Divide

Fall foliage along the Moose-Wilson Road

Snowshoe swan survey near Colter Bay

Thursday morning is filled with the scent of wet wood and the sound of the rain fly snapping on the tent. I wake up out of sorts from a fitful sleep, slip on rain pants and jacket, and crawl out of our sagging crypt.

Outside it's overcast, with a bracing wind. There's fresh bear scat twenty feet from the tent, but we find our food hanging safely in the bear tree far downwind. I'm glad we'll sleep in a cabin tonight. But our work isn't done yet. After breakfast, as damp wind batters our faces, we head up the west slope of Fossil Mountain. I'm sweating in my Gore-Tex. My swollen feet feel bound, like a Chinese woman's, and every muscle in my body burns. In my mind I dissect them all out: gastrocs, quads, hams, glutes, delts, traps, pecs. My face emits a furnacelike heat. I'm reaching my physical limits. At the saddle I stop. Can't climb another step. Put on all the warm clothes I have in the pack. Find a flat rock. Sit. Pick up binoculars. Glass the slopes.

Jace treks on, heading to the cliffs north of the mountain. I don't know how he does it. I painfully realize I'll probably never be the field biologist these guys can be. Is it just because I started doing this so late in life? What if my father had taken me hunting and fishing, like their fathers had? What if I'd backpacked all my adult life, like I wanted to? What if I'd stayed on course, and not let myself be sidetracked by marriage? What if I were a few inches taller, weighed a few more pounds, worked out more? What if . . . ? *Yadda . . . yadda . . . yadda.*

Bastante. Enough. I look down at my scuffed, filthy boots. I'm in the Grand Teton high country, doing a bighorn sheep survey. I *am* a field biologist.

A couple of hours later Jace returns, excited about seeing a ram with a full curl, which tells us it's more than six years old. Lunch is the rest of our pita bread, peanut butter, raisins, and M&Ms. I'm so sick of sweet stuff. I crave pizza, french fries, and juicy, plump things—tomatoes, cucumbers, oranges. And would somebody *please* squeeze fresh lemon into my water?

The six-mile hike back out Death Canyon is easy, but it rains much of the way and I'm chilled. We reach the patrol cabin just as my rain gear starts to leak. On the porch Mark splinters a log into kindling wood with a hatchet. We find Glen and Tim inside, draping clothes over the chairs to dry.

Used mainly by patrol rangers and trail crews, this log cabin measures about sixteen by twenty-four. A narrow stairway leads up to a sleeping loft with ratty mattresses and a closet full of army-issue sleeping bags. Downstairs—wood stove, propane camp stove, cabinets of canned and dried foods: beans, tuna, vegetables, rice, Bisquick, oatmeal. Dishes, utensils. Mismatched wooden chairs and a carved-up table. Generous evidence of a resident mouse population.

Mark has carried in a smorgasbord: tortillas, elk burger, jack cheese, salsa, tomatoes, green peppers, avocados, and a special treat—Courvoisier cognac. We whip up burritos and rice, and after dinner we sip cognac in coffee mugs. Even though my sore throat is long gone, the throat-soother excuse lands me a second splash. Soon I'm limp as a dishrag.

We laugh and gab by the light of an oil lamp. When I head to the outhouse with my Mini-Mag, I discover a dusting of snow on the ground, with more falling. "It's snowing!" I call back to the guys.

"Cool," I hear in response, along with some *yee-hahs* and *yippees*.

We have a slumber party in the loft where it's cool and comfortable. Feeling relieved and safe, the wilderness test now behind me, I nestle into my sleeping bag. Despite the snoring and rodent maneuvers going on around me, I fall into a deep sleep.

❦

The first sound I hear Friday morning is the lazy grate of a zipper. Jace bounds out of his sleeping bag, and the rest of the guys follow him downstairs to get a fire going. I'm left with the loft to myself so I can dress privately. By now all my clothes are dirty, so I reuse socks, underwear, shirt, pants. They feel coated and stiff against my skin. The gray wool hat Mom knitted for me covers my hair, which I haven't seen in four days. When I last touched it, I was reminded of a string mop. I vow to keep the hat on until I get to a shower.

Mark surprises us with a box of fresh blueberries, and we pig out on pancakes. I devour five and volunteer for the remaining two on the platter. This is after everyone else swears they can't eat another thing. They blink.

"Where the hell do you put it?" Tim asks.

"Hollow leg," I say, dowsing the pancakes with Aunt Jemima's and licking my fingertips.

Four miles back out to the trailhead in falling snow. I'm the first to bolt off the cabin step and head downtrail, leaving the guys behind. Without looking back I chug down the rocky streamside switchbacks and up the incline to the Phelps Lake Overlook. For some reason the song in my head is James Brown's "I Got You." No way was this a family sing-along tune, but its rhythm matches my zippy pace.

My boots are soaked through and mud-mushy when I reach the trailhead. The guys drop me off at my trailer, where I bow to my shower like a pilgrim at Fatima.

Clean, warm, and lighthearted, I go back to work for a few hours in the afternoon. I dart from office to office, searching for someone to share and process the trip with.

"Can we go over our sheep notes?"

"What was it like on Static?"

"How about Moose Basin, anything up there?"

But firm jaws and knitted brows prevail. Jace, Tim, Glen, and Julian all peer at their computer screens and type DOS commands, fingers humming keyboard chatter. No one has time to talk.

Back at my desk I go over my field notes and enter them into a dBase III database. My phone rings.

"You came out real high on the cert," says Larry Malone, a supervisor with the Fish & Wildlife Service at the Rocky Mountain Arsenal. "We'd like to do a phone interview."

This doesn't seem real. When I hang up the phone, I get jittery. Why would they want to interview me if they had the jobs wired for their own seasonals? I dip into the stash of York peppermint patties I keep in my desk drawer, hoping the strong mint will calm my rollicking stomach. I don't want to leave the Tetons. Not yet. But for the chance of a permanent job? If I worked only one day, I'd have status. Unlike Glen or Mark, I could apply for permanent wildlife biologist jobs, even if one opened up here at Grand Teton. It seems absurd that I could apply and these more experienced guys couldn't, but you gotta play by the rules. I fan my flushed face with an envelope.

Jace walks in with a packet of file folders under one arm. I just know he's come to chat, and I look up cheerfully. "Hey, Jace. Is Janet cooking you something special tonight to welcome you home?"

"I dunno," he says, frowning. Then he hands over the files. "I need you to Xerox these for a FOIA request we just got." He turns to leave, but I want to tell him the news before he's gone. "*Jace.* The Arsenal just called. They want to interview me by phone."

"Cool." He hurls the word over one shoulder as he walks out.

26

Search

"Mary Beth? I'm Jerry." He's blond, twenty-something, and dressed in typical Jackson Hole attire: jeans, plaid flannel shirt, hiking boots. He waves me inside. "Here's the living room. The kitchen's to the left."

I found Jerry's ad for a roommate in the *Jackson Hole News* classifieds. Already I'm disappointed. The apartment has dirt-colored shag carpet, tired walnut paneling, a gray sofa, and a TV hidden in a murky alcove. The kitchen's somewhat lighter, with avocado cabinets and a fifties-era chrome and vinyl dinette set, but the window looks out on the nondescript wall of the adjacent apartment building. The word that comes to mind is "dreary."

He opens two cabinet doors. "You'd have these cabinets for your stuff and whatever space you can find in the fridge."

"What do you do, Jerry?" I ask.

"I work at Jackson Lumber. And you?"

"I'll be laid off from the park in a couple of weeks, and ousted from my trailer at Beaver Creek. I'm looking for a job for the winter here in Jackson." And what might that be? Answering phones in a real estate office? Checking groceries at Albertson's? Cleaning toilets at the Antler Motel?

"Ah, that's tough," he says, winding his hand around his neck. "I worked seasonal with the Forest Service for a while, scrambled for jobs every fall. But when the lumber company offered me full time, I grabbed it for the chance to stay year-round." He looks away. "I still miss the forest though."

He shows me a room at the end of a narrow hallway. "This would be your room," he says. It has an east-facing window, a chest of drawers, a single bed. All encased by the ubiquitous gloomy paneling.

"Bathroom's here. You'd share it with Jill. She has this other bedroom. I have my own room and bath on the other side of the apartment."

"So another woman lives here, too?"

He nods. "I had a few guy roommates, but they were such slobs that I only have women now. They're a lot neater."

"What's Jill like?"

"Pretty quiet. In her twenties. Works at the hospital."

I wonder, where are the thirty- and forty-something-year-old women? The older divorced women who work in town and need help with the rent?

I ask about utility bills. *Yikes.* Tallying the numbers in my head, adding in the unused annual leave check I'll get when I leave the park, I realize I need to find a job pretty fast. "Have you had many calls?"

"Two. One decided to move away. The other one's supposed to let me know by Monday."

That gives me a few days. "I'll call you Monday," I say.

Mealy snowflakes snarl through the sky as I drive away. According to the *Denver Post* classifieds, an apartment of my own in Denver would cost me less than sharing one with two roommates here. But I shouldn't even think about that; the Arsenal jobs are taken. I don't want to move to Salt Lake. What other choice do I have? The Jackson job search is getting me nowhere. Been burying my nose in the want ads. Took some comp time to visit the local Job Service office. Filled out a mountain of applications at restaurants and stores.

Trying to psych myself, I'd decided on Shades Café. I love eating there; I'd love working there. I'd learn how to make those delicious breads and pastries. In a stained apron and rolled-up sleeves, I'd greet old friends and make new ones while serving up coffee and sandwiches. I'd nurture people with delicious food. During slow times I'd entertain the other workers by singing seventies songs by James Brown, Creedence, the Stones. We'd dance around the kitchen pumping our arms and waving saucers like the "Ain't Too Proud to Beg" scene in *The Big Chill.* After work I'd bundle up in my winter gear and mosey through the square. Friends would walk by with their dogs. We'd chat and throw Frisbees. It'd be great, working in town. This is what people do in Jackson. These are the sacrifices that people make for those three or four grand months of summer in the Tetons. But the Shades manager tells me they already have enough help for the winter.

I hear from several park people that the ski resort at Teton Village always needs people to clean condos, and they pay twice what I make at the park. But when I call the village, they're noncommittal. Call back in a month, they tell me.

The hand-wringing continues.

"Mary Beth? It's Greg Langer with the Fish and Wildlife Service."

My pen flies into the air. Julian frowns my way and leans down to snatch it off the floor. My heart's beating a bossa nova.

"I'm just touching base," Greg says, "to let you know there's a holdup on this end. You did great on the interview, but we still haven't filled the position. That's about all I can say now."

"O . . . kay." I'm tongue-tied. What's the point?

"But I'm going to send you some information about the Arsenal. And I'll tell you this: I've asked some people here who have big houses if they could spare a room until you could find a place to live."

I barge into Tim's office where he and 3-1-1 are scrutinizing a National Forest map. "You gotta hear this." I shake my hands as if to dry them, then relate the conversation to the backs of their heads.

Tim whirls around. "Sounds to me like they're gonna offer you a job. Congratulations."

3-1-1 leans back in his chair and steeples his fingertips. "There's probably some glitch in Personnel."

"What kind of glitch?"

"Like a veteran they're trying to get around."

And now, my parents. They've decided to take a cross-country trip and visit me in the Tetons. Just what I need. How can I deal with *them,* along with everything else? I know their reasoning. They're pissed at the golden boy for remarrying so soon. Bill has now fallen in status from Mr. Ne'er-Do-Wrong to Mr. Big Time Loser. This frees up their loyalty, which can now be focused on me. In their own warped but well-meaning way, they want to be here for me. As far as they're concerned Bill's upcoming marriage is the only thing weighing on my mind right now.

Julian shows up on my doorstep one night and drops this bomb: "I just don't know what's wrong with me. I fall for any woman who walks by. There were times out in the field with Rachel that I had to really control myself. You know—that body, that hair, those blue eyes . . ."

How much more of this can I take? First of all, he's talking about my best friend here, and second, he just described her as an assemblage of pieces. "Rachel's eyes are brown, Julian."

"No kidding?" He jams his hands in his pockets. The air between us is pudding-thick. He makes small talk, then leaves.

Shutting the door behind him, I create my own fortress of truths to protect myself: Julian is shallow, sexist, immature, insecure, and still surfs on adolescent hormones. And he's simple-minded—he truly thinks if it weren't for an incubating fetus and too few climbing partners, he'd attain nirvana, which I think to him means the freedom to spend days scaling cliffs and nights engaging in consequence-free sex with anyone who comes along. I, of course, am smart, mature, and light years beyond him in emotional and psychological development. But the fortress disintegrates when the inner babble starts. *How could I have been such an idiot to fall for him? Maybe this is my punishment for all the pain I brought Bill by divorcing him. That's it. It's karma. What goes around, comes around. I deserve it.*

⌘

A blast of cold air ushers me through the door of Dornan's bar. Katy and Patrick have invited me to a concert by singer-guitarist Bill Staines. Hard to believe I've become the type of woman who goes to bars alone. But this is the Tetons, and I know nearly everyone in here. I spot Katy and Pat who are saving me a seat. As I cross the room, Eric and Christy, friends of Elaine's at the Teton Science School, pull me aside.

"We're going to have a job opening up in January at the Science School," Christy says. "Year-round, permanent."

Eric's eyes bulge. "Oh, man, you'd be *great* for that job."

"*Wow,*" I say. The Teton Science School. That top-notch environmental education center across the valley, teeming with Birkenstock-clad enviro-granolas like myself.

"Call me," says Christy, "and I'll tell you more about it."

I take a seat at the table with Katy and Pat, Deb from Dispatch, and Mike, the new North District naturalist. We get drinks, settle in.

Pat wraps his arm around my shoulders. "Any news from Denver yet?"

I tell them about Greg's latest phone call, and what Jace said must be happening.

"Uh-oh," Mike says. "They *have* to hire a vet if one applies. If they don't want to, they can close the position, not fill it for now, and reannounce it later."

Pat sips wine and nudges me with his elbow. "Ya know, I can't say I'd be disappointed if you don't get that job."

"Me neither," says Katy.

Hesitantly, I tell them what Christy just told me about the Science School job.

Katy straightens. "Wouldn't that be *ideal?* And you'd get housing with it, too. One of those great log cabins."

"I say you're going to get that job. Here's to the Science School." Pat sweeps his wine glass around the table, and others clink against it.

"And in the meantime you could clean condos at the village," Deb says.

"You'd *love* the winter here, Mary Beth," Katy says. "We ski into the National Forest to cut down our Christmas trees."

Pat's blue eyes round, magnified through his thick glasses. "And on New Year's Eve we all ski to the Chapel of the Transfiguration to toast the new year and ring the bell at midnight." He mimes this last sentence, pumping his arms and bobbing his head like a cross-country skier.

I go limp and sappy picturing myself surrounded by friends in snowy darkness, the bell pealing through the cold, as we hug and greet one another with affirmations of joy and friendship. This is the quirky outdoor camaraderie I've always dreamed of.

"You got yourself a pair of Sorels?" Pat asks. "You can't spend winter in the Tetons without Sorels."

The others at the table chime, "*Right,*" and tip wine glasses all around.

I'm never leaving this place.

Bill Staines appears and speaks to us with his mellow guitar and soothing voice. One song grabs me.

Watch the moon, smiling in the sky,
Hum a tune, a prairie lullaby.
Peaceful wind, and ol' coyotes cry a song of home—
My sweet Wyoming home.

When she sees the tears slipping down my cheeks, Katy leans toward me and pats her heart. "You need to really listen to *that,*" she says.

27

Forever Love

I'm spidering my fingers around the park UTM map when 3-1-1 walks by.

"My folks are coming," I say.

He stops short, turns around, face clouded. "Uh-oh. How do you feel about *that?*"

What? 3-1-1 asking the counselor's premier empathic question? It just doesn't jibe.

"I don't know," I say. "A big part of me really wants to see them again."

"Good luck."

"Thanks," I say. Then, "Hey, Jace, is there any way I could volunteer for a few weeks after my job ends and stay in the trailer until I know where I'm headed?"

"I'll have to look into it," he says.

❦

The folks call from Dubois on Sunday morning. "How long will it take us to get theah from heah?" Dad asks.

It seems strange, my father asking me for information he could just as easily find on a road map and the AAA Trip-Tik he always travels with. "If you don't dawdle," I say, "about an hour and a half. But you'll probably hit some snow on Togwotee Pass, so be careful." I feel knowledgeable and competent, the daughter advising the parent.

Waiting for them at my kitchen table, all the hurtful things they said to me in the past year flood back. But when the green Plymouth van pulls up, those things scatter to the four winds, and clear feelings blow in like a clean high-pressure system. I rush into their arms. Moist faces against mine, they smother me with kisses.

When my mother's fine hair, the same consistency as my own, fluffs against my neck, I'm drawn back decades, to a few days before I had my tonsils out: "It'll feel like this," she'd said, gently placing a cloth napkin over my nose and mouth to simulate the ether mask. "They'll put a mask over your face. It'll smell funny, but it won't hurt."

Dad smiles the same strong-chin smile as mine as he pulls me to him. Burying my face in his thick chest, I smell bacon on his wool shirt, no doubt from a Dubois diner. His stout arms encircle me, protective and reassuring. All's right with the world.

Right here in my driveway, by my decrepit trailer, under an overcast October sky with the snow-stippled Tetons reigning above, I know I have my parents back.

They're charitable about the trailer, which I've scrubbed as clean as it could ever be. They stay in my room; I return to the small bedroom while they're here. Every morning I rise before the clackety-clack of the furnace wakes them so I can clean out all signs of nocturnal mouse maneuvers before they get up. I don't mention Julian or the angst I feel about the upcoming winter. I only want them to experience a bit of my life here, to understand why I came, why I want to stay. I take them to a meeting of the Native Plant Society and introduce them to Bob, Elaine, Jack, Katy, and Pat. I want them to see that I'm not alone, that I have lots of friends who are happy that I'm here. I overhear Mom thanking Elaine and Katy for being there for me when I was down.

We walk around the Fabian Ranch at dusk. We find an elk herd and listen to their bugling and the cracking of their sparring antlers. From the looks on my parents' faces, I know I don't have to try to convince them of anything. They get it.

When Dad starts to pant because of the altitude, Mom comes alone with me on a walk to Taggart Lake. The trail sports a thin layer of snow. As we near the Taggart barn Mom says, "So Bill's getting remarried already. What's wrong with him?"

I knew this was coming, but I don't want to play Whack-the-Ex with her. Putting on a happy face, I say, "He's found someone who's right for him. It's a good thing."

"It's a rebound. It's stupid."

"Probably, but he needs to be with someone. He can't handle being alone."

"We thought you'd be having a hard time. That's why we came out. We didn't want you to be alone on his wedding day Saturday."

I wince. They feel indebted to me now. They're trying to make up for their past behavior. "That's nice of you, but I'm fine. I'm not ready to remarry, but if he is, that's okay."

"I never thought I'd say this, but maybe you should live with somebody before you get married again."

What? My jaw falls open. Did I hear right?

"Your father and I can see now why you and Bill weren't right for each other. But we just don't want you to grow old alone, and so far away."

Never alone, never lonely.

We walk on. A cold wind blows off the lake, so we don't stay long. On the way back she says, "Do you have anything lined up for the winter yet?"

"I'm staying here. I'll find an apartment in Jackson. And I'll probably get a job cleaning condos at Teton Village."

She stops on the trail and glares at me. "*Cleaning condos?* With two master's degrees?" Her eyes are so wide they strain her cheeks.

"They pay twice what I make at the park."

"Yeah, but . . ." her voice trails away.

We walk further in silence. She's stomping her feet, hands clenched. As we approach the bridge over Taggart Creek, she says, "*Please,* Mary. Don't do it. Don't be a *maid.*"

"But why not? It's the best money I could make here."

"Because your great-grandmother and great-aunt were maids. It's a terrible job. You shouldn't have to do that."

All of a sudden I feel like I'm letting them down. This Teton trap of doing whatever you can so you can live in a particular place is incomprehensible to them. They worked hard for years to ensure their daughters were educated. To them, education was a guarantee we would never have to do demeaning work like our ancestors did, like cleaning up after other people.

"Maybe the job in Denver will come through," she says.

I wag my hands. "I *told* you they have people lined up for those jobs." *God,* she irritates me sometimes.

She pauses to kick a stone from her shoe. "You never know . . ."

I bring my parents to the office and introduce them to Jace and Tim. It's an interaction I never imagined: my macho Teton bosses shaking the hands of my self-effacing Portuguese parents. I sense their deference—their rounded shoulders and avoidance of eye contact—but Mom and Dad make me proud. They start to ask questions about wildlife and the Teton life, and then do what they do best: share stories of their own about wildlife they saw and people they met on long-ago hunting trips in rural Maine.

I say, "Tell them about the guy with the freezer."

"Oh, *jeez.*" Glancing at me, Dad grins sheepishly, embarrassed to tell the story, unsure of how it would be taken.

But I egg him on. "It was the guy down the road, right?"

And they step onto center stage.

"Yeah. Frye Edgecomb," Mom says, shaking her head. "Decides to buy his wife a new freezer for Christmas . . ."

Dad finishes her sentence. " . . . and it's too big to fit through the door of the house."

"So Frye, with his great ingenuity, solves the problem." Mom half-smiles, one eyebrow raised, and opens her chubby fingers toward Dad.

Knowing the rest of the story, I pin my gaze on Tim and Jace, primed to gauge their reactions. It's a gamble, urging my father to tell this silly story to these unpredictable lugs. I don't want it to bomb.

But standing tall in his green L.L. Bean jacket and blue-and-white-striped engineer's cap, Dad holds out his fists and yanks on an imaginary cord. "*Varoom—beddy-boom—boom—boom.* Fires up the chain saw. *Brz-z-z.—Brz-z-z—Brzzz.* Cuts a hole right through the bloody wall and kicks it in."

When Tim and Jace crack up in laughter, I'm spit-giddy. They get it. *They know me.*

In the afternoon, Mom and Dad head out to look for wildlife along the Gros Ventre Road. After a while Jace walks into the back room where I'm bent over a table flattening a stalk of dalmatian toadflax into a plant press. Contorting his face, he leans toward me and asks, "How's the visit going?"

"It's going well," I say. "They've come a long way."

His clear eyes meet mine. "Good. I'm glad to hear that."

"Thanks, Jace."

I don't know how many more gut-shocks I can handle in one week.

❦

The folks planned to leave on Sunday, after seeing me through Bill's wedding day on Saturday. But snow is forecast. I assure them I'll be okay, tell them they should head out tomorrow, Thursday, instead, to beat the storm.

Their last night in the Tetons we have dinner in Jackson. When the drinks arrive at our table, Dad stirs his Manhattan and says, "Ah, Mary . . . I, um, I know we didn't treat you very well in the past year."

My breath catches.

"When you told us you were getting divorced, we didn't know how to deal with it."

"We were shocked," Mom says.

"That's right. We were worried about you, and I thought I wouldn't be a good father if I didn't try to stop you."

My eyes pool up.

"I just want to say I'm sorry."

"Me, too," Mom says, taking my hand. "I'm so sorry for the things I said."

I'm moved beyond tears. "It's okay," I say. "It's okay." I'm so moved I consider throwing everything away and driving the twenty-five hundred miles back across the country with them, but only briefly.

Dad squeezes my forearm and smiles. "I should have known the kid of this Port-a-gee from the sout' end of New Beige would make out just fine."

"Thanks" is the only word I can muster as the waiter shows up with our food.

Buttering my baked potato, I ask Dad about his job as a draftsman at Brewer Engineering in the late fifties. His green eyes glow as he explains his work on atomic submarines and early warning systems, a story I've heard dozens of times. "It was fascinating work, and you know how much I admired Given Brewer."

Mom sets down her fork. "Given was the greatest. Your father got a raise every six months. And on our anniversary he sent a dozen roses to the house. Can you believe that?"

"He was really something," Dad says. "The smah-test guy I ever knew, and funny, too—had a great sense of humor. And that's how I got to come *heah*—to Jackson Hole. We were doing stress analysis work at the engineering lab over in Idaho, and we came to Jackson to ski. I'll never forget those elk." He saws into his steak. "You remember the slides I brought back?"

Mom palms an arc through the air. "Fif-ty-mil-lion slides of elk. How could we forget?" She blots her mouth with a napkin and laughs, eyes flowering.

How I've missed them!

"I remember," I say, giggling. "I wanted to come out here even then."

"No kidding?" Dad says.

"For years you've talked about how much you loved that job, Dad. Why did you quit?"

"Too much traveling. I was gone most of the time." He looks away. "I loved it, but I had you two kids. I couldn't be away like that."

I sigh, feeling spoiled and self-indulgent. He once had a dream like mine, but he abandoned it. For me.

28

Any Port

A few hours after the folks' tearful departure the sky silvers, the temperature plunges, and a fine snow salts through the air. But it's not really snow, Tim tells me. It's *graupel*—tiny, dry granules of ice that lay the groundwork for the serious snow.

That night there's a knock on my door, and Julian's in my living room. He starts in. No mention of Anita, who moved out of Beaver Creek last week. Pam's calling him all night begging to come back. He just can't be with her, never wanted kids, still doesn't, can't afford child support. *Blah-dee-blah-blah.* He goes on and on. I listen to him rave.

Finally, not knowing what else to say, I play counselor. "It's so obvious to me that she's not facing reality. She needs help. Is she getting counseling?"

Clenching his fists, he storms around the room. "You ... you ... just ... don't ... get it. You got too emotionally attached to me, and now you can't see this clearly."

"*Too emotionally attached?*" I go to the kitchen counter and fold up a rumpled towel until it's as thick as a Dagwood sandwich. "We hang out together, enjoy each other's company, laugh and talk, have great sex. And this is supposed to be shallow and meaningless? On the planet I come from, this is emotional intimacy."

"I'm different. I needed the physical relationship, but I couldn't handle all the intense, heavy stuff."

"Then I guess I don't get it." I clench my fists and stomp my feet. I rant, emphasizing words haphazardly. "And *you're* so self-centered and wrapped up in your own *ego* that you don't even care how *I'm* doing. Have you forgotten that the man I was devoted to for *nineteen years* of my life will marry another woman in *two days*? That *both* my job *and* my house will disappear in *one week*? Don't you think *I* might have things on *my* mind, and that I might not want to deal with this *shit* you're dumping on me?"

He stands by the door, hand on the knob, and studies his toes. "I know. Sorry."

"You need to leave."

I slam the door behind him, not bothering to turn on the porch light. In bed, I give in to the Creature, kick, rant, and whine. But I notice this Creature is not huge and terrifying. No. The Chihuahua is back—scrappy and snappy, but not deeply threatening.

"How're you doing today?" Julian asks the next morning. His head is off-center; furrows of concern radiate from his eyes.

I stand my ground. "How do you think I feel, Julian?"

"Uh, not too good."

"You're very perceptive."

"Sorry. I know it's a hard time for you, too."

"Yeah."

Fortunately, Tim asks me to run some errands in town so I get out of the office for a few hours. When I return after lunch, Julian's still there. On my desk is a malted milk ball on a paper towel.

"What's this?" I ask.

He turns to face me with a roguish look. "It's either a giant mouse turd, or a peace offering."

Call me a nitwit, but how can I stay mad at him? Doc was right about people who think they don't need anybody. More than that, I'm finding that men need women more than we need them. Popping the candy into my mouth, I remember how chocolate fixes everything.

We keep working. After a few minutes he asks, "Are you interested in pizza tonight?"

I go. We chow down at Mountain High Pizza Pie and laugh and yack like old times.

"So what's it like," he asks, "with your ex getting married to someone else tomorrow?"

"The weirdest thing for me is that he's throwing a big party and I'm not helping to plan it." I chase down an escaped mushroom. "I feel a door has closed. But I still miss *something*, I don't know what. Maybe my dream of a supportive, ebb-and-flow kind of marriage? Something we never had. But I still love him—I think I always will—and I want him to be happy." I set down my fork as a tall, swarthy man with a little girl tagging behind him passes our table. *That'll be Bill*, I think. Remembering Bill's honesty and loyalty, my throat catches.

In one of the universe's hole-blowing serendipities, Jace's wife, Janet, calls Friday night and invites me to spend the next day with her. I'm moved that Jace told her it was Bill's wedding day and I'd need attention. In the morning we go to Jackson for breakfast, then return and dig through hard ground to plant spring bulbs in their yard in Moose. Later their daughter, Elsa, helps us make cookies for her day-care center's Halloween party. When I return home, I find four "thinking about you" messages from Mom on my answering machine.

❦

Hours scurry by and clot into days that I spend writing reports: amphibian report, exotic plant report, swan report. I immerse myself in the tasks, trying not to project into the haze of uncertainty that lurks beyond my remaining days of work. To fill up the evening hours, I beg a carload of boxes from Albertson's and start packing. I'm holding Jerry off. (I've just unloaded one twenty-something roommate. The idea of having two gives me heartburn.) And despite the promise of big bucks, cleaning condos is losing its appeal. I've never felt so rootless, leaving so much to chance. But I call Elaine and Katy, and we make plans for winter. We'll ski Flagg Canyon. Soak in Grizzly Hot Springs. Spend a night at the Leigh Lake patrol cabin.

Two days before my job ends, 3-1-1 strolls into my office. "I cleared it with the powers that be," he says. "You can volunteer for two weeks and stay in your trailer."

I want to kiss his ring. Two more weeks in paradise. Two more weeks of housing. I feel reckless. I don't have to put up with roommates. Something urges me to just keep riding this bucking horse. I tell Jerry I won't take the room. Why live with strangers? I have friends, I rationalize. Worse comes to worst, I can crash at someone's place until a better living arrangement turns up.

After work I head home under a heavy, gunstock-colored sky. Clouds shroud the mountaintops, and a menacing November wind swats the treetops.

Storm's coming, I tell myself, but I think the words with carefree confidence. I'm ready for it. I walk past the deserted seasonal housing units. Beaver Creek is quiet and mostly empty. But *I'm* here. For two more weeks anyway. I get to live at least part of the winter in the Tetons. And I couldn't be happier.

Inside the trailer I turn on the heat and make tea. Humming "Sweet Wyoming Home," I unpack all the boxes, returning books to shelves, clothes to drawers, dishes and food to cupboards. I sit at the kitchen table with my journal. Outside three ravens flap by my front stoop as I write:

I will have rewarding, steady work and a cabin in the woods one day . . . and good friends . . . and among those friends will be a man—a kindred spirit, kind of scruffy but attractive, an outdoorsy kind of guy who hikes and backpacks but is also emotionally present and warm and sensitive and spiritual, who cooks healthy food and listens to classical music. Yes, I will have a beautiful, fulfilling sexual relationship full of delightful closeness and love and common ground . . . full of humor and romance and long talks, joy and music and dancing too. How I look forward to that!

Paciência. Patience. I close the journal, head to my room, and lounge in my bed as if I have all the time in the world.

29

Uncertainty Principles

When the phone rings before dawn, piercing the viscous morning quiet, I jolt awake, thinking, *What's happened at home?* I pad over the cold carpet to the living room and pick up the phone. Already a coarse worry-lump fills my throat.

"Ready for track counts?" Julian. The lump disintegrates.

"Huh?"

"It snowed last night. Glen's visiting friends in Bellingham so we gotta do the track counts. Meet me at the office in thirty minutes."

When the fall snows come, S&RM employees drive a planned route to count elk tracks before the sun melts them or the snowplows spray them with slush. Track count data is used to monitor the routes and timing of the elk migration that will end a few miles south of here at the National Elk Refuge, where truckloads of alfalfa pellets will see the animals through the worst of winter.

Swollen-eyed from stolen sleep, I flick on the porch light and peer out the window. The cup of yellow light shows three or four inches of fresh snow on the back step.

I haul out my winter clothes: green parka, wool hat, mittens, scarf. Technically I'm a volunteer now and shouldn't be wearing anything that sports the NPS arrowhead patch, like my parka. But I'm not going to take the time now to remove the shoulder patch. Besides, who else will be out on the park roads in the snow at six a.m.?

On the closet floor are my Sorels. If one were to set out with the goal of dreaming up the ideal footwear for winter in the north country, it would be the Sorel Pac, a big lug of a boot reminiscent of the L.L. Bean Maine hunting shoe, but on steroids. Made in Canada, Sorels have honking waffle soles, black rubber uppers to the ankle, then tan leather above to mid-calf. Inside are removable liners of beefy wool felt, thick as bread slices. Cords pass through wide metal grommets to lace up the boots.

Once dressed, I bumble about like the Sta-Puft Marshmallow Man. Julian drives with me a few miles up the inside road to show me how to do the counts. We creep along the road shoulder and peer out the windows at the snow. When we spot tracks we get out to count all the elk tracks that look like they're heading south.

I quickly learn the difference between big pointy moose tracks, tiny heart-shaped deer tracks, and blocky elk tracks. We count only the elk tracks, crouching to examine them, and do the best we can to separate out the tracks of one elk from another. We tally them on the worksheet, then rake over the snow to clear the palette for tomorrow's trampling.

After my lesson, Julian takes off to do the northern roads, leaving me to finish up down south. It's runny-nose cold, but I feel toasty in all my gear. I'm squatting at the base of the dugway on the Moose-Wilson Road studying depressions in the snow, my mittened fingers around a garden rake, when a red F-150 pickup pulls up.

Sam Billings's chestnut beard parts into a smile as he kills the engine and cranks down the window. He's wearing his green parka, too, and an NPS bomber cap with the ear flaps Velcroed up on the crown of his head.

"Stayin' warm?" he asks.

I grin through all the wool. "Trying to."

"How many tracks so far?"

"Eighteen at the last stop. None here. These are moose tracks."

He nods, opens his mouth, and presses his tongue into his teeth. *Is he going to say something?* I wait, but he doesn't. Finally I ask, "When does your season end, Sam?" My nose tingles with cold; I'm sure it glows like a stoplight. I cinch the ends of the scarf tighter around my neck.

"End of the month. They keep finding things for me to do. Today I gotta check out Elaine and Jack's furnace. Sounds like a rocket taking off." His laugh is hearty and contagious. Above his trimmed beard, his cheeks dimple.

"Oh, *no*."

"And we need to figure out what to do about beefing up some roofs in Colter Bay." He rolls his shoulders. "Last summer I'm up there checking out a roof on one of the trailers. It's so bad my foot goes through it. There's a seasonal ranger in the living room below me, and she's freaking out. So I yell down, 'You got air conditioning in there?' She says, 'No-o.' And I go, 'You do *now*.'"

By the story's end, we're both laughing—his an endearing sputter, mine a wide-mouthed cackle.

"Heard anything from Denver yet?" His expression is innocent.

"Nothing. Jace thinks they're trying to get around a vet."

His lips thin as he nods in slow motion. Then he leans back in the seat, presses one hand into the steering wheel and the other onto the shift lever. I'm sure he's getting ready to leave, but instead he stretches one side of his torso, then relaxes. "Great morning, huh?"

I noisily inhale a dollop of snot I feel dripping down one nostril. "*O-oh*, it *is*. I *love* the snow. It's so peaceful."

He nods at the mountains. "You wouldn't have *this* in Denver."

"It'd be hard to leave," I say, pouching out my lower lip.

"The things we do for a permanent job, huh?"

"You said it."

"Ah, well. Good luck." He reaches to the ignition and turns the key. "Hope everything works out for ya."

"Thanks, Sam."

His face seems to crumble on itself as he rolls on down the road.

That Sam Billings is such a nice guy. I throw the rake in the truck bed and climb into the driver's seat, floating.

⁓

The park elk hunt starts.

Jackson Hole elk, treated to alfalfa pellets at the Refuge, are saved from the starvation that normally trims ungulate herds in the winter. As a result more animals survive to reproduce in the spring, allowing the population to swell to range-damaging levels. Hunting in national parks is forbidden, but Grand Teton sidesteps the regulation. Every hunter who receives a Wyoming license to hunt elk in designated park areas is deputized as a park ranger. Come late fall, the park crawls with armed deputy Ranger Ricks.

To keep track of the park elk taken, S&RM collects, no joke, elk jaws. Hunters complete an information tag, attach it to a jaw from a killed elk, and drop the whole bloody, bony mess in a depository box at the Buffalo Fork Ranger Station. Julian and I drive up and retrieve two trash bags full of frozen elk jaws. Then, wielding pliers in a Beaver Creek garage, Tim, Julian, and I spend an afternoon plying teeth from 150 jaws. Coated with thawing elk blood, my hands freeze, but

I keep at it. We place the hunter's tag and a tooth from each jaw in a Ziploc bag to send to the Wyoming Game and Fish Department for aging. I hate the jaws with lips and tongues still attached, frozen into contorted positions like things in a slasher movie.

At the post office that afternoon, I retrieve a glitzy PR packet from the Rocky Mountain Arsenal—brochures and a 1993 calendar of professional, heart-melting wildlife photos. I learn that the Arsenal was established by the army during World War II to manufacture chemical weapons and was later leased to private industries for pesticide production. Forty years later, they found the place contaminated with mustard gas, nerve gas, pesticides, and other toxic wastes. In 1984, it was placed on the National Priorities List of the nation's most hazardous areas, now called "Superfund Sites." The US Fish & Wildlife Service became involved after bald eagles were found roosting on Arsenal land and feeding on its resident black-tail prairie dog population. Bald eagles are protected under the Endangered Species Act, which is overseen by the Fish & Wildlife Service.

This knowledge does little to comfort me. More than ever I'm certain I need to stay here, where I can walk barefoot on uncontaminated soils and breathe pure air without concern.

On a Wednesday morning, the day after Bill Clinton's 364 electoral votes gave him a landslide win over George H. W. Bush, a light snow scuttles down. I spend five hours on track counts with a spring in my step. After work I hike up the Lupine Meadows Trail, wending my way up to a point that overlooks the valley. Straight ahead, Blacktail Butte, with its timber-lined drainages and open meadows, rises from a white sea. Only the faint *skit-skit-skit* of snowflakes falling on the snow surface breaks the leaden silence. I think of bears snugging into dens, swans squabbling among themselves to compete for submerged *Elodea* plants, elk moving south. On my way down the trail, a mule deer doe watches me from the woods. She flicks her ears and wanders away, unfazed by my intrusion.

Later I tramp circles in the snow in my driveway. When my feet and hands go grating-cold, I head inside. The trailer furnace screeches; mice munch on taco shells in the cupboards. I turn on the radio to *All Things Considered*. Make chicken enchiladas. Wash dishes. Sit on the sofa.

Hours drag by. Since Daylight Savings Time ended, the evenings draw out into endless, creaky stretches of time that I have trouble filling, and I descend into a dark, hollow void. The Creature rears and paws the ground. My shoulders sag as if my chest cavity's filled with cement. I try to read a book, but I can only think of ugly things—frozen elk tongues, cygnet carcasses, betrayals, toxic chemicals.

I can't stop the monkey-chatter in my head: *If you hadn't been so headstrong and self-centered, you'd be sitting with Bill in a real house right now, making plans for Thanksgiving. But instead you're alone and depressed in this dump of a trailer. Bill had no trouble finding love again, remarrying only six months after the divorce. That's because he's an honest, kind, trustworthy guy, and you threw him away, like garbage. And look who you fell for! Hah! You'll never have a special man in your life again because you're so _____, _____ and _____ (fill in the blanks) that no decent man would have you. And here you are: nearly forty, jobless, and being considered for a job at a toxic waste dump. Soon you'll be homeless, having given up your only chance for housing in Jackson. Ready to crash on someone's couch like a college kid for an indeterminate amount of time.*

When I flop over and lean my cheek against the dirty sofa, my body seems to deflate. The book falls to the floor, pages ruffling. The Creature now pants at the windows, and when I look in that direction I swear I see its slobber glued to the glass in dribbly ropes.

No good. I need to be with people. With parka unzipped and jeans half-tucked into the tops of untied Sorels, I trudge around Beaver Creek seeking signs of life. I vow to knock on the door of the first place I find with lights on.

Outside it's quilt-still. New moon time. The Milky Way banners above, a gauzy canopy so full of stars it obscures the familiar constellations. With squinty concentration, I barely make out Orion and the smudgy nebula hanging off his belt. Pocketing my hands, I squeak through the snow. All the seasonal units, of course, are cloaked in darkness. Hedging my bets, I head first around the permanent housing loop. I pause in front of trails chief Rick Watson's commodious log home and sniff the homey scent of wood smoke wafting from the chimney. Light plays through one window—but it's the jitter-blue light of a television screen. I hardly know Rick or his wife, Judy. Do I really want to barge in on a happy, long-married couple cozied up on their loveseat watching TV? Can't do that. I head to the opposite end of the housing area until I'm standing before the only other house with lights on. The glow from the picture window pours onto the snow.

I think: *This is the last person I should be visiting.* Then I rap on the door.

The porch light comes on, the door opens. He's wearing a gray sweatshirt and his patched Carhartt work pants, with Sorel liners on his feet. When he sees me, his beard cracks, freeing a look of surprise.

"I was going batty communing with rodents and listening to my crotchety furnace," I say.

"You should have come sooner," Julian says.

We make popcorn in a dented pan, pour it into a bowl, then melt butter in the still-warm pan. Sitting on the sofa, we try to watch a program about reptiles on TV, but the reception is so poor we're really just watching shadows of turtles in a blizzard. We munch popcorn and wipe our butter-slick fingers on a flowery-blue dish towel. Electric baseboards click, and I feel my face flush. "It's hot in here," I say.

"I've only got one heater on low."

Head bent in amusement, he watches as I pull my wool sweater over my head, straighten my turtleneck, and run my hands over the curlicues of hair that levitate around my head with static electricity. We resume our side-to-side stance, eyes straight ahead, four unwavering headlight beams.

"You can lean on me if you want," he finally says.

That's all I need to hear. As I rest my head on his shoulder, the heat of his body, the softness of his sweatshirt, the hint of a musky smell draw me in. He pulls his arm free, wraps it around me, pulls me close. And suddenly my world is righted. I've got to be crazy.

We start to talk, which reminds me how easy it can be for us. He says we've put a lot of troubled water behind us and our friendship has deepened. I agree. And when he cradles my face in his hands and brings my lips to his, I melt.

He whispers, "Would you want to stay here tonight?"

By now my blood's simmering in my veins. As I open my mouth to answer, the phone rings, and a shard of anger bolts through me. "*Shit.*"

The way he huddles over the phone and murmurs into the receiver tells me it's Pam. Silently, I don my parka and Sorels and head back home. As I open the trailer door and turn on the light, a mouse blinks at me from the kitchen table before it runs down a chair, across the floor, and into a hole under the cabinets. I turn up the heat; in a few minutes the clucky symphony begins and hot air blows through a vent in the wall.

Am I nuts? I say to myself, spraying Windex on the table and wiping it down.

Not five minutes later, he's knocking on the door. "You left too soon," he says.

"She just can't let me go . . ." He goes on and on, but I've lost patience. I put it back on him. This is his problem. I'm truly sorry he can't deal with it.

I don't invite him to stay.

———⌒———

Three days before my volunteer stint will end, Greg Langer calls and offers me the seasonal employee's most coveted prize: a fully-benefitted PGJ with the US Fish & Wildlife Service. Right there on the phone I don't think twice. "I'll take it," I say. I must be dandelion fluff, the way I toss around in the breeze.

The news zings through the park grapevine. Everyone I run into in the course of my day—at Colter Bay, headquarters, downtown at Albertson's—rushes over to hug and congratulate me, and at the same time, express their disappointment at my leaving. With every good wish offered, a marble-size drop of my soul pulls away and disappears in the ether. But five little words I hear over and over fill me with hope: *You can always come back.*

———⌒———

I awake at five to a stone-cave silence. When I toggle the light switch up and down, nothing happens. No power. I stay in bed until a faint breath of light bleeds into the room before I call Julian to wake him for track counts.

Ten inches of snow dumped last night, embracing us in the true clasp of winter. The Moose-Wilson Road is pristine and lovely as I four-wheel through new snow in S&RM's gray Chevy pickup that I've dubbed "the Silver Bullet." A stunted morning light sets off the snow-softened peaks as I kill the truck engine and slide out the door. The cold is more pervasive, blunted, and insulating than any I've ever experienced. And when the sun finally peeks through a band of clouds, it's with a blinding, short-lived fierceness. A revelation.

I find few tracks, but I relish the serenity of early morning. It's about ten degrees and windless, but a blaze in my solar plexus warms me from within. Doffing my parka, I work only in sweater, hat, and gloves. I pull on the rake, loving the stretch and the exertion, breath misting from my mouth.

How can I leave this place?

After the counts Julian and I work in the office finishing up reports. There's no serious talk between us. I feel okay about it, I guess. But thoughts of our past intimacies haunt me. In my rootless state I long for a man's comforting touch. But he was such a prick. What will I settle for?

At three I turn off the computer and reach for my parka. "See ya, Julian."

He rolls his chair around to face me. "Hey," he says, squeezing his minuscule ponytail between his fingers, "I'm making lasagna tonight and just developed some wildlife slides. Want to come over for dinner and a slide show?"

Oh, jeez. "I'll have to think about it."

I wade through knee-deep snow to my trailer and call Elaine. She laughs. "Mary Beth, these are the nineties. You can let go of that old Catholic guilt."

I bite my lip.

"You can't expect monogamy from him, but so what? Have some fun before you start this next chapter in your life."

That evening a buried memory surfaces of Bill's father grinning, wagging his forefinger and teasing Bill and me as we headed out on a date: "*Não brincadeiras.*" (No playing around.)

Nonetheless, I head over to Julian's with a strip of condoms in my pocket.

———

On a frigid evening in mid-November I cram everything into my car—books, clothes, tent, backpack, cross-country skis. Fingers numb with cold, I lace the bike rack to Darcy's rear and hitch on the bike. Then I walk around Beaver Creek, snow creaking beneath my feet. A gibbous moon casts the mountains in an exquisite ice-blue light. Across the valley, the Gros Ventre Slide yawns through a black expanse of forest. Coyotes yip in the distance.

Thoughts roll as I wade through the snow around Beaver Creek. *I haven't changed that much. I've traveled a long and treacherous path, but I'm still me, I'm still everyone: seeking a full and happy life, searching for true love and meaningful work that both feeds me and serves a higher purpose.* I face the mountains. Although the thwarted light mollifies their sharpness, their staggering heights still lure me.

The next day I turn in my park keys at the Property Office. No more jangle of keys—those simple invitations into home, office, backcountry cabins, park gates, the lock on the Spread Creek weir—all intertwined and complementing one another, brass representations of a life full of purpose and belonging.

One key remains on my key ring—the one to my Toyota—and its sound is the Zen sound of one hand clapping.

Part 2: White Combs and Sweet Honey

Last night, as I was sleeping,
I dreamt—marvellous error!—
that I had a beehive
here inside my heart.
And the golden bees
were making white combs
and sweet honey
from my old failures.

—Antonio Machado
(Translated by Robert Bly)

30

Homing

April 1993. Capping its snow-swept bulk, the Teton skyline sawtooths through a slate-colored sky as a granular pre-dawn light washes over the Kelly Hayfields. Snow sheets over the ground and feathers up the mountainsides, lending a paradoxical softness to the landscape. Above and behind: a sliver of moon and Venus, the morning star. Straight ahead: Blacktail Butte, the rounded spine of a sleeping animal.

Beyond, bony mountain shoulders erupt through clotted snow: Buck Mountain, Static Peak, South, Middle, the Grand, Nez Perce, Mount Owen, Teewinot, Rockchuck Peak. Between them, Death, Garnet, and Cascade Canyons sleep under rock-dense wedges of snow. All here, heart-gripping, breath-stopping. Just here, being. Still. Silent. Humbling.

I couldn't stay away. I'm back in these mountains that have wormed themselves into my core, whose rivers and creeks now course through me as reliably as blood.

Cold seeps through the windows of the Silver Bullet. Steadying a pair of Zeiss binoculars on the steering wheel, I crank my neck into an S shape and peer through the eyepieces at a strip of bare ground in the distance.

Tim sent me here to count sage grouse on a lek, or strutting ground. It's an annual event. Sage grouse assemble before sunrise, and the boys strut their stuff to impress the girls. Driving out here half an hour ago in the dark, I nearly slammed into a bull moose on the Antelope Flats Road. Amid my squealing of brakes, he trotted into the sagebrush to join six more of his cohorts. Hyperventilating after the near-miss, I rechecked Tim's map. With headlights off I found the overgrown two-track and drove in a quarter mile to search for grouse.

I rotate the binoculars, ignorant of what I'm looking for. I've never seen a sage grouse, strutting or otherwise. The sage grouse strutting season had already passed when I arrived here last summer. All I see now is the nickel-colored ground.

There . . . I swivel the binocs back. A form moves slowly in the distance. I focus in. There's another . . . and two more. In all, eight moving things and three stationary blobs. Some fan pointy tail feathers.

I reach into my pack for my flashlight and the National Geographic *Field Guide to the Birds of North America* that accompanies me on all my work jaunts. Finding the dog-eared page, I reread the description of *Centrocercus urophasianus.* They're sage grouse all right. What else would be strutting around the Wyoming sage flats before dawn in April? I roll down the window and cup my hand to my ear to listen for the characteristic inflating and deflating of the males' air sacs.

"*Buddle-ee-oop.*"

The sound reminds me of a stone plopping into water at the bottom of a deep well. I watch and listen again. This time, a moment or two before I hear the sound, I see one bird's chest puff up full and flabby like a water balloon, then deflate.

Looking closely, I realize that the three stationary blobs are also sage grouse, but smaller ones, scratching and pecking at the frozen ground. Females. I write in my field journal:

Antelope Flats—4/20/93. 5:45 a.m. ~25˚, frosty, no wind.
8 strutting ♂s, 3 ♀s.

They make me smile. Men are always trying to impress women. Even plump birds with well-endowed chests. They're no different than the guys parading around the Cowboy Bar in Jackson or the Grizzly Rose in Denver.

Setting down the binoculars on the seat, I stretch my arms and yawn. *I'm back!* I'm home where I belong, doing real wildlife work. My whole body vibrates at the thought, or maybe it's just the cold.

I gave Denver a noble effort—I lasted five months. I rented a comfortable apartment and shipped out my modest belongings from Massachusetts. People were welcoming and fun-loving, and the job, while desk-bound and administrative, feathered my nest with securities: life and health insurance, retirement plan, even a TSP, Thrift Savings Plan, the government equivalent of a 401(k). While far removed from the field biology work I craved, the job taught me much about the intricacies of federal bureaucracy, as well as a few things about myself. Wearing the tan shirt and pottery-colored pants of the Fish & Wildlife Service, I worked in "Activities Coordination" as the liaison between the Fish & Wildlife

Service, the US Army, and its hazardous waste cleanup contractors. Army contractors called me when their work needed to take them into the BEMA, the restricted Bald Eagle Management Area on the Arsenal, and I made the decision whether to allow or deny entry, based on time of day, eagle activity, and whether the birds were likely to tolerate disturbance. I caught on quickly, and soon I was handling problems, smoothing over disagreements, speaking out at meetings. My supervisor, Greg, often called me into his office to ask my opinion on how we should do things. One day I stepped back in amazement and beheld the get-it-done, confident, outspoken, and professionally respected woman I'd become. A long and prosperous federal career stretched out before me, mine for the taking.

But at what cost? The mountains hung out there, intangible, like a picture on the wall. On occasional drives through the Arsenal I watched eagles, burrowing owls, jackrabbits, and whitetail deer, but these did little to satisfy my wilderness craving.

I enjoyed a lively social life, making many friends at work and on ski trips with the Colorado Mountain Club. Shortly after my fortieth birthday I joined three CMC women at a Vietnamese restaurant one Saturday night. All attractive middle-age women, they wore eye shadow and lipstick and neutral-colored woolen coats with patterned scarves threaded through the collars. Passing a platter of spring rolls, I looked around and saw in their tired faces my future self. They all were on lucrative career paths, living in city apartments. They were partnerless, having long ago given up on lasting love. Every one of them seemed lonely and empty, grasping for connections with other lonely, empty women.

Right then I decided this wasn't the future I wanted. I didn't leave a marriage and move out west to live in a city with a smoggy view of distant mountains. I didn't want to waste my remaining years of good health on a worn path to a cushy government retirement. I decided how and where I spend my days is more important to me than job security.

But despite my relief to be back in the Tetons, doubts flourish. I gave up a future of security for a seasonal job. Sure, I tell myself, everything's fine during the summer. But what about the fall? What then? What a *tola*, an idiot. (The Creature is bilingual.) But while I've given up permanence and security, I *have* gained one thing that could make all the difference: *status*. By working a few months in a permanent government job, I now have federal employment status for the next three years. This means I can apply, without competition from non-status applicants, for most federal jobs. With luck, a permanent wildlife biologist position will open up at Grand Teton during that time.

I need to quit ruminating. I want to live in the moment and not anguish over what's passed by or what's yet to come. I want to accept *what is* with love and peace in my heart. Be *present* and open to life.

Through binoculars I see that the sunrise has chased the sage grouse back into hiding in soil depressions and under sagebrush overhangs. I start the pickup and back down the dirt road until I hit pavement. Driving back to the S&RM office, I study the tangle of peach-colored summits brushed by tenuous clouds.

Never again, I realize. It will look like this only once. *Now.*

Hermit Crab

The raptors are back. Julian and I sit on a rise overlooking the Kelly Hayfields and peer through binoculars. April is the busy time for raptor research, and Mark has engaged us to help out.

One of the office hamsters runs frantic circles in a bal-chatri trap about seventy-five meters away. Used by falconers as well as biologists, the trap consists of a hardware cloth box covered with monofilament slip-nooses. When a raptor spots the moving rodent in the box and swoops down for the kill, the loops tighten around the bird's feet. The rodent, called a "lure animal," is left unscathed, albeit terrorized.

A southwest wind nips the back of my neck. Overhead a tepid sun skitters in and out of clouds dense and textured as tapestries. Despite bulky layers of clothing and letter-sized sheets of Ensolite foam insulating our backsides from the frozen ground, we shiver. Our arms occasionally scrape together, making a *zip* sound, and still, I have to admit, a *zing* in my middle.

"Look, there," I say, pointing. "What *is* that?"

He parallels his binoculars with mine. "Swainson's."

"Oh, yeah. The dark bib."

"And there's a rough-legged."

I check my field notebook on the ground beside me and read my cryptic notes:

Rough-legged—*Buteo lagopus*. Tail—wht @ base, dk band @ end. Blk patches—wrists & wing tips.

A white-rumped raptor dips by. "Harrier," I say. Overhead, a much smaller one, with pointy wing tips. "And there, a kestrel." I'm *stoked*. Last summer I didn't have a clue how to identify raptors on the wing. Now I have a smattering of bird sense.

Julian notes our observations on a clipboard. The chasm between his eyebrows is especially deep these days, so deep I fear his skull might crack open and implode right down the middle of his liverwurst-pasty face.

I'm still kicking myself for getting romantically involved with a coworker, especially so soon after my divorce, especially with his ex still in the picture. I could handle this better if we had some geographical separation. But like it or not, Julian's *in my face.* We still work at adjacent desks, and I now live in the barracks house across the street from his place.

And what's the first gossip I heard when I got back from Denver? That Pam is moving back to Beaver Creek with the baby this summer. Julian hasn't said word one to me about this and it pisses me off. Every day in the office he sits beside me and types silently, his face tense and pleated. Through slitted eyes I watch him clench his hands, huff, *phew,* hit the delete button, wriggle his shoulders. From time to time he shoots from his chair to the file cabinet where he yanks open drawers, *tsks,* then slams them shut. Whenever I ask him a question about wildlife, he rolls his eyes as if he's never known someone so ignorant, then grunts the answer in monosyllables.

In three hours many raptors pass over the hayfields but not one shows any interest in the hamster. Cold numbs my hips. "I'm freezing," I finally say through chattering teeth.

"Me, too. Let's move on."

We pull the trap and drive up to the Kelly Butte loop for a repeat attempt. Driving past lavish log homes, we spot a red-tail on a telephone pole, stop, and set out the trap.

"So if we catch one of these guys," I say, "what'll we do with it?"

"Band it and check it for skin and blood parasites."

I'd love to learn how to restrain a hawk and draw blood from it, but I don't want to give a hamster a lifelong phobia. It's a moot point though because as we cut the truck engine the red-tail flies off to the southwest.

"*Damn,*" Julian says. He drives to the end of the loop and parks where we can overlook a grassy expanse. We resume our glassing. When I glance in his direction, I notice bands of tension in his neck. His teeth must be clamped in a death grip. Jagged lines mar his cheeks, and the dry cold has turned his hands pink and scurfy.

"Lunch time," I say after an hour, reaching for my pack. Opening up my thin sandwich, I examine the splinters of jack cheese with a few dabs of salsa. "My food stash is dwindling," I say. "I need to head to town tonight."

Julian sighs audibly, pulls off his stocking cap, and adjusts his ponytail. Then he leans back and pinches the bridge of his nose between two fingers.

"You okay, Julian?" Why, why, why after all his shenanigans do I still fall into the caring counselor role?

Another heavy sigh as he clenches the steering wheel and arches his back. "Pam's moving back from Dallas with the baby in two months."

Finally. Dousing the smoldering ember in my gut, I force nonchalance. "Is that what you want?"

"Of course not."

I snort. "So why's she coming back? You've been saying all along you guys are over."

Julian fiddles with a Doritos bag, mouth corners drawn into his beard. "Because I feel like I *have* to let her come back." His voice is low and hoarse. "She doesn't have a job. What else can I do? It's my kid. I'm—ya know—feeling responsible."

"Look—two juncos," I say.

"I still say she stuck pins in the condoms."

"*Ppfft.* Isn't it too late to matter?"

"I suppose. There's another kestrel."

"Two nuthatches in that cottonwood."

After a period of silence Julian looks at me askance. "I had hoped you and I could still be friends, but Pam doesn't want me hanging out with you."

"Fine." I stash the sandwich bag into my pack and reach for an apple. "Does she know we have to do work projects together?"

"This is a professional relationship. She has to understand that."

Hours pass, during which my lunch jabs in my stomach like a cat in a pillowcase. Still no aerial attacks on the hamster; I keep my relief to myself.

Julian checks his watch. "Let's call it a day."

We dismantle the trap. The hamster's toenails scratch on fabric as I drop him into my jacket pocket.

Back at the office I return the hamster to his mate in the aquarium and drop in a few peanuts and sunflower seeds. Both hamsters stuff them into their cheeks. Leaning on the rim of the tank, I reach down and scratch each furry head. The odor of urine is overwhelming. "I'll clean out this pigpen tomorrow, guys. I promise." Then, with a sidelong glance at Julian, I say, "These babies need names."

"Oh, *God* ... "

"I know," I say, wagging my forefinger. "I'm anthropomorphizing again. Unforgivable."

"That's right."

"Tansy and Salsify."

"That's appropriate, naming them after weeds. They're worthless."

Fuck off, Julian. I skim through a stack of handwritten notes, and, finding nothing pressing, slide them under a book.

"See ya tomorrow." I turn to leave.

"Hey."

I look back.

Julian's stretched back in his chair, fingers interlaced behind his head, eyes creamy-soft. "I need groceries, too. You want company going to town tonight?"

Air hisses through my pursed lips. "I thought Pam didn't want you hanging out with me."

"She doesn't. That's why I want to do as much socializing as possible before she gets here."

God, what a prick. "No, Julian. I don't want company."

Minutes later I'm heading down Windy Point on my way to Jackson. Steely clouds brace the sky. Over the Gros Ventre, veils of rain fall from clouds and appear to hang tangled in midair like Einstein's hair. It's called "virga" and it's common in dry climates where rain often evaporates before it reaches the ground.

Julian's words zip through my head like pinballs: "I want to do as much socializing as possible before she gets here." How, exactly, does he define "socializing"? Will the grocery shopping be followed by *howaboutdinner, mytreat?* And later, *wouldyouwanttostayheretonight?* My chest heaves, portending a spurt of volcanic anger. At him, of course, but also at myself, for not seeing through him, for succumbing to his charms.

Forcing my attention back to the present, I peer into the sage flats eager to see gray-green spots of open ground that might herald the emergence of the first spring flowers—bell-shaped yellow fritillaries or the legendary steersheads everyone talks about—thumbnail-sized beauties resembling cows' heads, horns and all. But bare spots are few; snow still reigns in the valley.

The gloom and gray weigh on me. Returning to the Tetons was supposed to be all stars and sunshine. I thought I'd grown beyond this nonsense with Julian and was ready to be on my own for a while. Now all I can think of is whether I'll ever have sex again.

Just past the Chapel of the Transfiguration the speed limit slows to 15 mph through the park entrance gates. I spot Doug Bonner and Sam Billings painting the log kiosks. As I drive by Sam sets down his brush and waves for me to stop.

He strolls over and I roll down the window. All smiles, he rests his forearm on the car roof and blinks at me through yellow-tinted sunglasses. "Welcome back."

"Thanks, Sam. I couldn't handle Denver. I missed *this*." I nod in the direction of the mountains. "Cities aren't my thing."

"I hear ya."

"You guys giving the kiosks a face-lift for the *tourons*?"

He throws his head back and bursts out a gut laugh that balms my troubled heart. "The *tourons*, yeah. Gotta spiff up the place for the tourons." He hooks his thumb into his belt. "Hey, I'm heading to Utah for a few days next week to visit the grandparents. I was wondering if you could check on my cabin and water my plants while I'm gone."

We do this all the time—help other employees with house or pet care when they travel. I don't know Sam very well, but what the hell? "Sure," I say. "Be happy to."

He gives me cursory directions. "Great. Stop by sometime. I'll show you my exotic species."

"You growing pot?" I ask, eyes scrunched.

He chuckles. "Just musk thistle."

A ray of sunlight follows me to Jackson.

~~~

Despite its hapless location in the neighborhood, I'm delighted with my housing this season. After spending my first few weeks in another grungy trailer, I moved to Beaver Creek 56, a sunny CCC barracks—two bedrooms, lots of windows, wood floors. The refrigerator has an efficient bottom freezer that was stocked with packages of antelope meat when I moved in.

According to the Grand Teton Housing Office, I have a roommate, Carol, who works at Park Headquarters. But HQ Carol, being engaged to marry Maintenance Jeff in June, spends all her time at his trailer at the opposite end of Beaver

Creek. (As a permanent employee Jeff scored a higher-end trailer than my last year's firetrap, so high-end, in fact, that it's known as "The Taj.") Jeff shot the antelope last fall, and Carol left some stew meat and burger in the freezer for me.

Despite a few cracked windowpanes, peeling mustard-colored walls, and the ever-present mouse issue, my barracks house is luxurious. I can see the Grand from my bed, and I have a spare room for company. After Carol's wedding in two months, the park will assign me a new roommate. I try not to think that far ahead.

This chopping of time and viewing of my future in week or monthlong segments is a challenge to me. In the past year I've moved four times: to Moose, to Denver, back to Moose to a trailer, and then to the barracks. Luckily I don't have much to move anymore; I've left my meager home furnishings in a Denver storage unit and returned to the Tetons with just clothes, bedding, a few dishes and books, a bike, cross-country skis, and camping gear. Who knows when I'll see my grandmother's rocking chair again, the oil of a bear cub my sister, Nancy, painted for me, the tab curtains Mom made, the pine desk Dad built? All these treasures were supposed to accompany me to the Tetons, to my new life, to my dreamed-of log cabin in the woods with the view of the Rockies. Turning forty just before I left Denver made me crave more than ever a nest of my own. I hadn't planned on getting all of my life's accoutrements together, then leaving them somewhere else while I moved on. *It's only stuff,* I tell myself. But its absence from my life is symbolic of this transience that so grates on me. But this house, like this life, is mine for a while, and that's all anybody can hope for.

32

Stewardship

Her eyelids float dreamily in the late afternoon sunlight. She lies prone, relaxed, legs splayed out behind her, in his embrace. His arms, tucked in the soft hollows of her armpits, hold her close as his strong thighs encircle her hips. As her body writhes, his pelvis rolls to match the motion . . .

I feel like Pee-wee Herman at a peep show. I'm hunkered down on the shore of Schwabacher Pond, waders binding in the backs of my knees, watching two boreal toads in "amplexus" position in the shallow, silty water. Although I've been finding egg masses and tadpoles, I've never seen toads "do it" until now.

After a while the female extrudes two rows of eggs strung like black pearls in gelatin sheaths that will drape around blades of sedges and rushes.

"Each female produces an average of twelve thousand eggs," Chuck whispers, chewing on a Hershey bar. Shaded by a tan porkpie hat, his round face is fringed with unkempt gray-brown hair that brushes his collar. "And they'll go at it for hours. Those poor females!"

Chuck Peterson is here from Idaho State in Pocatello to spend a day in the field with me. He picked me up in his blue Dodge van at the office at seven-thirty this morning to drive out to Half Moon Lake, where last year Rachel and I found the baby boreal toads. This year we found no sign of toad egg strings; the area was dry. According to Chuck, they'd moved on. Next we got back into his van and headed to Togwotee Pass, east of the park boundary. There we found a pond busy with chorus and spotted frogs, with several softball-sized masses of spotted frog eggs.

Backing away from the pond, I turn to Chuck, seated on a lichen-crusted rock surrounded by gear. He checks his watch. "Almost four. We should head over to Taggart." He unfolds off the rock, brushes off his baggy khaki pants, and starts stuffing the myriad pockets of his fishing vest. When he's done, every pocket and pouch bulges with doodads: aquarium fish net, measuring tape, thermometer, tape recorder, plastic bags, flashlight, hand lens, paper, pencils, candy bars. The thing hangs lopsided from his shoulders. As we slosh through the muck, he steps into a hole and would have capsized had I not grabbed his arm with both hands.

"*Jeez*," he says, adjusting the vest around his chest. "I feel like a Winnebago in this thing."

A day in the field with Chuck is a scrumptious treat, worlds away from the office egos and Julian's moods. When I first met Chuck last summer, I pegged him as the *Far Side* kid grown up: a chubby, freckle-faced guy who spent his boyhood chasing snakes and frogs and never outgrew it. As unaffected as the moon, he eagerly shares his knowledge and is supportive of my fieldwork. We talk nothing but shop. After knowing him for a year, I still know nothing about his personal life. He's just Chuck the Herp Guy, in his Winnebago vest. "I'm so glad you took over the amphibian project," he tells me, "because if you didn't, the work just wouldn't get done."

We park at the Taggart lot and head down the trail for the mile-and-a-half walk to the pond. Besides the vest, Chuck lugs a black bag of camera equipment over one shoulder. With all his paraphernalia, he swishes and clatters as he walks.

For late May the day is warm. Unrelenting sun bears down through charred lodgepole pine boles left behind in the 1985 fire that burned a thousand of these acres. Sweat trickles down my ribs. Shade is elusive; it combs the trail in thin stripes.

We hear chorus frogs, the familiar fingernail-scraping-over-a-comb sound, as we approach the pond beyond the lake, but they fall silent as we get closer. We drop our packs and sit on a log to wait. Soon one brave frog calls from across the pond, then another closer to us, then another, until we are surrounded by screeping frogs. Sitting as motionlessly as possible, I scan the water with my binoculars while Chuck switches lenses on his camera. Bulbous frog eyes seem to float on the satiny water. I watch one frog inflate its throat to a translucent marble, a remarkable feat when you consider that the whole frog is smaller than my pinkie finger. I imagine pricking the gossamer-thin throat with a pin and watching the frog spiral backward into the air with a *pf-f-f-t* sound, like a popped balloon.

(These are the sick things that run through my mind these days. It frightens me.)

Last summer the Elk Refuge biologist told me about his elk calf research. He'd thrust out his chest as he explained how, when they swoop down in a helicopter into a group of cows and calves, the cows run away, and the babies cower down under the draft from the blades. Then it's easy for him to jump out of the chopper and snap radio collars on them.

"My *God,*" I said. "Talk about stress . . ."

He stroked the crown of his head, as if there were still hair there. "It's wild-life biology," he said. "We're getting great information."

It's so *yang,* I thought.

Now *I'm* thinking about sticking frog throats to watch them zing through the air like Zizz-Boom firecrackers.

By the time Chuck gets the photos he wants, the sun has disappeared behind the mountains. "Let's take a walk around the pond," he says, "before it's too dark to see anything."

I'm getting tired and my legs ache, but, hell, I'd walk through fire for this guy. Using lodgepole sticks for balance, we head in opposite directions and search the shallow water near the shore. Almost immediately we start to find spotted frog egg masses, blobs of what look like pea-sized, gelatinous eyeballs.

The water varies from ankle- to thigh-deep, with occasional deeper holes to dodge. The worst area is the far shore, where we have to maneuver through and climb over intersecting logs. As I sit on a high log and swerve my legs over it, something plops into the water nearby. In the shadow I see movement. *Catch it. Catch it.* I guide my hand slowly into the water and clamp my fingers around a bony, slimy body.

"What is it?" Chuck calls from across the pond.

I turn the animal upside down in my hand. Orange coloring covers its lower belly and thighs. "He's wearing orange pants," I say, "so he's a spotted frog."

Not fair, I think, the little thing is so helpless, and no threat to me whatso-ever. I cup my hands around it. Is it any less afraid of me than the elk calves are of the helicopter blades? I wish it peace and abundance, then I reach down and release it. As I open my hands it digs its rear feet into the heel of my hand and peels off.

Chuck and I come together on the opposite shore. We return to the starting point, pack up, and head out. Silently we kick along the dusty trail back to the van, cool dusk settling all around.

The next day I run into the chief ranger's wife in Moose. "I saw you at Tag-gart yesterday," she says. "What were you doing in the water?"

"Looking for frogs."

"You guys are so strange," she says, head zigzagging.

33

Cabin Fever

My car jounces over a lumpy two-track. Where the hell am I going? This seems like the end of nowhere. I try to remember the directions. Left at the aspens, then right after the bridge? Or right then left?

Ahead of me a couple walks through the sagebrush. The man is tall and gray-haired, the woman petite, her hair in a dark bob.

"I'm trying to find Sam Billings's cabin," I say, pulling up beside them. "Am I on the right road?"

"Yes, you are, but you missed the turnoff." Shielding her eyes with her hand, the woman gestures back behind me.

"So I should turn back there?"

She nods, then winks. "I hope you're his girlfriend because he sure is *cute!*"

My face heats up several degrees as I force the shift lever into reverse and head back. He *is* cute, I think, but right now, still with a heart chewed raw by Julian, I don't see Sam as a "possibility." Nothing really draws me to him; he seems just another all-head, no-heart Teton man. I'm sure we have little in common besides a love of the Tetons. But I'm willing to water his plants for him. Maybe he'll turn out to be a good friend. I need one of those.

The driveway ends in a cul-de-sac, and beyond it stands a log cabin. I swoon at the simple structure with its peaked cedar roof, walls of sun-baked logs, and porch cluttered with snow shovels, a ski pole, firewood, a bent golf club, elk antlers. Under the cabin's north gable is a window. Are those lace curtains? Can't be. Sam isn't a lace curtain kinda guy.

The "yard," an overgrown expanse of sagebrush, grasses, and wildflowers, is stippled with firs, lodgepoles, and aspens. In a tuft of willows stands an authentic tepee, white canvas painted with Indian symbols. Behind it all, the bellowing Teton view. I gape. Then, with an idiotic grin plastered on my face, I arch my back, spread my arms, and pirouette on one foot, ballerina-style. Of all times for Sam to appear from the back door with a can of polyurethane in one hand and a brush in the other. I, *quick,* drop my arms to my sides. For the second time in less than ten minutes, my face burns. I hide my cheeks with my palms.

"Don't be embarrassed," he says with a laugh. "This place has that effect on people." He sets the can down on the back step and balances the brush on the rim.

"My *God,* Sam, this is *heaven.*"

"The best, isn't it?" His hazel eyes glow.

I peer behind him through the open door. "What are you working on?"

"A lodgepole bed. Jeff and Carol's wedding present."

He waves me to the doorway of a tool-filled room that smells of sawdust and polyurethane. Leaning against a workbench is a headboard, a curved pole of wood with vertical posts, all butter-colored and slick with wet sealant.

"You *built* this?" I squeak. "It's *gorgeous.*"

He's wearing an outrageous cap—yellow with magenta and turquoise orchids—and a stained "Moosely Seconds" T-shirt, faded jeans, and Hi-Tec hiking shoes. The left shoe is split on the side and a bit of white sock shows through. I can't help noticing his muscular shoulders and sculpted glutes.

He nods to the east. "Counted fifteen elk by the river this morning with a coyote running through them. Two bald eagles in those cottonwoods yesterday. And look—the dunce caps are coming in."

"Dunce caps?"

Taking my shoulders in his hands, he turns me around to face a stalk of chest-high purple blossoms with deeply split leaves, then quickly drops his hands. "Mary Beth, meet dunce cap. Dunce cap, meet Mary Beth."

He wheels around and heads to the front of the house. "In the winter, starting around Halloween, the driveway becomes impassable," he says, "so I park out on the road and ski in and out."

I'm smitten with this idea. "How deep does the snow get?"

"Oh, more than halfway up the windows in a normal year," he says, brows raised and chin angled in cocky nonchalance. "I have to shovel off the roof to keep it from caving in."

Here's that mountain man essence, that prideful love of hardship I've seen in so many guys here. It comes with an air of ownership and satisfaction that this type of life can only be endured by a select, hardy few.

After pointing out the thriving musk thistle crop in the meadow, he leads me into the cabin. The interior is dark, cluttered, and dusty, but cozy. It's obvious a man lives here alone, with a pair of antelope horns and a Charlie Russell print on the walls, a rickety rocking chair, and a geometrical-print Naugahyde recliner. I peruse titles on his bookshelf—books about wildlife and hunting, *Black Elk Speaks,* an array of novels. The bottom shelf holds a row of vinyl albums in blue covers, all nine Beethoven symphonies.

"Classical music? You don't seem the type, Sam."

"Ya know, the winters are long out here. I got hooked on NPR's classical music at night. When I first heard the symphonies I loved them. Decided I wanted the whole set. So I bought them all."

I spot a book, *The History of Opera.* "You're into opera too?"

"*Hell, no.* I bought that at a garage sale so I could put it on my bookshelf and look smart."

I'm touched by his contagious, self-effacing humor. Not a word leaves his mouth that isn't couched in a smile. He laughs often, a pulsating, full-body laugh, with animation and fervor.

The cabin, he explains, was part of an old dude ranch, the Circle H, whose owners sold out to the park sometime in the sixties or seventies. "But they have a lifelong lease, so they've been renting this cabin out to low-lifes like me over the years. We usually had two or three guys living here at a time, but I got it all to myself now."

Scraggly plants cover one side of a huge table. He points out each one and explains their watering needs, then nods at the picture window by the table. "We had some wild times here. One winter a bunch of us skied up 25-Short and came back here after. Somebody had a snowmobile and a coupla guys're tooling it around the meadow.

"The rest of us're drinking beer in the living room when we start hearing yelling and the snowmobile getting louder. Before we know it, the goddamn snowmobile plows through the window here and lands on this table, *brum-biddy-brum-brum-brum,* and finally conks out. The guys'd bailed off in the yard. So here we are with this snowmobile on the dining room table, and a hole the size of Nebraska in the front of the house."

Opening a door by the kitchen, he leads me up a stairway, covered with cracked linoleum, to an attic. I notice a hammock full of unrolled sleeping bags, a bench with ammunition reloading equipment, a fly-tying setup, and a row of seven or eight backpacks along the wall. While he describes everything in great detail, I finger a sleeping bag on the hammock, one that looks familiar. It's a goose down bag, a North Face "Blue Kazoo," the same kind I have. I notice his has a right-side zipper. Mine, I know, zips on the left.

Finally we head to the room with the window I spotted from below. Sure enough, they are indeed lace curtains. They're deteriorating from hanging here a while, but they're still lace. Owl-eyed, I tiptoe around the room and finger the log roof supports, the raggedy curtains, the bedcover—a faded quilt with specks of meticulous stitching. Images kaleidoscope through my mind. This room is a portal to dreams, and already I'm being drawn through. It's a room out of *Anne of Green Gables*. Sam babbles on, but I'm barely listening. I peer out the window at Blacktail Butte, Shadow Mountain, and Buck Mountain.

Yes, yes, yes! It clicks into place, one of those puzzle pieces. I'm sure of one thing: This is the cabin I'd seen in my mind's eye when I read *Dot and Dash* over thirty years ago.

34

Grizzly Distinction

Tim arranges for ranger Jim VanDyke to join me on a survey for harlequin drakes in Berry Canyon. Bearded, self-reliant, and wiry-strong, Jim seems to be just another Teton mountain man—cranked-brow serious—who prefers wilderness muscle-flexing to hobnobbing with bipeds. His job title, "backcountry ranger," is like "wildlife biologist," in its ability to elicit angst and longing among regular folk, causing them to question their own life paths.

As Jim motors us across Jackson Lake, I resign myself to the fact that this will be an almost silent, all-business day. No small talk from this guy. From what I've learned about his ilk, I can expect to spend much of the day hiking alone because he'll be far ahead of me. I know little about him and don't expect to know much more after this work excursion. I'll be cordial, do my job, and go home tonight with scribbled notes about duck sightings.

We beach the boat in the willows and assemble our gear. Jim hoists his mammoth gray pack onto his slender, muscled frame. He's in summer field uniform: green shorts, gray shirt, ball cap. Because we're unlikely to run into park visitors so far from the popular canyons, I'm out of uniform in shorts and T-shirt, my ponytail tied with a green scrunchie. I pull my foolproof bear repellent—the V-8 can of pebbles—from my pack.

On this stellar day, sky and plants gush in rainbow colors. We bushwhack through the willows to the trail. My legs feel strong and pliable, with my pack's weight just enough to make me aware of my back muscles. Binoculars hang around my neck, ready for action.

When we pass the Owl Canyon turnoff, Jim turns and says, "So you were married too?"

Now here's a shocker. That Grand Teton news line! I immediately lighten up. His question tells me he wants to talk, that we might have a chatty, companionable hike ahead of us, my favorite kind.

"Yeah. Divorced now."

"Me, too."

"Pretty awful, isn't it?"

"The worst," he says, grimacing.

We pause to watch a sandhill crane in a clearing. It does a slow motion dance, deep-bending one leg, then the other.

"My ex is already remarried and settled again, but I'm still in turmoil." I explain my winter move to Denver and back. "I don't know if I did the right thing, leaving a permanent job. I love being back in the Tetons, but I just turned forty. No home, no partner, and back working seasonally. I don't know what I'll do when I get laid off this fall and get kicked out of park housing again."

"The seasonal dilemma. I bought a little place over the hill in Idaho, so at least I have somewhere to go."

"You're smart." Maybe I should buy a place in Idaho? Driggs or Victor, across Teton Pass. More affordable than Jackson.

He looks at me, eyebrows arching over his sunglasses. "Hey, come fall, if you're still homeless, I got an extra bed and a room to store some stuff. You're welcome to crash at my place for a while if you need to."

I'm taken aback, because I hardly know this guy. "Thanks, Jim. That's really nice of you. I'll keep it in mind."

In flower-studded meadows we find bear diggings, mounds of loose soil dug up where the bears have been feeding on roots, corms, and bulbs. I've learned that only grizzly bears leave these diggings. Black bears seldom dig for food; they swipe berries from branches and scratch on logs for insects instead. But hiking with Jim I feel safe and relaxed. He stays by me, doesn't rush ahead to show off. I jiggle my bear can from time to time, but talking so loudly, we're unlikely to surprise any bears.

Periodically we bushwhack through sage and willows to the creek to search for ducks. When the trail veers toward the creek and enters a stand of conifers, I spot the pile first. It's huge and moist and threaded with vegetable matter.

"Look, Jim. Bear scat."

"Hm-m-m. Looks pretty fresh. And *big*."

We keep on. Water thunders by at the peak of spring run-off. I'm leading us on a narrow section of trail through a wooded area when Jim says something I can't make out.

"What'd you say?" I turn my head to face him. "I can't hear you above the roar of the creek."

"I was just asking how long you were married."

"Oh. Fifteen years."

"Long time."

"Too long. How about you?"

WOOF!

The sound comes from uptrail. I spin around just in time to catch sight of a brown furry body, then a black one, both the size of Pomeranians, about twenty feet away. I pluck off my sunglasses for a closer look. Emerging from a tangle of shrub juniper just off the trail is a Texas-sized bear.

My breath catches in my throat as I register: shoulder hump, massive head, dish-shaped snout. Electric sparks surge through my body as synapses fire.

Beside me Jim stage whispers, "*Grizzly! Grizzly!*"

"*Holy shit.*" Without thinking, I scoot behind him, grab his shoulders, and leap onto his back, but his pack is in the way and I slither off, my chest dragging along rip-stop nylon and plastic clasps. (How embarrassing! Whatever possessed me to do such a stupid thing, I'll never know.)

The bear snorts and swats at her cubs, then herds them up a hill to the north, plowing through shrubs and snapping branches in her path. Jim dumps his pack and fumbles with the zippers. "My video camera . . . it's in here somewhere." I tear into the pack with him and we strew clothes and gear until he finds it. With camcorder in hand, he runs up the hill after the bears.

(These Teton guys. I'll never understand them.)

He turns back after the bears disappear over the crest of the hill. "I think I got some footage of them as they took off," he says, picking his way back down. "That's the closest *I've* ever been to a grizzly." He stuffs everything back into the pack and swings it onto his back. "And with cubs, too. *Damn.*"

I suck in air so sharply my eyes cross. My heartbeat finally winds down to a slow drum roll.

"Let's go on," he says, "and see what we find."

We head into the juniper shrubs where we first saw the sow.

"Ah-hah." He points. Hidden behind some brush is a carcass, probably a moose calf, with the meat around the ribs still moist and bloody.

"*Fuck,*" I say. Then, touching my hand to my mouth, "Oh, sorry."

"Don't be." He grins. "That'd be the word I'd choose, too. Let's remember to be on the lookout when we come back through here later."

Back on the trail, I look down to be sure my feet are still touching the ground. My whole body buzzes with the aftermath of fight or flight. Bears are naturally defensive around carcasses. We were damned lucky this bear was still so unfamiliar with humans that she rallied her cubs and took off in fear. All this is running through my head when Jim turns to face me.

"Six years," he says.

I blink. "Huh?"

"I was married six years."

By the end of the day we've found only three harlequin drakes, aptly named for their clown colors and patterns, but we've seen six bears. Besides the three grizzlies, we've also seen a black bear with two cubs foraging on a faraway hillside.

The sky blackens as we hike back. We're still about two hundred yards from the boat when a deluge comes. We pull on rain jackets and start running. Despite a silver wall of water streaming from the sky, Jim easily finds the boat in the maze of willows. We pile in and shove off.

A hard pull on the outboard motor cord yields a throaty gasp. "Uh-oh," he says, "The prop's tangled up." He leans over the stern, grasps strands of slimy vegetation, slings them aside.

Peering under the gunwales, I find what we need. "No problem," I say, snapping the oarlocks into place and setting the oars into them. I move to the center of the boat and face aft. "Pull up the motor." Part of me is astonished I would shout an order to a park ranger. Another part of me is shocked that he tilts the motor up without question. Yet another part, the new, more confident part says, "My Granny taught me how to row, and I'm gonna do her proud." I pull hard first on one oar, then the other, and guide us through the choking vegetation to open water.

"Good job, Mary Beth," he says.

Back at the office eyelids shrink back when I tell them about the bears. I've come closer to a grizzly bear family in the wild than anyone else in S&RM, and I relish the status, albeit self-bestowed, that it gives me.

35

Gift

I'm rinsing lettuce at my kitchen sink and staring out the window when an unfamiliar green Subaru goes by, brakes, starts again, and finally comes to a stop in front of Julian's house. A petite woman climbs out; shorts and a tank top show off a striking body. She opens the back door, dips inside, and emerges with a baby, a round-faced carrot-top, in her arms.

It's his, all right.

Hurrying to the bedroom for a better view, I hide behind the flowery curtains I've made out of bedsheets. With the baby on one hip, the woman fiddles with the car hatchback until it springs open. She hangs an overstuffed purse on her shoulder and hauls out a duffel bag. No sign of Julian. I know he's inside because I saw him go home right after I did. With a determined slant to her head, the woman heads to the front door, wrests a hand free, and tries the knob. It doesn't open.

What an ass. He's actually got the door locked, something no one ever does at Beaver Creek. She kicks it with a sandaled foot until it finally yields. A disembodied hand appears and takes the duffel bag, and she disappears inside.

Oh, man. Even with all the heartburn Julian's given me, I still feel for him.

When I get to work the next morning, the Bronco's gone from the lot and Julian's not at his desk. He must have skedaddled into the field early this morning. No big surprise.

I can't focus on the amphibian data I'm trying to enter into a database. I'm hashing instead. Pam—this woman—this third leg of the tripod—is now living across the street from me in Beaver Creek. We're bound for a wreck sooner or later. As a counselor, I'm bothered by this. I can't just pretend everything's fine. I know I should initiate a talk with her *before* we run into each other in the laundry cabin. But it's the last thing I want to do. Just thinking about it feels like anesthetic wearing off. I want to avoid her, and I'm sure she feels the same way about me. I wish she would just go away.

But at lunchtime I head over and knock on Julian's barracks door. After a second knock I hear an impatient "Come on in." I find her sitting on the sofa, patting the baby over her shoulder.

"Hi, Pam," I say, extending my hand. "I'm Mary Beth."

"Hi." Along with her greeting, her handshake is half-hearted.

Pale with wisps of pearly-blond hair, she reminds me of a cloud, but there's a heaviness about her. Clasping the infant around its middle, she wiggles him on her lap and coos at him, ignoring me. Babies are great diversions.

Now what? A cold sweat mists my sternum; my heart races. Finally I say, "This must be Max. He sure is a cutie."

"Thanks." Her voice croaks; her tone is bored.

Talk. I scoop in a breath. "Pam . . . I just want to say that I know we're both uncomfortable about all of this, but I hope we can get beyond everything that's happened. I don't hold any bad feelings toward you, and I hope the past won't cause us any more pain."

Still focused on the baby, she shrugs. "Sure."

Reading the contempt in her voice, I turn and let myself out.

Julian's in our office when I walk in. Turning on my computer, I say, "I just visited Pam."

He'd have been more relaxed if I'd dropped an A-bomb on his paper-littered desk and he had to ride the mushroom cloud through the roof. Reeling to one side, he stomps his foot on the floor to keep from capsizing his chair. He stares at me, eyes ablaze, face bleached of color. "You did *what?*"

"Somebody had to break the ice so we wouldn't be obsessing about each other."

His left eyelid quivers, still quivers even after four or five power-blinks. "What did you *say* to her?"

"I said I didn't have any bad feelings about her and hoped the past wouldn't cause us any more heartache."

"Oh, *God.*" He sniggers through his nose, slices his fingers through his beard. Despite his obvious discomfort, his mouth tweaks in wobbly amusement. "I can't *believe* you did that."

I shudder in exasperation. "We live across the friggin' street from each other. Were we going to ignore each other all summer?"

"No, I mean . . . well . . . how did she respond?"

"She didn't say much. Seemed okay with it."

"It shouldn't matter. I told her she's just here temporarily until she gets a job and an apartment in town." He chops the air with his forefinger.

He's lost it. He knows it's near impossible to find jobs or apartments in Jackson at the beginning of the tourist season.

I sort a stack of wildlife observation forms and start entering information into the database. I let several minutes pass, then ask, "So, if you guys aren't together, are you going to date other people while she's here?"

He peers at me with raised eyebrows. "That depends on who's around," he says, lips pursing into a teaser smile.

Back to the keyboards—*tik-tik-tiddle-iddle-tik-tik-tik.*

"So," he says, "has Sam Billings asked you out yet?"

⌁

On a show-stopping June day, Carol marries Jeff at the Hunter Ranch. I spend the ceremony standing behind the rows of folding chairs, choking back tears. I always cry at weddings, moved by the innocence of fresh, open hearts. To me a wedding is life's crowning ritual—the serendipity of having found that special person in a whole sea of mediocre fish, such pure love and eagerness to dive in and commit. But this is my first post-divorce wedding. As soon as I see Carol, full of youth, her veil fluffing about her head in the breeze, and Jeff in his tux so proud and handsome, both of them looking like they'd each found the world's greatest treasure, my mind jets back to that long ago December day when I recited similar vows. It seemed so right at the time, but there were nuances I missed. That's okay. I was young. But why did I stay so long? I should have left while I was still young, come out here, maybe had a chance to find someone more appropriate. Now, as silver hairs wind through my dark mane, I realize my odds of finding another husband are slim. According to much-touted statistics, I have a greater chance of being shot down by a terrorist.

Oh, *man.* I've stuffed myself in the blender today and pressed the "Puree" button.

Snap out of it. I glance around at the mountains, the people seated in the chairs. Most are fellow park employees; several are good friends. This is my new life, and these, the people who fill it. This realization comforts me until I spot scowling Julian slouched in a chair with legs and arms crossed, and Pam beside him in a tan shift dress, their gooey-faced baby on her lap. And the tears start dribbling down my cheeks again.

Plastering a tissue to my nose, I spot Sam Billings eyeing me with a sympathetic frown from across the crowd. Last night as I primped for this year's Spring Fling, there was a knock on my door. Tightening the sash of my flannel bathrobe, I opened it to find Sam standing in the entry. He was hunched over, seeming to hide behind his brown felt outback hat. On the floor by his booted feet sat a plastic ice cream bucket with two chunks of russet soil, each holding a prickly pear cactus, one blooming pink, the other yellow.

"What's this?" I asked, crouching by the bucket.

"I wanted to bring you something to thank you for watering my plants last weekend. I dug these up at Grandpa and Grandma's farm."

I was touched. "They're beautiful. That's so nice of you, Sam."

When he left, the wooden screen door slamming him in the heels, I flapped my arms to air my dripping-wet armpits.

He sure is cute, I think, smiling across the wedding crowd at him. But Sam seems so different from me, from anyone I've ever known. He works in the park's Maintenance Division, on the "Quarters Crew." He fixes anything broken in the park housing units and builds whatever they need. His skills, it seems, are limitless—plumbing, wiring, carpet laying, cabinet building, house remodeling. I've heard he's had special training in log work; he built the oft-photographed Taggart Barn, a striking log structure at the base of the mountains, and the ranger patrol cabin in Upper Berry Canyon. This is a guy who skis to his cabin in the winter, puts in firewood, and hunts elk and antelope for food. What interest would this QTMM (Quintessential Teton Mountain Man) have in a forty-year-old, scrawny, divorced easterner who can barely open the Resource Management garage doors?

After the wedding ceremony Sam saunters over. He's wearing fancy western garb: clean new jeans, white shirt, red tie, black vest and sport coat, cowboy hat and boots. Unruly brown hair flecked with gold licks his shoulders. The feral look trapped in dressy clothes intrigues me.

"You okay?" Warm-caramel eyes shine clear and curious under the brim of his hat.

"I'd be fine if I could stop crying," I say. "First wedding after my divorce. Too many memories."

"Ah," he says, raising his chin and turning away to face the mountains. He stuffs his hands into his pockets. "Sorry. Sorry to hear that."

For a few minutes we stare silently at the silver-blue peaks as other wedding guests mingle in small groups around us. In my peripheral vision I notice him slowly shifting his weight from one foot to the other. *He's squirming. Another Teton mountain man who can climb rock pillars and ski down vertical cliffs but can't handle emotion.* I decide to let him off the hook and be done with him. "What a view, huh?" I say cheerily, giving my nose one last satisfying blow.

"The best in the world."

"Well, see ya." I turn to leave.

"You going to the reception at the Highlands? I'll walk you back to your car."

To my dismay the skin of my forearm tingles under the hurried brush of his fingers. We walk past the lingering guests, by a row of lilac bushes in bloom. "Ah-h." I bury my nose in a blossomy bundle. "My favorite flower."

Someone calls out, "Hey, Billings, can you head up to the Highlands now and help set up some chairs?"

Sam turns to me. "Gotta run," he says, and lopes away.

At the rustic Highlands hall, we spend a relaxed afternoon full of food, drink, and conversation. After dinner, I head out to join a group on the porch and claim a lawn chair next to Tim and Jennifer. Sam sits before us on the porch railing. Now he wears only his jeans, boots, and shirt with his sleeves rolled up. A bottle of Heineken is tucked into the crook of his knee.

"Tim and I were trail dogs back then," Sam says. "Must've been when, eighty-eight or so?"

"Eighty-seven. Before the Yellowstone fires." Tim licks cake frosting off his thumbs and grins. "I think I know this story."

"Yep, you sure do, *butt-hayed.*" Sam throws back his head in a gut-spewing laugh. "Right. Eighty-seven. Anyways, one afternoon we head up the south fork of Cascade to fix some rock walls on the switchbacks near Hurricane Pass. We were in fire training all day so we got a late start. The plan was to camp that night and start working early the next morning. Man, it was hotter than hell that day."

I can't help smiling. His voice is loud and animated with bursts of laughter barely contained beneath the surface. *This is his milieu,* I think, *the humor, the audience.* I envy his confidence and poise.

"And of course we're lugging the tools—the crowbars, the Pulaskis, the shovels," he says, "plus food and camping gear."

"And don't forget the honey bucket," Tim says, raising a plastic cup of wine.

"Oh yeah, the honey bucket." Sam slaps his knee. "My pack felt like a friggin' loaded U-Haul. We get to camp about seven-thirty at night and dump everything on the ground. I'm sore as hell, smelling like a goat. All I'm thinking about is a dip in the creek when this guy says, 'Man, that beer is sure gonna taste good.'

"I start dancing around. '*What?* You brought beer up here?' and he says, 'No. *You* did.'"

Roars of laughter from the crowd.

"No shit! So I start pulling stuff out of my pack, and sure enough, there's six Buds wrapped in my sleeping bag. By this time I'm laughing so hard I almost piss my pants."

At the conclusion of the story, I join the rest of the crowd in throwing back my head and laughing uncontrollably.

When the party breaks up, Sam waves good-bye to me as Elaine, Jack, and I walk back to our cars. She takes my arm. "Do you have something you want to tell us, Mary Beth?"

"What?"

She bats her eyelashes. "Like something involving Sam?"

I'm learning that park employees love gossip, especially gossip about liaisons between seasonals. *Seasonal Affairs,* we call them, after the park's Seasonal Affairs Committee that deals with housing and other seasonal employee issues.

"No." I swing open the car door. "It's too soon, Elaine. I'm still grieving my divorce. Then there was the last debacle." I nod toward Julian who's running to intercept Max as he speed-crawls across the yard toward a fire pit. "I need to give it some time."

Her lips wrap around her teeth. "Sure. That's probably a good idea."

But when a dazzling gift drops in your lap, you don't pitch it into the river and walk away.

36

Mudpuppy Love

Late that night the phone jangles me from a deep sleep. "Mary Beth, it's Sam. I hope I didn't wake you up, but I thought I'd call and see if you'd want to go on a hike tomorrow."

Butterflies lick at my ribs, and all my previous misgivings up and hightail. "I'd love to."

When he picks me up at seven-thirty the next morning in his pickup truck, I notice a limp sprig of lilac on the dashboard. "What's this?" I say.

"Oh," he says, turning on the Inside Highway. "Just a piece of lilac I picked for the cabin and forgot about, and now it's dead."

We drive north, up the Pacific Creek Road, out of the park, into the Teton National Forest where we park at a trailhead. As we're putting on our packs, I decide to try something. Drawing in my chin, I say, "'We're a hundred miles from Chicago. We got a full tank o' gas, half a pack o' cigarettes. It's dark, and we're wearing sunglasses.'"

He frowns, holds up his thumb. "Hit it," he says gruffly. Then he wings his arms, steps a tap dance, and sings, "Da-da-da-da-DA—da-da-DA . . ." The song from the *Blues Brothers* movie.

"You *got* it!"

He passed. Extra credit for the song rendition. *Wow.*

Summer in the lower backcountry is in full, cacophonous swing, the sunlight viscous and blinding. Big clusters of arrow-leaved balsamroot and lupine edge the trail. Birds sing complex mating melodies from thin spires of subalpine fir and Engelmann spruce. I feel lighthearted and full of purpose as I set one hiking boot ahead of the other.

"When I die," I say, "if heaven isn't like this, I'm coming back."

Sam launches into a full-body, staccato laugh. "I'm with ya! Hey, look." He points out a plant with lacy white umbrellas of flowers on a branched stem. "Yampah."

"Looks like what we call Queen Anne's lace back east," I say. "Carrot family, I think."

"Yep. You gotta be careful with carrot family plants. There are some poisonous ones. But this one's safe." Sam kneels and, with clawed fingers, digs in the dirt around the plant's root. Then he eases the whole plant, roots and all, out of the ground. Using a Leatherman tool from his pocket, he deftly slices off the stem and rubs the thick roots on his shorts to clean them. "The Indians and mountain men loved these. Here." He cuts off two pinkie-sized pieces and hands me one.

I trust he knows what he's talking about, so I bite into it. The taste is nutty with sweet undertones, not bitter at all. "Like a sweet potato," I say.

His eyes roll back as he savors the taste. "Mm-m-m."

As we hike, dirt from the trail coats our boots, socks, and shins. I seem to fly uphill, pumped with energy, despite yesterday's emotional ride. The Creature seems pillbug-sized today as it skitters through forgotten mental detritus. Around noon we reach a silty pond and settle into a shady spot along its shore.

"I brought lunch," he says, hauling things from his pack and setting them on the ground—two sandwiches, bananas, apples, Doritos, M&Ms. I feel a bit selfish that I've only brought enough crackers and cheese for myself, with one pear, and a Snickers bar. But I did plan on splitting the candy bar with him.

He hands me a peanut butter sandwich on wheat bread, then peels a banana. "Wanna split this?"

"Sure," I say, expecting him to slice it with his knife.

Instead he breaks the banana in half and passes one half to me. He holds the other in his fingers. "You know how many sections a banana has?"

"No. Never thought about it."

He squeezes the fruit with his fingertips; it cleanly separates into three fleshy spears.

"Three," he says as he lays each section on my open sandwich.

Something slithers in the pond. "Sam, *look*. Mudpuppies."

"No way! Where?"

We peer into the murky water, the hairs of his arm pleasantly commingling with mine. I take his elbow. "There. See? That grayish-brown squooshy thing with the gills? Looks to be about eight or nine inches long. Just to the left of that submerged log."

"*Oh, yeah.*"

"Chuck Peterson, the herp guy from Idaho State, told me about these. It's a larval form of a tiger salamander that hasn't transformed to an adult. They stay in water habitats and grow bigger than normal adults." As I wave a stick through the water near the animal, it slinks away, stirring up a cloud of sediment. "Sometimes they even breed in the larval form. Then maybe two or three years later they'll turn into adults. Could be the seasons are too short here for them to become adults in one year like they do in other places."

"I think we should name this place 'Mudpuppy Pond,'" Sam says.

After lunch we sit side by side, our shoulders and hips touching, as he talks about his grandparents and their farm in Utah, where he spent summers as a child. "To me growing up, Grandpa was a real hero. He taught me how to hunt and fish. How to build things. How to fix things. How to tan leather from hides."

My spine zings with a taut vibration. I'm marveling at not only his clear head, uncomplicated lifestyle, practical know-how, and wilderness savvy, but also his admitted love of his family. I remember the words I wrote long ago—*a man—a kindred spirit, kind of scruffy but attractive, an outdoorsy kind of guy who hikes and backpacks but is also emotionally present . . .*

It's a small thing, but I noticed Sam was the first person I met out here who seemed to recognize and easily pronounce my last name. I ask him to explain.

"Jean Baptiste Charbonneau," he says, munching on his sandwich, "was Sacajawea's son. A real mountain man."

"*No kidding.*" I had no idea I shared a name with such an impressive lineage.

When we stand up to leave, Jace's words from last summer's sheep survey come to mind: *Men love to be pursued by women.* My legs go weak as I face Sam and hold out my arms. "Can I give you a hug?" I ask. "I like to hug my friends in beautiful places."

He leaps into my arms like he's been zapped by lightning. My cheek slides along the sun-warmed skin of his neck, and my nostrils flare with the heat and musk of him. It feels very, very good.

"You needed one of these yesterday, didn't you?" he says.

"I sure did."

We disentangle, shoulder our packs, and hike back down the trail. Near a cluster of boulders, a mule deer with a spotted fawn trains her eyes on us as we pass. A hermit thrush trills from a fir tree. After passing a marshy area full of shooting stars and elephant heads, Sam turns to me. "Can we do that again?" He holds out his arms and I fall into them.

"I wanted *so bad* to hug you yesterday," he says. "I just didn't think it was appropriate—didn't know how you'd take it."

I dip my head and smile.

"Remember that lilac sprig in my truck?" he says. "I picked it for you yesterday at the Hunter Ranch after I left you behind. I was going to leave it in your car. But I lost my nerve. I'm sorry I didn't do it now."

He stops at a spray of Indian paintbrush. "Hey," he says. "Do you know how to get honey from Indian paintbrush?" He plucks off a tubular, green bract from under the crimson ones. "Stick out your tongue."

He touches the bract to my tongue. I smack my lips at the pinprick of sweetness. "Yum."

Right then a sparrow twitters from a pine tree as a marmot skirrs across a rock. Everything seems so right, so simple. It's been a long time since the colors seemed so vivid, the birdsong so melodious, the light so pure and life-giving.

37

Dog Days

Driving down a dirt road that parts the sea of sagebrush near Cora, Wyoming, a road crisscrossed with Oregon Trail ruts, Sam and I once came upon a stationary horse, brown with strokes of cream painted over its hefty rump. Our eyes fixed on its front legs, hobbled together with a knotted, frayed rope. Speaking smooth, level words, Sam glided his hand down its chest and foreleg and sliced through the rope with his pocketknife. I remember the fiery nugget of eye as the horse showed off with a feisty buck and trotted away.

I feel that same newfound freedom as I find myself the shining star in the life of a QTMM. My life now takes a quirky, delicious turn into a world I never dared imagine.

"There! There!" Sam points at the concentric circles wrinkling the water. I aim and cast the fishing line where I saw the fish jump, but I miss by a car's length.

We're sitting on a rock by Phelps Lake after sneaking through the woods of the JY Ranch, the Rockefeller place, to get here. This part of the lakeshore is closed to the public, but we're out of view of the ranch buildings.

Sam is patient with my lack of skill. "Try again," he says. "You'll get it. Arc your arm wider, like this." He swings his rod to the side in a graceful stretch. *Zizz-z-z*—the line unfurls, and his grasshopper bait plops far out into the lake.

I cast again and again with varying degrees of success. Sam keeps saying, so softly, "That's good. You're getting it. Try again."

After a few more tries, I set my rod down and inch behind him on the rock, both to give him more space and to watch him. Once more he casts the line. Full shoulders and firm biceps plump out his T-shirt.

I'm remembering coming out of the shower at his cabin last night, and finding the clothes I'd cavalierly dropped on the floor neatly folded on the bathroom counter. Lying on them was an oxeye daisy from the yard and a business card–sized piece of paper. "Sam's Drying Service," it read in fine, crooked letters. "Call me when you're all wet."

As romance blossoms at an intensity I've never known, I wallow in that painfully ephemeral, mesmerizing space where I love everything about him: his thinning, shoulder-length hair, his reddish beard, the paradox of his hands—so rough, yet so gentle. But most of all, I admire his absorption in life. The set of his mouth and the intensity in his eyes tell me he's not thinking about whether he'll ever be able to retire comfortably, what we'll be eating for dinner, or what insult his boss dished out to him yesterday. He is 100 percent *here*, with the lake, the mountains, and the endless sky. He *is* the lake, the mountains, the sky—seamless, indistinguishable from them. I envy him that.

"My dad didn't fish enough," he says, reeling in the line.

"You mean your dad's not alive?" I can't say *dead*.

His beard puckers as his lips fold over his teeth. "Died at fifty-six. I was twenty."

"I'm so sorry. How . . . ?"

The line whizzes out again. "Keeled over of a heart attack. Sitting at his desk at work. He was a geologist."

Leaning closer to him, lichen crusts abrading the seat of my shorts, I stroke his arm and wait for him to go on.

"High stress job. I don't think he liked it much. Always told me, 'Do what makes you happy in life.' He never pushed me to go to college, so I didn't. But, hey, I live in a log cabin in the woods like I always wanted to, and I work at *the* most spectacular park in the National Park System. I think Dad would have been proud."

I frown. What kind of parent wouldn't encourage a child to go to college? But as I think about it, two master's degrees haven't brought me the happiness I hoped for. At forty, I'm still floundering. Have I lost sight of what matters in life? *He's* got it figured out. I chalk one tick on the plus side of the "Long-Term Relationship Potential" chart.

I go out on a treacherous limb. "How long have you had a crush on me, Sam?" I expect him to say "a month or two."

He starts. "Since last year."

"*What?*" I peer into his eyes.

Laying the pole on the rock beside him, he launches into one of those one-man comedy acts he excels at. "Last summer Jeff and I're lugging a roll of carpet into the superintendent's cabin at Beaver Creek," he says with a jerk of his thumb, "and I see some movement up on the hill behind the cabin, and there's this *babe* in skin-tight NPS coveralls, with a ponytail bouncing through the back of her ball cap. She's pushing an orange wheely-wheel up the hill out back."

Oh, yeah. The day I struggled with the distance-measuring wheel through the grouse whortleberry bushes behind Beaver Creek. I must have walked right by him and Jeff as I headed up the hill, but I was too focused on the job to notice. Not being the type of woman that usually draws the attentions of men, I'm finding this revelation incredibly funny.

"I don't know why, but when I see a woman in coveralls doing manual labor, I go nuts. No girly-girls for me. No gaudy jewelry or war paint or big hair. No siree. Give me a woodswoman that can swing an ax any day.

"So I stop short and Jeff keeps walking. Classic Three Stooges move. His end of the carpet slips out of his arms and slams on the ground. 'Fuck,' I say. 'Asshole,' he says. 'Oops,' I say. 'Who *is* that?' And Jeff says, 'I dunno. Some new seasonal, I guess.'"

By now I'm laughing so hard I'm pounding my knees with my fists, relishing this story, but in the back of my mind is an issue we haven't addressed yet. I pick up my fishing rod and fiddle with the line.

"I have to tell you, Sam," I say tentatively, "I'm forty years old. If you want kids, I'm not the woman for you."

He pinches one eye shut. "Mmmm . . . ," he says, "I'd rather have a puppy."

At this moment above the aquamarine water of Phelps Lake, my heart's edges, unable to contain a sizzling burst of love, splinter and crack open.

That night at the cabin, after he cooks a splendid dinner of grilled trout, salad, and baked potatoes, he sprints upstairs to the attic and returns with an armload of soft, white nylon—a parachute—that he arranges on the bed. In this cloud-nest we make love and fall asleep twined together like puppies. In the morning he takes my hands and leads me out the back door where we stand together, naked bodies gleaming in tangy sunlight, and gaze at the glaring belly of Sleeping Indian.

38

Niche

Poking around the woods all day, and still no sign of the bear. Calves aching, feet burning, I collapse, cross-legged, onto the flat rock below Inspiration Point. The water in my nearly empty water bottle is warm and tastes like plastic, but I drink it anyway, then bring the binoculars to my eyes once more. Nothing but trees and shrubs, with the occasional scampering chipmunk.

On any other day at this time, park visitors would be swarming down the trail, tired and thirsty, eager to catch the last boat across Jenny Lake. Today, though, Cascade Canyon, Grand Teton's most popular, is closed.

A few days ago a report came in from a Boy Scout claiming a black bear had torn his pack off his back. Another visitor said it had licked sunscreen off her legs. This is the type of bear that gives park officials heartburn: one that's lost its fear of people. Jace and Tim agreed with the superintendent that we have to get the bear out before someone gets hurt. The culvert trap, hauled in by helicopter two days ago, now stands in the woods near Hidden Falls, the fish bait rotting and stinky. I've been checking the trap daily, but either the bear is trap-shy, or the bait didn't appeal to him.

Early this morning Tim, Julian, and I crossed Jenny Lake on the boat, and we've spent the day searching for the bear. We once glimpsed it far away in a cluster of thimbleberry bushes, but it scurried out of reach while we were picking our way over some blowdowns. Since then, we've scoured an ever-widening area, coming across a track or pile of scat from time to time, but no bear.

After lunch we split up to cover more territory. In my multiple traverses of the hillside between Jenny Lake and Inspiration Point, all I found was a day-old scat with a shred of paper in it, a sure sign of the culprit. About an hour ago, Tim radioed that he was heading into Cascade Canyon and sending Julian up Hanging Canyon.

I've eaten all my trail food except for two peanut butter crackers, and I'm weary. Will we be wandering around here all night? When do we give up and admit the bear outwitted us?

My radio hisses to life.

"MB. Where are ya?"

It's Tim, calling on F-1, the local channel. We can be more informal on the local channel because the signal doesn't go through the repeater on Signal Mountain, and the rest of the park won't hear our conversation.

"Just below Inspiration Point."

"Anything going on?"

"Not a thing."

"I'm about a half-mile above you. I'm gonna head down. Be there in a few minutes."

"Hey, guys, it's Leo." Leo Larsen, one of the Jenny Lake climbing rangers, comes through on the radio. "We're hanging out down at the boat dock with a litter if you need it."

"You bet."

Sliding my radio back into its holster, I breathe in the forest smells of decaying vegetation and subalpine fir. As the sun dips behind Symmetry Spire, a chilly shadow slips over me; I pull on my NPS fleece jacket.

The sound of a Swainson's thrush fluting from the treetops is so clear and true that it prickles my arms with goosebumps. Then, hearing a faint *hoo-hoo-hOO*, I cup my hands around my ears to amplify the sound. There it is again: a great horned owl, its hooting almost lost in the gurgling of Cascade Creek as it tumbles into Jenny Lake. If I listen purposefully, I hear music in the water: there—something like Dvorak's *New World Symphony*. Now—Beethoven's Ninth, a chorus singing *Ode to Joy*. And there's Mozart's *Requiem*. I swear I hear the voices—from the thundering *Dies Irae!* to the poignant *Lacrimosa*.

Then it's Sam's voice I hear saying my name, his eyes fixed on mine. The sweetest sound in the world is the sound of your own name, and the way Sam says mine melts me. Never trust a man who can't look you in the eyes and say your name at the same time. Sam's teaching me how to trust men again. He's teaching me what's possible in love. We're so different in some ways, such deep-blood soul mates in others.

Gravel crunches behind me and Tim appears. "Kind of a wasted day, huh?" he says. Kneeling down beside me, he takes the dart gun from its leather case to remove the tranquilizer syringe. "Guess we won't be needing this."

Munching on a cracker, I say nothing, but I'm relieved that our bear might have a chance to get away and avoid an unpleasant fate.

As Tim finishes his task, he glances up. "Well, well," he says. "Looky here."

I look up to see a bear heading down the trail.

Santa Barbara. This must be our bear, the way it's so fearlessly approaching. My heart booms in my chest as I study its form, its narrow, rounded nose and big, doglike ears. Definitely a black bear, although it's caramel-colored. This guy is probably wondering where all the park visitors are with their easy loot. Remembering the Boy Scout, my altruism toward the bear vanishes as I stuff the remaining peanut butter cracker into my mouth. No goddamn bear's gonna get food from *me.* I rise to my feet, and unsnap my radio holster, foolishly thinking I could bonk the bear off the head with the radio in a pinch.

"Are ya scared yet?" Tim grins in my direction.

I flash my eyes at him.

"Let's keep it entertained," he murmurs, tossing the gun case in the bear's direction, "while I put this thing back together."

As he reloads the dart gun, the bear sniffs the case, arcs its head around, and continues toward us with its pigeon-toed gait.

Damn. It must smell the peanut butter. And now it's gonna rip my friggin' belly open to get it.

"Don't let it get too close," Tim says. "I need some distance to dart it."

I clap my hands. "Hey."

From fifteen feet away, the bear looks me up and down, nostrils flaring.

"That's far enough. Git!" I stomp my foot.

It keeps walking. Ten feet away now.

"Tim, he's not stopping." I frantically clap my hands. "I said *GIT.*"

The bear keeps coming. At about six feet from my toes, it stops, raises his head and starts popping its jaw in a typical bear dare.

Fuck. He's gonna charge. He's gonna charge.

I know in my head that it'll probably be a bluff charge, but my jellying knees and clamping gut tell me otherwise. Everything in me wants to bolt, to turn and run down the slope, but I know that would only trigger the bear's predatory instinct. Chest thumping, I stand my ground and slowly reach for the radio.

CHOOMPH!

The bear staggers and backs away, then runs up the hill into the woods, a white plastic dart dangling from its rump. I breathe. While I was communing with the bear, Tim had been slowly backing away to get enough shooting distance between them.

Tim barks into his radio. "We got him. He's on the run. Julian, see if you can intercept him on the hill above Inspiration Point."

"I see him," Julian says. "He's staggering. . . . Still moving. . . . Oh . . . oh . . . easy, boy. . . . Ah, he's down."

Leo comes through on the radio. "We're on our way with the litter."

We find Julian crouched over the bear, a few yards off the trail. "He's out," he says. "Pupils dilated. Oh. It's a female."

Kneeling down beside her, I run my fingers through her fur in what's become a ritual for me. This job humbles me in so many ways. How could this little girl have caused so much trouble? By now I know the routine. While Tim plows through his pack for tooth-pulling tools and a workup sheet, I take vitals, then curl back the ears and check for mites. I silently christen her "Jenny."

As we're finishing up, Leo shows up with Ron Steffans, a fire management seasonal, and the litter, an orange cage that would fit an average-sized person. They loosely lash the bear into it with climbing ropes.

Not wanting to just stand by and watch, I volunteer to carry.

"Ever haul a litter before?" Leo asks me.

"No."

"This bear's pretty small and will be easy to balance, but we gotta go slow and keep the litter horizontal at all times so she doesn't slip out."

Tim and I station ourselves on one side of the litter, Ron and Leo on the other. Leo and Tim, being taller, take the downhill end. Julian follows us, prepared to relieve anybody who needs a break.

Piece of cake, I'm thinking as we start down the trail. Even though the bear's weight tugs at my shoulder socket, I feel strong and in control. I step carefully over rocks as we move slowly and in rhythm. Tall conifers close in overhead. Beyond them the night sky gobbles up a Jell-O-pink sunset.

As I stumble over a rock near the Hidden Falls bridge, a sharp pain pierces my left shoulder. I bring my right hand around to hold the litter with both hands. Soon I'm gritting my teeth to keep from focusing on the pain. My arms feel like they're lengthening with every step.

Crossing the wooden bridge, our feet stomp clear and rhythmic as a marching band: left-right, left-right.

Finally as we pick our way down the trail in near-darkness, Tim says, "Left here."

We turn onto a grassy swath that leads to the culvert trap. Julian secures the door open, and we slide the bear inside. She's still asleep when we ease the door back down and lock it. Leo radios the helicopter pilot. Within minutes he's chopping overhead—*whump-whump-whump*—and dropping a line that Tim clips to the top of the trap. The last thing I see silhouetted against the violet-streaked sky is the helicopter swooping away, dangling the three-hundred-pound trap like a Tinkertoy on a string.

The next morning I skip up the hill to the office. I hardly slept last night, flushed with excitement. This is it! This is my calling. I want to work with bears.

Jace sits catatonically at his computer as I come thrashing into the room.

"Got a minute, Jace?"

"Give me a few minutes."

I'm sitting at my desk, feet tapping, when he shows up half an hour later.

"What's up?" he asks, sitting in Julian's chair.

"I just wanted to tell you how much I loved being in the backcountry looking for that bear yesterday. I really think bear management is my niche."

Jace leans back, checks his watch, then crosses his arms over his chest. "Yeah?" His face shows no expression.

I start jabbering. "So I'd like to be involved in any bear work that comes up. I'd like to go out with you guys whenever we have a problem bear, and, you know, get more experience with it."

He looks into the hallway, then rakes his fingers through his hair. "Have you had any wildlife courses?"

What? He *can't* be serious. "Jace, I have a master's in wildlife, just like you do."

He flicks his hand. "Oh, yeah, I knew that. But your research was a sociological study, not a scientific one."

Ah. So that's what this is about. My research wasn't macho enough to make the grade.

"My research," I say, stiffly, "was on human-bear interaction."

"Right." He strokes his goatee. "Well . . . to be honest, Mary Beth, I don't see you ever immobilizing bears at this park."

I haven't asked to do the actual immobilizations, but I know where this is heading. "Why not?"

"We only need two people to do them, and Tim and I already have the specialized training for it. We don't need anyone else."

Stale air plugs my craw, but eventually dissipates. "But you never know. Maybe someday I'll get a job at Yosemite or the Smokies." I flutter my fingers to distract him from my raspy voice. "I could get the training there."

He shrugs. "Sure."

"In the meantime, though, I still want to help out with bear management."

"Uh-huh." He self-ejects from the chair and walks out.

Only need two people. He and Tim already trained. Besides, they're both hunters and are skilled at shooting animals. I guess it's reasonable. I'll still get to help out and be part of it.

Then these words fizz up inside me: *She divorced her husband and moved to Wyoming, and now she works with bears at Grand Teton.*

How many Portuguese farm girls from southeastern Massachusetts get to say *that?*

39

Opening Day

Light intensifies and dims, wildflowers progress to fireweed and asters. Cygnets grow gangly. Someone finds a tiger salamander under a bubbler in the Colter Bay maintenance garage. Bears get antsy and elk start bugling at dusk.

One day in early fall, I'm gloating because I've just backed the bear trap into the S&RM garage without hitting anything, and the dreaded call comes. Mark Kelleher, the park housing officer, radios to tell me he's moving a roommate into my house. A few days later my tranquil home explodes with blaring radio and TV every non-working hour. My bathroom fills up with cosmetics and hair dyes. My cozy nest, where I could journal through crisp nights to the sounds of bugling elk and yipping coyotes, and stretch into yoga postures in the enchanting stillness of dawn, is now assaulted by strident, vapid chatter. A few weeks later I jump with glee when she finally moves out and heads to some polluted concrete forest—Houston? Vegas? L.A.? They're all the same to me.

Soon come the sunny banners of aspen and cottonwood leaves along river and creek bottoms, and on the undulating ridges of Shadow Mountain. Sam and I drive up Ditch Creek to cut firewood for his cabin. When we're done cutting down dead trees, toppling them end over end down a hillside, and loading them into his truck, he nails paper targets to a tree stump and we take turns shooting them with his .22-caliber rifle.

Fall is my favorite but most unnerving season, the time when I must make reluctant changes. Only this year isn't as hectic because Sam softens everything. Moving to the cabin with him isn't an option yet; we've only been together three months and I'm not *that* flaky. I want to live on my own a while longer, and Sam respects my wishes. At the same time I'm certain that someday I will call that log cabin on the bench of the Snake River home.

Five in the morning. Sam, newly deputized as a park ranger with his elk hunting license, drives us north through the matted darkness and parks his truck in a roadside turnout. A thermos of tea stashed behind the truck seat. "Dream Weaver" on the radio. Dashboard dials like liquid dream images. Curtailed sleep like grit in my eyes.

It's my first hunting trip, but I don't carry a license or a rifle. This is Sam's show. I'm a spectator, I confess. But not just any spectator: the wildlife biologist. All the S&RM guys grew up hunting. They're as comfortable with a rifle as I am with a blender. They all hunt together and serve up elk roasts at the office parties. Now Sam is opening this door for me. I'm eager to learn how it's done and to help field dress the carcass.

Raindrops spit from the sky as we enter the lodgepole forest, stepping on a skim of snow now turning to slush. "This is good, this rain," Sam says. "It'll soften the leaf litter and muffle our footsteps."

We head east following at first a thin game trail, barely visible. A few years ago, a microburst funneled through here, snapping off many of the trees, so that their trunks now lie willy-nilly across our path, like pickup sticks. I wrench my foot from under one log, lift my knee to climb over another. Fog stirs up and we walk into it, up a hill. I'm totally lost in this opaque, motionless space. We meander around willows and huckleberry bushes, up, down, and around logs. We climb hills, skirt patches of woods edging grassy meadows sprinkled with sagebrush.

Sam plans each footstep carefully before planting it soundlessly ahead of him. Abruptly he stops and points downward at two elk tracks in the slush. Eyebrows raised, he gives me a thumbs-up sign, then turns and continues his mindful walking. Drops of water plop from overhead branches.

This is Sam's world. He's standing on the stage and drawing the curtain aside to reveal it, stretching his hand and inviting me onstage, and I'm loving it. I watch him in his nubbly wool pants and shirt, gaiters, felt outback hat, and hiking boots, with his thirty-ought-six Winchester slung over his shoulder, tucked against his backpack. Rain pelts his hat. This is his element. I am enamored of it, and of him within it.

Stopping just ahead, he turns, beckons me to him. As I approach, he angles his arm around my neck and whispers in my ear, "This is where I saw a herd yesterday, just beyond this little hill."

We twist from side to side, watching, listening. Rags of fog dance around us, alternately blanking and revealing various sections of the clearing. In the distance, trees line up like stoic sentinels. We resume our turtle pace. Matching his stride, I can smell the wet wool of his shirt as we inch up the hill. He stops again.

"See anything?" I mouth.

He shakes his head, then tilts it back and sniffs. "But I smell them."

What does he mean, he smells elk? I don't smell anything but decaying wood. I scrunch up my eyes at him.

"They smell a little like horses."

My nostrils cool and flare and I think maybe I smell a hint of barn odor. Then he stiffens, nods. "*There.*"

At the edge of the mist, a shadow moves, then a form emerges. It's a cow elk, and behind her are three more, all grazing the meadow grasses and moving slowly to the north.

I gasp. It thrills me that one of these animals might be my winter's food. But then I pull back in solemn gratitude. This elk might give its life that we might be nourished. Unlike other animals I've eaten, this one isn't suffering through life in a filthy cage or feedlot before being shipped, shaking in terror, to an abattoir. But nonetheless, this elk, because it happens to be grazing in this meadow on this October morning, might sacrifice its life to us.

I want to fall to the ground in humility, but instead I glance at Sam. He nods, and we hold our collective breath. In one smooth motion, he slides the rifle off his shoulder, eases off the safety, pulls it to his shoulder.

I flinch. I love elk, and here I am, about to witness the death of one. My gut goes crampy. I shudder, my insides wail, *Why did I give up vegetarianism? Why can't we all be vegetarians?* Then my science mind goes to work. *This is life. Nature is cruel. People rarely kill their own meat anymore. Most people are removed from the realities of life, from nature, from natural processes. This is natural.*

Then I seal my ears with my forefingers.

Before me Sam is on auto-pilot. He's motionless, but I know his synapses are effervescing and his brain waves are as focused as sun rays through a lens. His head is cocked as he peers through the scope and waits for the animal to turn slightly, so he can aim at a spot right behind its shoulder to enter the heart/lung area.

Can I watch it go down? What if he misses? Or worse, what if he cripples it?

In the end I close my eyes. I'm actually standing there with my fingers in my ears and my eyes pressed shut. Some wildlife biologist.

But the rifle never fires. Hearing rustling, I open my eyes to see the animals wandering away.

"I can't get a good enough shot," Sam says, unloading the rifle. "And they're moving on. I think they smelled us."

The surge of disappointment I feel surprises me. "Should we keep on?"

"No, they're scared now. I don't want to shoot one that's scared. I want to catch it totally unawares, so it'll never know what's coming." He shoulders the rifle. "Most of the time they just look up after I've shot them as if to say, '*What was that?*' And they just keel over."

"We all should be so lucky when the time comes."

"No kidding." He touches my cheek. "Let's go home and I'll cook you a nice breakfast."

For the first time, I notice how hungry I am.

Back among the blowdowns, he stops and points. "Bear scat."

"Ooh! Let's see what it ate." I just can't help myself. I grab a stick and start poking through the pile of bear shit. "Here are some buffaloberry seeds. They like those. And look, there's some fine hair. Must have eaten a rodent of some kind." I'm totally absorbed in the task, not at all thinking that this might be considered freakish, bordering on sick, behavior by about 99.9 percent of humanity.

When I look up, Sam's shoulders are shaking with stifled laughter. "I'm so glad you moved out here where you belong." He encircles me with a wooly arm and we head out, now into stark sunbeams peering around lingering clouds. Only a few blazing yellow leaves still cling to the cottonwoods and aspens, reluctant to release into winter.

As we drink our tea before we leave, the truck cab heats up in the sun. We peel off layers.

Sam winks at me. "I'm thinking we'll take a little detour. What do you think?"

I shrug, wondering what he's conjuring up in his devious little mind. Something tells me it could involve nudity. He heads back down the highway and turns onto a dirt road that loops through the sagebrush flats and ends at a gentle rise peppered with trees, overlooking the whole glittering Teton Range. It's a view of the valley I've never seen before. Taking my hand, he leads me to a grassy spot. On cool earth, with our clothes scattered on the ground, we wrap in the safe chrysalis of one another's arms, as sun and fervor draw crescents of sweat from our skin. Pine needles press into our shoulders, knees, and hips. Together our bodies open and fill and crest and shudder into that blissful, velvet space, while all around us waft pungent smells of sage and pine, and the mountains thrust into the sky with an intensity born of fire and ice.

⌒

Jace manages to extend my season until mid-November. I settle into the S&RM fall routines: elk jaws, track counts, reports. Only this year I'm staying in the Tetons for sure, no matter what, and this fact soothes me like balm. I know *something* will come through. I trust that a path will open for me.

Eventually it does, but it's a path with a price. Mandell Thompson comes through with a plan—an offer of half-time work with a month-long furlough in March, which would allow me to stay in Beaver Creek 56 through the winter. But there's a catch. I'll be working as an office clerk, in other words a secretary, for S&RM.

It's not the work, I tell myself. *It's about being here.*

Walking home from the office, I pause to watch the sun nestle into a splendid lavender quilt wrapped around the summits, and I shiver, but not with cold.

Here.

40

Borealis

Winter spools me in with a relentless magnetism I have no desire to fight. The first snowstorm comes one Monday night while I'm at a chorale rehearsal. When I head home from Jackson, snow is dumping in earnest and blowing in great arcs across the highway. Darcy bucks loyally through it. I soon learn the value of the reflector posts that approach each junction. The first post has three green reflectors, the second has two, the third—at the junction—one. When I sense I'm nearing Moose Junction—all the road signs are obliterated—I peer into the sheeting snow. On blind faith, when I see the one green disk illuminated by my headlights, I turn left and miraculously I'm heading toward Beaver Creek on the Inside Road. Beyond the park entrance gates the wind ramps up, whipping up the snow into a complete whiteout. I can barely make out the roadside as I creep along. Soon I see three green disks, and, suddenly, one. I must have missed the two-disk marker. I turn, plow through deepening scallops of snow, and sigh in relief as I find myself in the Beaver Creek compound.

That night the storm drifts a cubic yard of snow dense as cement against my front door. I call Mom in the morning. "I'm trapped in my house," I say.

"Oh, my God!" she shrieks. "What are you going to do? How will you get out?"

I know she's thinking I'll be stuck until spring, but I'm confident, relaxed. "Don't worry. I'll call Sam."

"Good," she says. "Oh, hold on, your father wants to talk to you before he leaves. He's heading over to Frank and Yvette's to set up the stereo cabinet he built for them."

There's a shuffle on the line. "G'mawnin', Maeh," Dad says. "Hey, you know why the Portagee has TGIF printed on his shoes?"

I'm laughing already. "Can't be 'thank goodness it's Friday?'"

"Nope. *Toes Go In First.*"

My giggling fit fades to a feeling of poignancy. I miss being part of their day-to-day lives. As we exchange small talk, I hear scraping on my front step. "Hey, Dad," I say, looking out the window. "Tell Mom she doesn't have to worry anymore. Sean, the ranger next door, is shoveling me out."

This is the winter that will draw poetry from me. Having assured work and housing in the Tetons, with Sam nearby to ease predicaments and squelch loneliness, frees my creative impulses, and I discover the intense joy of stringing words together on the snapshot-sized monitor of a borrowed Mac computer. A pleasing routine develops: work four hours every morning, write every afternoon and into the night, with frequent breaks for skiing or shoveling snow. At Julian's suggestion, I bring Tansy and Salsify home in their aquarium to spend the winter on my coffee table, and I truly don't know how I've survived this long without pets. I turn them loose to run around the living room floor. Then I ply them with peanuts that they stuff in their cheeks until they look like mumps-infected homunculi.

December. Snow falls day after day after day. It accumulates gently, sweeping into dips and crevices, quiet and unnoticed. Trees froth up while mountains sink under a great white weight. To get to my car parked on the street, Sam helps me shovel a path from my door through hip-deep snow. On my metal roof snow piles up and advances downslope like a glacier to overhang the eaves in solid waves. It generates yard-long, wrist-thick icicles, some defying gravity and pointing inward toward the windows. I snowshoe around the house and break them off before they puncture the glass as they have on other Beaver Creek houses.

Diaphanous green sheets of an aurora borealis shimmer in the northern sky when I drive out one evening to go caroling with the chorale at the homes of elderly shut-ins. We sing "Joy to the World" and "Deck the Halls" on doorsteps, and when the doors swing open, we file into sweltering hot houses and sing more carols. It makes me sad, singing for these old folks as they watch with such intense focus and sing along with us. I ache for all those painful human commonalities—loss, uncertainty, fear—and how we appeal to music, like dance, to briefly suspend them. I see myself in those tired eyes, and I wonder: *Did they follow their dreams? Or does the pain of regret weigh on their shoulders?* One laughing eighty-five-year-old requests "Jingle Bell Rock," and we sing it for her, palming the rhythm on our thighs. This one, I realize happily, probably walks unencumbered.

Part 3: Light Inside My Heart

Last night, as I was sleeping,
I dreamt—marvellous error!—
that a fiery sun was giving
light inside my heart.
It was fiery because I felt
warmth as from a hearth,
and sun because it gave light
and brought tears to my eyes.

—Antonio Machado
(Translated by Robert Bly)

41

Sharpshooter

April 1994. "Welcome back, Mary Beth." Jace meets me at the S&RM office door as I enter, surprising me with his chirpy greeting. His face glows cherry-red this chilly morning.

"Thanks, Jace. It's good to be back."

I'm returning to biology work after a month-long furlough that followed my winter secretarial gig. The familiar smells of the Resource Management office—dry wood, stale carpeting, frozen animals—delight me. I'm back in my world, doing biology work, on a par with the guys again.

Jace follows me to my office. "I need to talk to you a minute."

"Sure."

He slides his hands into his pockets to assume the Cool Dude salute. "I, uh, I just wanted to tell you that we sent Glen to bear immobilization training last month."

Blood drains from my innards and into my fists. I try to sound indifferent. "Oh, really."

"Yeah," he says, "I decided we needed one more person after all, and Glen was the obvious choice with all his experience."

Jace reminds me of Dennis the Menace trying to explain to Mr. Wilson next door why it was his particular baseball that broke the window.

My eyes swell. *Damn!* To occupy my shaking hands, I pick up *Weeds of the West* from my desk and walk it to the bookcase across the room. I file it in a row of Code of Federal Regulations books where I'll never find it again.

"But we'd still like to keep you involved," Jace continues.

"Uh-huh." I kick at a loose carpet thread.

"We're having a brush-up training on the sedatives today, and you're welcome to come if you'd like to learn more about them. Then after lunch we'll head over to the rifle range at the airport pit for some shooting practice."

I want to tell him to fuck off, but I say, "Sure. That'd be great. Thanks."

He walks out.

Okay, now what? Should I be pissy and start slamming doors and drawers? Then when someone asks me what's wrong I can bare my poor, persecuted soul? But no, I decide. I'll play nice. I'll go to any training they offer, learn things, be patient. Maybe this is for the best.

They've set out bottles of veterinary sedatives, Ketamine-Rompun, Telazol. Glen and Tim sit close to Jace with notebooks and pens and murmur among themselves.

Jace looks up. "Come on in, Mary Beth."

I drag up a chair, sit down outside their circle. It's clear I'm an observer, not a participant.

"Of course, it's a lot harder when the bear's not in the trap," Jace says, fondling his goatee with a curved forefinger. "When we're free-range darting we have to estimate the animal's weight from a distance."

Tim nods so vigorously the scraggly hair quivers on his head. "When I look at a bear, I ask myself, 'How does it compare in size with my black lab, Jasper?' Jasper weighs about ninety pounds." Tim reclines in his chair, chest puffing.

Following suit, Glen leans back, crosses one lanky leg over the other, and places his hands on his middle. "Cool. And since it's usually the younger bears that get into trouble, I'm betting it's unlikely we'd deal with a bear much bigger than that."

"Hah . . . don't count on it," Jace says, with a huff.

Glen backpaddles. "Oh, sure, Jace. You're absolutely right. We never can be sure what we'll find."

It's a trained seal act, a finely choreographed dance, the way they ebb and flow to accommodate Jace's ego.

After lunch, in sporadic drizzle, we ride together in the king cab Ford to the airport pit, a hollow depression in the sagebrush where ammunition can thud into piles of sand. The guys burst out of the pickup and engage in frenetic activity. Tim and Jace haul out the firearm cases while Glen stands a wooden pallet on end against a sand pile and wedges a plastic bottle cap between the slats. Tim paces out twenty yards from the target and heels a line in the dirt.

Folding my arms over my chest, I lean against the truck, ball cap low over my eyes, ponytail thrashing in the wind. Again, the observer. But it's a great show. And free, too.

"Let's start with the Cap-chur air rifle," Jace says. "We each get two tries. Why don't you start, Glen?"

Unzipping his jacket, Glen stands at the line. First comes an elaborate pre-liminary ritual. Shoulders roll in exaggerated circles and draw up to alternate ears. Neck spirals around like an owl's. Then he props the rifle to his shoulder. Mouth corners turn down. Elbows wriggle like wet wings. Legs plant, unplant, replant. Scapulas squeeze and relax.

I want to scream, *Just* shoot *the damn thing*.

Finally he pulls the trigger, and we all squint at the target, which is still there, but a fresh divot in the pallet wood catches our eye.

"You're about eight inches off," Tim says.

He fires again.

"Looks a little closer," Jace says.

"Not much." Glen storms off the line in disgust. "*God*. I'm rusty."

Tim follows. He strips off his rain shell and rolls up his shirtsleeves, then steps up to the line and shoulders the rifle. Takes it down, checks out the firing mechanism. Aims again. Waffles a bit, then finally pulls the trigger.

"I don't even see it," says Glen.

Jace tugs at his cap. "Try again."

Same ritual.

"Looks about six inches off."

"My turn." Jace takes his place. He stretches out his arms, rolls his shoulders in figure-eights. Inhales a big one, then brings up the rifle.

I watch. He assumes a marksman's stance—left hand holding up the barrel, cheek against the stock, finger on the trigger. And he waits. And waits. Before long, the gun barrel starts to waver. When he finally shoots, the target still sits securely on the pallet.

"Not even close," Glen says. "Try again, Jace."

Same performance. This time he hits the pallet about seven inches from the target.

"Good job," Tim says.

Okay, I've got nothing to lose. I know they won't let me shoot, but I ask anyway. Glen and Tim raise their eyebrows in Jace's direction. They all shrug, in unison.

"Sure," Jace says. "Why not?"

I'm not even anxious when I take the rifle and step up to the line with six macho eyes boring into my back. Without thinking, I nestle the rifle into my shoulder, peer down the sights, line up the little ball in the V, and squeeze the trigger. The pellet pings off the pallet three inches from the target.

I feel the silence like a pall behind me. I don't turn around, don't say a word. Again I lift the rifle, line it up, shoot. The bottle cap zings off the pallet.

"Holy shit," someone murmurs with a chuckle.

Stone-faced, I turn around, resist the urge to blow imaginary smoke from the barrel, and hand the rifle back to Jace. He laughs like he's got something caught in his gullet. "Oh, yeah. *Now* look who's gonna be the best shot of the group."

"Oh, she didn't hit it," Glen says. "She just knocked it off."

"No, Glen." Jace yanks off his ball cap and tousles his hair. "She hit the target." He arcs his head around, watching the darkening clouds.

Glen replaces the bottle cap. We keep shooting, next with a pistol, then with a rifle using real tranquilizer darts and gunpowder charges, at thirty, forty, and fifty yards. My shots are more consistent and closer to the target than theirs, at all distances.

Now a light rain patters the sand and gutless thunder thrums over Sleeping Indian. No one speaks as we pack up the firearms and load them into the truck. I've surprised myself more than any of them, and I'm keenly aware that I've earned some new respect or at least blasted some egos.

As I pass Jace and climb into the truck, he says the unimaginable: "Good shooting, Mary Beth."

At dinner I relate the story to Sam. He leaps from his chair, grabs his knees, and guffaws. "That's the best story I've heard in *ages*."

42

Swan Lake

Just north of the Elk Ranch reservoir, on the sunny slope of Uhl Hill, clusters of tiny pink *Claytonia* and nodding yellow *Fritillaria* dot the ground. Through binoculars I'm seeing that, far from the boisterous singles hangout of past years, the reservoir is nearly empty this year, save for a pair of swans swimming and feeding together at the east end.

It's a good sign. Trumpeter swans haven't nested here in many years. But there's a problem. The raised area where they historically nested is nearly inundated with water. I recall Tim's comment two years ago about Herbie Doyle over-regulating the water flow from the dam.

But rather than sneaking upstream to the weir and shutting it down, I track down Herbie, cheek full o' chaw, behind one of the barns.

Stabbing his shovel into the ground, he strides over to meet me, his tanned, leathery face split by a wide grin. "How ya doin', Mary Beth?" He clasps the crown of his sweat-stained cowboy hat and tips it. Herbie knows how to greet a lady.

"Sure is a lot of water in the reservoir," I say, peering into his face to gauge his reaction.

Herbie turns and spits, then faces me. "Been awf'ly dry," he says. "I'm afraid we won't have enough water. I got the dam wide open trying to fill it up before the cattle get here."

Hm-m-m. I have to step gingerly. I don't want angry ranchers burning swan effigies in my yard at Beaver Creek. "Yeah, it's been real dry this spring. Nothing like last year."

"You said it."

Take it slow. "We got a pair of swans."

Herbie's face brightens. "Sure do. Maybe they'll build a nest and have a brood of young 'uns."

"I'm worried there's too much water, though. The nest platform's nearly covered and they aren't going near it."

"Huh. Maybe we ought to slow it down a little. I'll do that this afternoon."

"That's a *great* idea," I say, smiling up at him.

Three days later, while the flow has lessened, the reservoir is full and water still burbles over the spillway. But I don't want to be a pest. This time I take the matter into my own hands and drive up to the dam. I unlock the padlock on the weir with my park master key and close two gates of the dam completely. The middle one I leave open about eight inches. When I'm done, there's very little water flowing through, less than one-tenth of a cubic foot per second, according to the gauge. I lock it back up and take off.

The next day both swans appear to be asleep on a low mound far from the original nesting area. I tell Tim about it at lunchtime.

"That's no good," he says. "It'll get flooded out as soon as Herbie opens up the dam again. We need to get them back on the higher nest site."

We return that afternoon with clippers and loppers and cut bunches of cattails and willow branches. Tim tells me, "Go to bed early tonight, and set your alarm. I'll pick you up at three tomorrow morning and we'll go canoeing."

The sky is wooly black and pin-pricked with stars at three-thirty a.m. Chorus frogs stop their screeping as Tim and I paddle across the reservoir with our cuttings and two bales of straw stuffed in the canoe. This, I realize, is wildlife management at its bluntest.

Tim scans the lake with binoculars. "I see two white blobs at the far end. We gotta work fast."

At night and from this vantage point, it's confusing. We paddle around several mounds until we find what we think is the original nest site. Sliding into the water in our waders, we quickly and quietly unload our cargo and place it on the mound. We work hunched over, keeping low profiles. When we're done we hop back in the boat and paddle-scamper out of there.

Damn! I think, scoping the area later that day. From Uhl Hill in daylight, I see we've missed the nest site by about twenty meters.

"No problem," says Sam when I tell him about it after work. "We'll go out there tonight and fix it."

At nightfall in the meadow by the reservoir, a snipe *woo-woo-woos* as a porcupine waddles by. Sam and I hide until dark, then skim out in his canoe and move the cattails, willows, and straw to the correct site.

Just over a month later, I look through the Questar and behold a miracle. The pen stands over our reconstructed nest with spread wings, showing great interest in what's happening beneath her. As I watch, a quivering gray ball shakes free of an eggshell, and a tiny cygnet head emerges. The baby thrusts up, teeters on weak legs, and stumbles back down. At least two more eggs are visible, and eventually two damp cygnets thrash out of them and catapult forward. Tears flow down my cheeks.

In all, seven cygnets hatch at the Elk Ranch Reservoir, the largest trumpeter swan brood ever recorded in the Tri-State area. I'm ready to pass out cigars.

43

Bearing Up

If only to assuage Jace's guilt, I still score enviable bear management assignments. He sends me out to inventory all the Dumpsters and garbage cans in the park so we can replace them with bear-resistant ones that have swinging mailbox-type lids. I plan my swan and amphibian surveys around my "Dumpster survey," which takes me to all the park concessions areas—not only the lodges and restaurants, but also the out-of-the-way, hidden picnic sites used for float trips, chuck wagons, and trail rides. Wielding a staple gun, I attach a laminated card describing the Dos and Don'ts of camping in bear country to every picnic table I can find. On my computer I make a neon yellow sign titled You Are In Bear Country, and have it printed on large sticky sheets that I press onto every Dumpster and trashcan in the park.

I get to know all the campground hosts and show them my foolproof bear repellent. "It really works," the white-haired host at Jenny Lake Campground tells me, after he used his soda can of pebbles to chase a recalcitrant bear out of the campground.

One early morning Julian and I walk the forested trail south of Emma Matilda Lake. Sunlight filters through pine boughs overhead and dapples the trail. I'm edgy and iron-tense. Every step confirms our suspicions as we pass fruit-droopy branches of buffaloberry, huckleberry, thimbleberry, and gooseberry.

Somewhere in here yesterday a jogger was mauled by a likely grizzly bear, the first ever recorded bear mauling in Grand Teton history. Jace has sent us on a mission to assess the quality of bear habitat in the area, and it's looking really, really good.

The victim, a tourist from Utah, was doing practically nothing right— jogging on this trail in the early morning hours, silent and alone, through a berry patch. He told rangers he heard crashing through the brush behind him. When he turned around, the bear was coming at him full speed. It knocked him to the ground and tore into his abdomen, thigh, back, and head with teeth and claws. Suddenly the bear stepped back as if it heard a noise, turned, and ran off. While the victim has no broken bones, he does have severe lacerations and faces lengthy surgeries to reattach muscles in his leg.

Julian walks silently while I talk, whistle, clap, and keep my radio on high volume. If that bear's still around, I don't want any part of it. We find piles of berry-filled scat, and in a muddy section of trail, three clear tracks with claw marks more than two inches from the foot pad—definitely grizzly tracks. But is it a mom with cubs? We keep looking but don't find any smaller tracks.

I point at a lodgepole trunk. "Look at this, Julian." Several long hairs bristle from the tree's bark. Holding them against my hand, I see they are two-toned, black, with silver edges.

"A rub tree," Julian says, slipping the hairs into a Ziploc bag.

My stomach's turning cartwheels, but we keep on, all the way to Pacific Creek. There are no further reports of aggression, and the guilty bear is never found.

———

This sweltering summer of 1994 becomes one of other newsworthy disasters. Temperatures rarely reach ninety in the Jackson Hole Valley, yet this summer passes the mark several times. No rain falls for weeks; vegetation pales and curls. Wind swoops and thunder groans while dense, rainless clouds brood overhead. Our beloved ice-blue skies fill up with sinus-stinging smoke, blurring the mountain view. Startling red "fire moons" rise through thick dusks, while the sun, a seething, orange ball, backlights smoky clouds into spectacular sunsets. I blink my eyes, trying to clear my vision, but a haze remains.

The west is cooking. On July 6, fourteen wildland firefighters are killed in one incident on Storm King Mountain in Colorado. This is the highest number of wildland firefighter deaths in a single incident since 1937, when fifteen firefighters lost their lives in a wildfire northwest of the Tetons in the Shoshone National Forest.

On July 27 a fire burns near Two Ocean Lake. I bring my radio to Sam's after work and we listen through the evening. Certain he will be called out tonight, Sam sets his fire pack, Nomex shirt, hard hat, and boots by the door.

Hearing the radio crackle with familiar, frantic voices fills me with excitement and dread. Rick Lichtenhan, who danced with me at my first Spring

Fling, shouts, "How many do they need?" He's making sandwiches for the firefighters.

"Is there someone on the lake?" The voice is Jim VanDyke's. "I left the Lower Berry cabin in such a rush I forgot to shutter it up against bears."

North District rangers jump in. "We need road barricades. Can someone bring them to the Colter Bay garage?"

Sam and I are snuggling in bed when we hear the panicked voice of a Colter Bay ranger. "More crews! We need more crews." They already have four crews, twenty people each, on the fire.

"This is it," Sam says, jumping out of bed. "I'm heading over there."

They don't need Sam, and this fire is soon contained, but a month later on August 28, a rogue bolt of dry lightning ignites vegetation on Mormon Row. What would become known as the "Row Fire" spreads northeast through thirsty grass and sagebrush, consuming six log buildings on the historic Pfeiffer home-stead on its way.

By Monday morning the fire is declared contained, but at noon, as I crest Lozier Hill and train a telemetry antenna on my quarry, a red-tailed hawk, my radio erupts. The fire has reignited, and Engine One from the Moose Fire Brigade is dispatched to the scene. Sam is probably driving the truck.

On the way back to Moose, I spot the vortex of smoke to the southeast. Near the ground, dense white cumuli encompass pink flames, then, wind-goaded, boil up and thin to translucent gray puffs that obliterate a teasingly blue sky. Even from miles away, the acrid smell lodges in my throat, singeing my olfactory nerves.

At home there's a message on my answering machine. "I'm heading out on Engine One," Sam says. "Don't know when I'll get in."

After dinner I join a line of gawkers to watch the fire from a turnout on the Outside Highway. We stare, bedazzled by the spectacle. I'm struck by the sound-lessness, occasionally pierced by the clicks of camera shutters. I expected pops, cracks, booms, like fireworks, but this is a grassland fire so far, and trees aren't exploding in the heat. Tongues of flame lick the sky and creep toward Shadow Mountain and Ditch Creek.

I'm saddened to see the smoldering expanse left in the fire's wake. But if I could see the future, I wouldn't be concerned. This fire, which now seems wan-ton and senseless, will enrich the soil with plant nutrients from its ashes. Next spring, Antelope Flats will thrust up the most luxuriant crop of lupines we've ever seen, covering the burned area with vibrant flowers like purple rockets, and bison will nudge one another's shoulders to compete for the thick, nutritious grass underneath.

But now, all I can think is this: *Sam's in there somewhere.* The thought fills me with blood-draining terror. I have little knowledge of wildland fires, how to fight them, or how to stay safe fighting them. All I know is that Nomex firewear and the infamous one-man foil "baked potato" tents seem dangerously inadequate.

The crowd watches until darkness falls. I head to Sam's cabin for the night. On his answering machine I find a staticky message from a prototype mobile phone saying he's calling from Shadow Mountain and he loves me.

I pace back and forth and eat chocolate. Time seems to collapse on itself. Twice the phone rings. Above the static, I think I hear Sam's voice yelling, far, far away. I hate this helpless feeling.

The Teton Science School is evacuated. I'm sure the Hunter Ranch barn, where Sam and I waltzed so tenderly to "Ashokan Farewell" at this year's Spring Fling, is gone, and probably several homes near Shadow Mountain, one of which belongs to singer Tom Rush.

Head buzzing and limbs trembling with anxiety, I finally fall asleep after midnight. In the dark, early morning hours Sam enters the bedroom; I bolt awake and leap into his arms. He reeks of smoke. I'm surprised to find him wearing not the Nomex shirt and Red Wing boots of the wildland firefighter, but the bulky garb of the structural firefighter—heavy, insulated fire pants and coat, with folded down rubber boots flapping around his calves. Soot smears his face, hands, and clothing.

"We saved Tom Rush's house," he says. He describes how, with burning lungs and choking fits of coughing, he and fellow park employees Mark Kelleher, John Courtney, and Colin Clark hosed down the house all night with water from a pumper truck. A twelve-foot-high wall of fire surrounded them, surging at the bulldozed firebreak twenty feet from the house, before charging up Shadow Mountain.

I'm in awe of the park firefighters, of their skill, tenacity, fearlessness, and devotion. More than ever, I yearn to be part of this Park Service family, to be a career employee with a real PGJ at Grand Teton. I want to dive into the blustering fray, work with a team for the greater good, whether it's searching for grizzly tracks, carting around road signs, or preparing food.

"Oh, you'll be happy to hear," Sam says, turning back to me on his way to the shower, "the Hunter Barn pulled through."

44

Growing Pains

For weeks Sam types on his Standard Form 171 government application for a permanent carpenter position in the Maintenance Division. I tell myself: *With his work ethic, craftsmanship, and twelve years of seasonal experience, how can they turn him down?* But they do. They hire one of his less experienced coworkers.

But Sam stays upbeat. He keeps up his skills, does his job every day, volunteers for special projects. And when a higher-level maintenance position opens up soon after, he jumps right back in to tailor his application to the job requirements. But it's not until another year passes, after two false alarms and a sixty-five-page SF-171, that I finally will rig up a paper towel banner reading Congratulations, Sam! across the cabin porch to welcome him home one day, and his high school buddy Doug Bonner will tell him, "*Wow.* You're gonna be an *old* mo'-fucker when you retire!"

Like him, I need to brush off setbacks and keep up the momentum. If I ever hope to get a permanent biologist job here, I have to dive into the deep end of the pool. I need to be knowledgeable about the park's wildlife and learn the necessary skills so I can do any S&RM task that comes up. I can handle four-wheel driving, canoeing the lakes, and navigating the backcountry on foot. I've already shown them I can shoot. But I still don't know anything about motorboating on Jackson Lake. While I grew up sailing on Buzzards Bay, I never learned anything about outboard motors. That was Dad's realm.

When I ask Glen to show me where the raptor nests are along the shore of Jackson Lake, he Vs his eyebrows with suspicion. I know I'm treading on forbidden ground. Raptors are his domain; he wants them all to himself. Like me, he's also itching for a PGJ, but because he doesn't have federal status, he needs to maintain authority in certain areas. Nonetheless, he reluctantly agrees to take me along on his next raptor survey.

Under morning clouds of liquid opal, Glen steps into the boat at the Colter Bay dock. He uncovers the Johnson outboard, pulls out the pin, and hinges the propeller into the water. This is when I make known my ulterior motive.

"Why don't you let me drive? I want to learn how to run this thing," I say, climbing into the blue and white cup of boat with him.

"You can drive when we get out of the harbor."

"But I want to learn how the motor works." I stand over him, hoping he'll ease out of the way and let me drive.

But he won't budge. As his chest inflates, his mouth draws into an O. "All you do is flip this switch, pull this thing out, and pull the cord." The motor roars to life. "That's it."

Exasperated, I flop on my seat as he twists the tiller grip for more power and steers us from the dock. He putters us out of the harbor, craning his neck from side to side. "The first osprey nest is about fifty meters from the point here."

We head south along the lakeshore. At each site we stop and glass the nest for activity. When we spot incubating females in the nests, we note them on our clipboard data sheet and move on. About a quarter of the way around the lake I say, "Okay. Let me drive from here."

Glen shoots out a breath of air and moves to one side so we can switch seats. I grasp the vibrating phallic lever. Can't be much different from learning to drive a car, only that took many months. I play around with the tiller, pulling it left, pushing it right, seeing how the boat responds. *Maybe I'll learn to love this.* We reach the next nest in about ten minutes.

I slide the shift lever to neutral and pull up the binoculars. "There's a female on the nest."

"Good. There was no productivity here last year."

I continue creeping along the lakeshore.

Finally, forcing a smile, he says, "It'll take us all day to do the whole lake at this rate. I need to drive."

I feel like a child begging to grow up but Big Daddy can't handle the competition. I'm tempted to whack that patronizing look off his face with the clipboard. But instead, I slink back to my place as he zooms us to the next nest.

When we complete the circuit, he turns back into Colter Bay. I try again. "Let me at least pull up to the dock and practice parking."

"*Parking?*" He snorts through his bottom lip.

"What else do you call it?"

"Pulling up to the dock."

Asshole. My patience with him is fading.

He jerks the motor into neutral. We switch seats again. Just ahead, water swirls in soft ribbons from the dipping paddles of two red kayaks making their way between moored sailboats.

"Watch out for the kayaks," he says. "And this boat here."

"No shit." I'm already giving wide berth to the kayaks and the green and white sloop, emblazoned with the name HOLE ENCHILADA on its stern.

"You're gonna have to head to the shore, then turn left to pull in parallel to the dock. Just as you get there, cut the motor." Mustache twitching, he watches my every move. As we approach the shore, I push on the tiller. The bow veers around and we head to the dock.

"Cut the motor. *Cut the motor,*" he shouts, lurching across the space between us and cutting it for me. "Why'd you wait so *long?*"

I'm still pushing on the tiller but the boat maintains its momentum as it drifts closer, closer, closer, and finally crashes obliquely into the dock. Water splashes over the gunwales. I'm mortified as I look at him moon-eyed.

"*Jeez.*" He grabs the dock with both hands. "You practically took out the damn dock." He leans over the gunwales to check for damage. Finding no dings in the fiberglass, he absorbs himself with securing and covering the motor.

Grabbing the bow line, I jump up on the dock and head for the brass anchoring cleats. With an absorption born of embarrassment, I wrap the line around the cleat, then make a loop, flip it over, and tuck it neatly under one arm of the cleat so it's snug. The remaining line I twirl and pat into a neat spiral the size of a Frisbee. I then take the aft line to repeat the procedure on the other cleat.

"What're you doing?" Glen's standing behind me, arms full of gear.

"I'm tying authentic nautical knots, like my dad taught me. Don't want these things to work loose now, do we?"

He shudders, pivots, and heads up the ramp.

"There's a dead bison on the road to the Moulton Barn," Tim tells me one afternoon. "We could use a leg or two of it to bait the bear trap. You'll need an ax."

"Sure," I say. The task sounds simple enough. No big deal.

At the Maintenance building, I pass Elaine at her desk. "*Mary Beth,*" she says with a cheery smile. "What a nice surprise!"

"I need to borrow an ax," I say.

"*What?*" She winds her red hair behind her ears, as if to hear me better.

I tell her about my assigned task.

"You've *got* to be kidding," she says. "Why do they send *you* out to do their dirty work?"

My hands hover. "I do it all, Elaine. Can't give them any reason to think I can't handle this job."

She nods, knowingly.

I find an ax in the tool shop and head out to the Moulton Barn. Before I even see the bison, I smell it. A hoard of flies buzzes through Nellie's open windows while I rush to roll them shut. Inching along the two-track I finally see the bloated carcass lying on its side and swarming with flies, its rigid legs forced into unnatural angles by the distension of its belly. The fetid odor of death clogs my throat. But I *can't* go back empty-handed. Holding my breath as long as I can, I slide out of the truck, ax in hand. All I need is one leg—I can handle this. Just sink the ax into a shoulder joint and rip it outta there. *Oh my God.* So disgusting. This stink will cling to my skin, hair, and sinus passages for the rest of my life, I just know it.

Three ravens fly off the corpse as I approach, gagging, yet feeling a twinge of sadness. This cow was killed a few days ago by a car on the Antelope Flats Road, and the park's Road Crew hauled it out here to get it out of view of park visitors. Now here she is, so undignified, so unlike those regal, prehistoric-looking animals we see munching grass along the roads. And I have to further defile her by cutting off her leg.

Taking shallow mouth breaths, I lean over the animal. *Does she have a calf?* I wonder. *If so, what will happen to it?* Her belly, with its unlikely black sheen, is stretched further than what seems physically possible. I nudge the ax into the dry armpit and saw it back and forth. Then I take a few feeble swings. The skin is tough as, well, buffalo hide—*duh!*—and I can't even pierce it. Maybe I should get my knife out of my pack and make a slice first? Then a thought horrifies me: *Contents under pressure, you idiot!* Cutting a hole into this thing could shoot me to the moon, drenching me in slime and putrefaction and unimaginable vile grossness.

Okay, that's it. I'm going back and explaining this to Tim. To hell with him if he thinks I'm a wimp.

Back at the office, Tim's eyes roll with impatience as he agrees to go back with me. As we roll up to the carcass and the stench and flies again fill the truck, he brakes, prunes up his nose, and clamps his eyes shut. I hoot in relieved laughter.

"I think we can find some better bait for the traps," he says.

———— ✦ ————

It's a bane of American culture: We all want to make our mark on the world, rise above the masses, shine in some unique way. I felt different from other women; I'd never fit into mainstream culture. I had to do something big, something extraordinary. I had the itch, and the wild, persistent dream.

I wanted to believe that all the drudgery and angst I'd endured in my life would eventually pay off, and I'd collect a return on my investment, a permanent biology job at Grand Teton. I'd paid my dues—the necessary education, years of marital repression, family rejection, a move across the country, years as a seasonal, a move to and from Denver to get the coveted government status, secretarial work—these sacrifices, I thought, should one day earn me a glittering chest of riches. In my forties, I should be reaping the benefits of those hard-sown seeds, my past efforts sustaining me far into the future.

But the day finally dawned when I realized that the strong message of my culture and upbringing—that hard work and perseverance would bring the sought-after reward—was not going to ring true for me here.

Jace tells me, "The assistant superintendent really likes you. She told me if we make Glen's job permanent, she'd hire *you* in a heartbeat because you're more pleasant."

Smart woman, I'm thinking. It's no secret that the park honchos aren't crazy about grumpy Glen, but I don't know why Jace is telling me this. "She's right," I say. "I *am* more pleasant."

But when funding for a permanent biologist job finally came through, Jace turned it down. He had to, of course, because he knew there'd be pressure from HQ to hire me over Glen. I didn't understand it then, but Grand Teton wildlife biologists are a special breed. Like the Jenny Lake climbing rangers, they set high standards for themselves. Jace needed an insufferably athletic, muscley worker.

While I was tougher than the average woman, could put people at ease, and talk the shirt off anyone, Jace knew he wouldn't be looking for me when he needed someone to shimmy up a cliff to band peregrine falcons in a nest. Glen fit the bill, but the higher-ups would have nixed him.

The new chief of S&RM one day calls me into his office. "We're getting funding for a permanent secretarial position. You should apply for it. Get your foot in the door."

—❦—

One night I dream I hold a prestigious position in some government agency. My uniform is a handsome navy blue dress with a white bolero jacket made of Kevlar. I'm rushing to get to my sister's wedding, but obstacles keep popping up. At the airport I'm stopped at a security checkpoint. With great fanfare, I remove my jacket, hook my finger through the collar, and swing it under the guards' noses. "This is *Kevlar* you know," I declare. They nod knowingly and say, "It'll take a while then." When the jacket finally clears the red tape, I don it again and run to the next station, only to go through the same rigmarole. I arrive at the church just as the wedding party prepares to walk down the aisle. Pushing my way ahead of them, I parade to a front pew in my impressive uniform. But the guests don't fawn over me in admiration. Rather, they seem annoyed.

When I wake up, I glance around my bedroom. On my desk sits my Motorola radio in its charger. A uniform shirt and ball cap with their arrowhead patches hang on the back of the chair. Worn hiking boots that I've just treated with water-repellent mink oil sit on the floor by the door. Instead of Kevlar, I realize, these are my trappings, along with bear traps, spotting scopes, and telemetry gear. Symbols of engagement and hard work, they legitimize me, float me above mediocrity. More than that, they protect me, like Kevlar, from the sobering well of meaninglessness that gapes beyond certainty. But what important things will they keep me from?

45

Woodswoman, Reprise

Through the spotting scope, they're big as military tanks—two frosted brown beauties with massive, concave faces and shoulder humps dark like stoles. They shudder and list as they dig in the ground for bulbs and roots. Slowly traversing the Moose Basin meadows, they're heading north, toward the divide, where I spent the day alone yesterday glassing for sheep on the rocky slopes leaning from Owl Peak.

Moose Basin. I've heard this is where, decades ago, Olaus and Mardy Murie and their small children spent months at a time studying elk, using the tiny Moose Basin Patrol Cabin as their base camp.

By now sheep surveys are as familiar as toast: the nine-mile uphill hike into Webb Canyon, fitful sleeps on mouse-nibbled mattresses alongside coworkers, endless hours of sitting on the ground, my spine forced into a surreal curve around binoculars or spotting scope, with sporadic leaps to my feet to jumpstart the circulation in my numb legs.

For this year's survey I'm here with Jace and Ann, a volunteer who helps us out with fieldwork. Jace, feeling sniffly and achy this morning, decided to avoid the higher areas today and stay close to the cabin.

After an unproductive day of searching for sheep, Ann and I have just reentered Moose Basin through Horse Thief Pass. Far below us, Bitch Creek meanders through a willowy maze, with aptly named Carrot Ridge beyond it. We've spent the last two hours traversing the steep slopes of two buttes west of the park boundary. While I love the talus slopes now, they still scare the hell out of me. We tackled the loose, ball-bearing rocks slowly, calling out encouragements to each other as we dipped, slipped, scrambled, and barely missed a number of rocky face-plants. Now, back in Moose Basin, a passing cloud squirts a tantrum of icy raindrops, then cold sunlight spears down on us. New snow glistens on the surrounding peaks—Doane, Rolling Thunder, Moose, Elk, Owl.

The bears are probably three-year-old siblings, pushed out of their pregnant mother's care so she can tend to the new litter she'll give birth to in January. They're roaming, searching for a place to begin their adult lives. It's frightening, breaking the ties, striking out, taking those first shaky steps of a new life. This I know for sure.

Beyond the bears is our destination: the dark cube of the patrol cabin, two miles away in a pocket of timber.

"Jace sure picked a good day to be sick." Ann laughs nervously and dismantles the spotting scope. Her black hair swirls around her ski cap in the gusty wind as she straps the scope to her pack and hands me the tripod.

"The bears are downwind, so they've probably already caught a whiff of us," I say, lashing the tripod to the side of my pack. "But we'll still have to detour way to the south."

"And make a lot of noise."

All neurons fire up to Red Alert as we step down a game trail. We hoot and crow as we skip from rock to rock, past curled-up leaves of green gentian, through clumps of snow here and there on the gravely soil.

"*Hey, bears, we're coming through . . .* " My voice rings out. I feel agile, light-footed, invincible.

"*Look at this!*" Ann yells.

There's a giant bear scat, still steaming, and a knee-high mound of upturned soil.

"*Holy crap!*"

A track in soft earth—I don't stop to make sure, but it seems I could place my whole forearm, from elbow to fingertips, within its outline.

"*Oh, man!*"

Time goes static. The peaks to the west eclipse the sun, draining light and confidence, but we charge ahead through the palpable, ashy light of dusk.

"*Yee-hah!*"

The scent of subalpine fir fills our lungs as the cabin comes into view. Ann and I jog the remaining distance before collapsing into each other's arms, shrieking with relief.

The cabin door creaks open, and Jace, bundled in fleece, comes out to greet us. "I heard you all the way down," he says, eyes twinkly with amusement.

Smiling, I squeeze his arm and stride past him, feeling strong and tall.

Truly, it's enough.

46

Dream Story

Shortly after I move into the cabin with Sam in November, a skim of snow falls in the night, and we find in the yard dozens of grassy ovals where the snow had melted. They're elk beds, and I'm comforted to know we were protected all night by a herd of elk, a circle of living wagons, as breath from their velvety noses swirled through the air.

We ski to Grizzly Hot Springs through a cottony net of falling snow. The trail is buried, but Sam leads intuitively, and I'm happy to follow. On the way we frighten a coyote off a deer carcass. The deer's spine arches backward; bloody ribs claw through the snow. Around the carcass are the coyote's tracks, red with blood, roses in the snow. I step back and peer into the snowfall. About fifty yards away the coyote sits patiently, snow gathering between its erect ears, eyes trained on us, waiting for us to move on so it can resume its feast.

Soon we spot steam rising from a small pool as the smell of hot sulfur bristles our noses. We strip out of our sweaty ski clothes and fold into the water. Sitting on a barely submerged stone, I'm scalding from the waist down while snowflakes dapple my shoulders and melt into my skin. *What a miracle,* I think, sitting naked under snowfall, in water whose heat is generated by thermal processes in the very heart of the earth.

I glance around, taking everything in: the spring-green blobs of algae on the water surface, the cold creek gurgling beyond the pool, the roiling mist, the evergreens sifting snow through their feathery boughs. Absentmindedly picking dabs of scum from his chest hair, Sam lounges in the water on one elbow, wearing only his ball cap—this one watery blue with green fronds and goldfish.

When my upper body stings with cold, I scrunch down, leaving only my head above water. My shoulders turn lobster-red as they go under, tingling as

Sam glides his hands over them. I reach out and touch the stones around the sides of the pool.

"It's been engineered," he says, massaging my backbone with his thumbs. "People find smooth rocks in the creek and move them around to hold the hot water and to make seats."

"It's a 'circle of stones,'" I say.

"Like that book you just finished?"

I nod. He's referring to *Circle of Stones* by Judith Duerk.

"What was it about?"

I wonder how to describe the book's message about the sacred Feminine. "Have you ever heard of the goddess-worshipping cultures?"

"Yeah," he says, "I'm in one."

❦

We're one ragtag group, standing in our skis by the Chapel of the Transfiguration, taking turns pulling on the bell rope. As we count to ninety-five, cold-metal clangs jar the snow-muffled night. All that's visible lies in the thin columns of light from our headlamps; they tangle through the darkness in complex webs, illuminating falling medallions of snow and shafts of body parts. There's a black ponytail polka-dotted with snowflakes, blue parka arms holding the rope, a glint off someone's glasses. There's Maggie sniffing the ground for crumbs, Patrick popping a champagne cork, Bob holding plastic cups, and a gloved hand, Katy's, with a fork, stabbing pieces of kippered herring from a jar and draping them on crackers Sam holds for her.

"Have one," Katy says to me. "It's supposed to bring you lots of money in the New Year."

Windfall or not, *I'm here,* I think, as the salty fish slides down my throat. *I'm here*, I realize, as snow finds an opening in my scarf and sears my neck with cold. *I'm here.* This I know deep in my bones, sure as my ski-booted feet standing solid on many feet of snow, sure as the earnest mountains looming before me.

❦

I drive home at midnight after an evening with women friends at a Teton Science School cabin. With light snow sprinkling down from thin clouds, I park in the wide spot along the road, pull on headlamp and skis, and climb the snow bank to the ski trail. Just as I start out, two yellow disks flash in my headlight beam. A moose is bedded down just ahead on the trail.

No doubt it's "LaVerne." This is the name we've given an ornery moose that lumbers around the area with her calf "Shirley" in tow. According to Sam, LaVerne has an ongoing case of PMS, "pissy moose syndrome." She once galloped after him on the road as he ran to his truck, and skidded to a stop just as he wrenched open the door and hurled himself across the bench seat.

Angling off the trail into swishy, thigh-deep snow, I hear crashing ahead and I freeze. I make out the silhouette of a second moose trotting away, deeper into the forest.

I'm in no hurry. Snapping off the headlamp, I pause, rest on my ski poles, and look up into a hushed cathedral of black evergreens. Intermittent snowflakes spatter my face with cool specks. A statue-still quiet engulfs me like a kinesthetic meditation, dense as a monsignor's cape around my shoulders. Snow, I've always believed, is a great comfort to the earth, a cleansing invitation to slow down, conserve energy, shelter the sleeping animals below, and be at peace. To me, this piercing intensity of blue-gray snow, cold, and silence is as achingly precious as the fleeting blush of springtime.

I'm here. The mountains called, and I came. I found my way home. I created my own piece, albeit a scarred and dimpled one, in the wilderness puzzle. In this world of mountain, snow, and sky, I finally feel the power of my life, and it matters.

Some of us are blessed, or cursed, with a dream, and have to bare claw and fang to claim it. To anyone with a diehard dream I want to say: Put aside all the kneading and fretting. Choose your trail. Jump. Watch a moose as it paws through a great depth of snow to get to the antelope bitterbrush underneath (you want to grow that kind of persistence). Deflect naysayers for now; they'll come around in the end. Be open to the sturdy graces that show up. Welcome friends, regardless of species. Beware of trappings; they tend to transmute into traps. *Trust thyself.*

In the end, you know, it distills to this one thing: In your own deep quiet, the only-left-with-you times, can you rest still in your cup of peace while emptiness laps at the rim? If your answer is yes, rejoice.

I don't pretend to understand it all, but this I know: Dreams won't die, no matter how hard we try to slay them. Somewhere near here, where mountains' purple tongues scribe stories of eternity on starlit skies, are remnants of a dream story, buried in the woods. They endure under layers of fragrant humus and forest duff, impervious to microbes and beetles, rodent teeth, and cloven hooves of elk.

The clouds dissipate and clean moonlight illuminates a maze of fir branches drooping under pillows of snow. I plod through it until I emerge from the forest. At the far end of the meadow, a light gleams on the cabin porch. High in the eastern sky hangs a bold moon, a pearly peach ripe for the picking. My skis train on it like a compass as I pull into the snow and glide home.

Author's Note

I sincerely hope that those who recognize themselves in these pages will understand that I wrote this story from a place of love and gratitude for all of you who crossed paths with me during this magical time of my life. The events in the narrative did occur. Whether others will recall them as I have is debatable. To protect privacy, I changed some names, genders, physical identifiers, draft numbers and birthdates, radio call numbers, and other finger-pointing characteristics, and I created a character to take the heat. Some local place names have been changed.

A chronology of events does not a memoir make. To create narrative flow, I reconstructed dialogue, scrambled chronology, and compressed time. To keep the book to a manageable length, some people and events had to be left out.

Acknowledgments

Whether they realized it or not, numerous people and organizations helped to nurture my creative vision into tangible form. Kim Wyatt and Erin Bechtol of Bonafide Books published a variation of Chapter 18 in the anthology *Permanent Vacation I: Twenty Writers on Work and Life in Our National Parks.* I've used short passages from longer essays that were previously published in *Wyoming Fence Lines: An Anthology of Prose and Poetry* and *Copper Nickel: A Journal of Art and Literature.* Thank you!

The Wyoming Arts Council has honored me with two Frank Nelson Doubleday Awards, and with a 2014 Creative Writing Fellowship. My sincere thanks go to Neltje, who funds the Doubleday Awards, and to Mike Shay of the WAC for his ongoing kindness, support, and encouragement. I'm also grateful to Wyoming Writers, Inc., Women Writing the West, and the Authors Guild for inspiration and community.

The Jentel Artist Residency Program in Banner, Wyoming, kindly provided me with a room, stipend, and cozy nest of a writing studio by a frog-filled creek in May 2009. Thanks go to Mary Jane, Lynn, and the rest of the Jentel staff for going to such great lengths to keep us residents comfortable and happy, for keeping snakes out of the residence, and for lending out their dogs like library books to accompany us on our hikes. My Jentel "littermates"—Dave, Manya, Forrest, Cerese, and Johntimothy—provided stimulating conversation and gut-wrenching laughs during our daily cooking fests, and great company during our walks to check on the owlets and on our trips to town for shopping, Cajun dancing, and bluegrass jams.

In October 2011, I had the opportunity to spend two creative weeks at the Brush Creek Artist Residency in Saratoga, Wyoming. I'm grateful to Katie Christensen for her conscientious care and feeding of our motley group of artists, musicians, and writers: Tricia, Stanka, Michael, Mary Frances, Morgan, Elisa, and Kelly.

In his course "Write Your Novel," Jackson novelist Tim Sandlin convinced me long ago that I truly could write a book-length creative work. Many years later I befriended another Jackson novelist, Tina Welling, who continues to encourage me. Vicki Lindner helped steer my course to writing memoir. Alyson Hagy and Bob Southard generously provided valuable advice. My thanks to all of you.

Julene Bair once invited me to join the now-defunct Silver Sage Writers Alliance in Laramie, an event which set my life on yet another auspicious course. Thanks, Julene, for many years of friendship, outdoor adventures, writing advice, and emotional support through times both bright and dim.

I owe a heap of gratitude to my TwoDot editor Erin Turner for her willingness to take the leap with me, and also to Matthew Mayo who opened the gate. I'm also thankful for the keen eyes of the many other editors at Globe Pequot Press who sifted through my words to polish the manuscript.

Many thanks to Shirley Craighead for the use of a photo and to Bill Staines for permission to reprint the chorus of "Sweet Wyoming Home." Wesleyan University Press allowed me to reprint a portion of Antonio Machado's fitting poem. Thomas Dunne Books and HarperCollins Publishers granted permission to quote from Jack Turner's *Teewinot* and Annie Dillard's *Pilgrim at Tinker Creek,* respectively.

I'm grateful to my manuscript readers for their thoughtful insights: Richard Allen, Mary Pat Curran, Catherine McLaughlin, Beth Buskirk, Katy Duffy, Sarah Dabney, Pam Galbreath, and Diane Panozzo. Your feedback was invaluable and prevented me from trying to foist an unfinished manuscript on a critical public.

Colleen Mekeel generously provided writing space at her Teton condo in 2008. Also, my old friend Bob Wemple continues to invite me to write at his Teton home while he travels the world. I'll keep the plants watered, Bob.

Dorly Piske was a great help with Portuguese translations, spelling, and *proverbios. Muito obrigada, a minha amiga!*

A number of gentle women and men did not make it into the pages of this book, but their listening ears, love, and understanding, as well as home-cooked meals, letters, phone calls, and in-home stays, helped keep me afloat during the period covered by this memoir: Chuck Domermuth, Claire and Hank Duckworth, Leigh Anne Dunworth, Mike Giles, Chris and Gary Gomes, Greg Gomes, Richie Iovanni, Nancy Kehoe, Rick Mulligan, Roberta Rivet, Cathleen Saunders, Linda Schworm, Janifer Smith, and Sue Wolf.

And lastly, fondest thanks to Mom, Dad, and Nancy, whom I will always hold close in my heart, and to LMG who launched me, ARW who floated me, and RDA who caught me.

Bibliography

The Tetons and the West

Baxter, George T., and Michael D. Stone. *Amphibians and Reptiles of Wyoming.* Cheyenne, WY: Wyoming Game and Fish Department, 1980. Second Edition copyright 1985. Reprinted 1992.

Betts, Robert. *Along the Ramparts of the Tetons: The Saga of Jackson Hole, Wyoming.* Niwot, CO: University Press of Colorado, 1978.

Dorn, Robert D. *Vascular Plants of Wyoming.* Second Edition. Cheyenne, WY: Mountain West Publishing, 1992.

Haderlie, Carrie. "Bark Beetle Epidemic Has Infested 4 Million Acres in Colorado, Wyoming." *Laramie Boomerang,* January 26, 2011, 1.

Hansen, Skylar. *The Trumpeter Swan: A White Perfection.* Flagstaff, AZ: Northland Press, 1984.

Herrero, Stephen. *Bear Attacks: Their Causes and Avoidance.* New York: Lyons & Burford, 1985.

Hough, Donald. *Snow Above Town.* New York: W.W. Norton & Company, Inc., 1943.

———. *The Cocktail Hour in Jackson Hole.* New York: W.W. Norton & Company, Inc., 1951, 1953, 1956.

Huffman, Mark. "Grizzly Is Suspected in Attack on Runner." *Jackson Hole News,* August 17, 1994, 6A.

———. "Gumption, Skill Saves Homes." *Jackson Hole News,* August 31, 1994, 1A, 15A.

Kershaw, Linda, Andy MacKinnon, and Jim Pojar. *Plants of the Rocky Mountains.* Edmonton, Canada: Lone Pine Publishing, 1998.

Koch, Edward D., and Charles R. Peterson. *Amphibians & Reptiles of Yellowstone and Grand Teton National Parks.* Salt Lake City: University of Utah Press, 1995.

Murie, Olaus J. *The Elk of North America.* Harrisburg, PA: The Stackpole Company, Wildlife Management Institute, 1951.

———. *A Field Guide to Animal Tracks.* Second Edition. Boston: Houghton Mifflin Company, 1954; Second Edition copyright 1974 by Margaret E. Murie.

Murie, Olaus, and Margaret D. Murie. *Wapiti Wilderness.* New York: Knopf, 1966.

Righter, Robert W. *Crucible for Conservation: The Struggle for Grand Teton National Park.* Boulder, CO: Colorado Associated University Press, 1982.

Scott, Shirley L. (editor). *Field Guild to the Birds of North America.* Second Edition. Washington, DC: National Geographic Society, 1987.

Shaw, Richard. *Plants of Yellowstone and Grand Teton National Parks.* Salt Lake City: Wheelwright Press, Ltd., 1974 and 1981.

Shelton, Christopher. "Teton Spark Turns into Major Blaze." *Jackson Hole Guide,* August 31, 1994, A1, A15.

Simpson, David. "National Park Logs First Grizzly Attack." *Jackson Hole Guide,* August 17, 1994, A7.

The Wilderness Society. http://wilderness.org/bios/former-council-members/mardy-murie.

Turner, Jack. *Teewinot: A Year in the Teton Range.* New York: Thomas Dunne Books/St. Martin's Press, 2000.

United States Fire Administration. "Analysis Report on Firefighter Fatalities in the United States in 1994." Federal Emergency Management Agency, 1995.

United States Geological Survey, Northern Rocky Mountain Science Center. "Amphibian Disease." http://nrmsc.usgs.gov/rarmi/amphibdisease.

United States National Park Service. "NPS-43: Uniform Wear Standards." Date unknown.

Whitson, Tom D. (Editor), Dave Cudney and Robert Parker (Assoc. Editors). *Weeds of the West.* Ninth Edition. Newark, CA: Western Society of Weed Science in cooperation with the Western United States Land Grant Universities Cooperative Extension Services, 2000.

Wingate, Janet L. *Rocky Mountain Flower Finder: A Guide to Wildflowers Found below Tree Line in the Rocky Mountains.* Berkeley, CA: Nature Study Guild, 1990.

Yoon, Carol Kaesuk. "Thinning Ozone Layer Implicated in Decline Of Frogs and Toads." *New York Times,* March 1, 1994, www.nytimes.com/1994/03/01/science/thinning-ozone-layer-implicated-in-decline-of-frogs-and-toads.html.

OLD FAVORITES

Abbey, Edward. *Desert Solitaire: A Season in the Wilderness.* New York: McGraw-Hill, 1968.

Allen, Durward L. *Our Wildlife Legacy.* New York: Funk and Wagnalls Co., 1962.

Brockman, C. Frank. *Trees of North America.* Racine, WI, and New York: Western Publishing Company, Inc. and Golden Press, 1968.

Caras, Roger A. *North American Mammals: Fur-bearing Animals of the United States and Canada.* New York: Galahad Books, a division of A&W Promotional Book Corporation, 1967.

Core, Earl L., and Nelle P. Ammons. *Woody Plants in Winter: A Manual of Common Trees and Shrubs in Winter in the Northeastern United States and Southeastern Canada.* Pacific Grove, CA: The Boxwood Press, 1973.

Dillard, Annie. *Pilgrim at Tinker Creek.* New York: Harper's Magazine Press, published in association with Harper & Row, 1974.

Emerson, Ralph Waldo. "Self-Reliance." Essays by Ralph Waldo Emerson. New York: Thomas Y. Crowell Company, 1926.

Giles, Robert H. Jr. (Editor). *Wildlife Management Techniques.* Washington, DC: The Wildlife Society, 1969; Third Edition, 1971.

Leopold, Aldo. *A Sand County Almanac and Sketches Here and There.* New York: Oxford University Press, 1949.

Peterson, Roger T., and Margaret McKenny. *A Field Guide to Wildflowers of Northeastern and North-central North America.* Boston: Houghton Mifflin Company, 1968.

Thoreau, Henry David. *Walden, or Life in the Woods.* Boston: Houghton, Mifflin & Co., 1893.

AZOREAN CULTURE, HISTORY, AND GEOGRAPHY

Barnes, Jennette, João Ferreira, and Joseph R. LaPlante. *A Nossa Vida: The Portuguese Experience in America.* New Bedford, MA: Southcoast Media Group, 2006.
Marsh, Terry. *The Azores, Globetrotter Travel Guide.* London, UK: New Hólland Publishers, 2009.
Santos, Robert L. *Azoreans to California: A History of Migration and Settlement.* Denair, CA: Alley-Cass Publications, 1995; www.library.csustan.edu/bsantos/azores.html.
Tyson-Ward, Sue. *Portuguese Verbs & Essentials of Grammar.* Second Edition. New York: McGraw-Hill, 2008.
Wright, Carol. *Portuguese Food.* London, UK: J.M. Dent & Sons Ltd., 1969.

MISCELLANEOUS

Bly, Robert (Translator). *Times Alone: Selected Poems of Antonio Machado.* Middletown, CT: Wesleyan University Press, 1983.
Montgomery, L. M. *Emily of New Moon.* New York: Frederick Stokes Co., Lippincott edition, 1923.
Perrottet, Tony. "John Muir's Yosemite." *Smithsonian Features,* July 2008, 48.
Waller, Robert James. *The Bridges of Madison County.* New York: Warner Books, Inc., 1992.

About the Author

Still a mountain woodswoman at heart, Mary Beth Baptiste lives with her husband in southeast Wyoming, where she continues to add to her checkered job history. A two-time winner of the Wyoming Arts Council's Frank Nelson Doubleday Award for Creative Writing, she has published her work in a variety of periodicals and anthologies.